THE TRAILMAN'S HANDBOOK

For Navigators and Adventurers

SECOND EDITION

Belton, South Carolina

THE TRAILMAN'S HANDBOOK
Published by Trail Life USA, Inc., dba Worthy Trailman Press
10612 Augusta St
Belton, SC 29627
www.TrailLifeUSA.com

This book or parts thereof may not be reproduced in any form, stored in a retrieval system, or transmitted in any form by any means—electronic, mechanical, photocopy, recording, or otherwise—without prior written permission of the publisher, except as provided by United States of America copyright law.

Unless otherwise noted, all Scripture quotations are from English Standard Version.

Book design: Anna Jelstrom
Cover illustration: Ken Raney
Cover photography: Stephen Jones

Copyright © 2019 by Trail Life USA, Inc.
All rights reserved.

International Standard Book Number: ISBN# 978-0-9912316-6-9

While the author has made every effort to provide accurate telephone numbers and Internet addresses at the time of publication, neither the publisher nor the author assumes any responsibility for errors or for changes that occur after publication.

Second edition, second printing.

19 — 98765432

Printed in the United States of America.

THIS BOOK BELONGS TO

Trailman _____
NAME

A member of Troop # _____, a ministry of

_____
CHARTER ORGANIZATION

in _____
CITY, STATE

ACKNOWLEDGMENTS

This handbook is a collective work of both volunteers and Trail Life USA staff who share a commitment to the mission of Trail Life USA to guide generations of courageous young men to honor God, lead with integrity, serve others, and experience outdoor adventure.
While it is impossible to point to any one person's contribution, each would give all due glory to God, Who gave us the outdoors.

SENIOR EDITORIAL STAFF
Project direction: Laura Burton
Project coordination: Seth Morrow
Contributing Authors: John Burkitt, Tim Owen, John Stemberger, and Mark Hancock

Dedicated to the adventure
of growing in the image of God
in God's great outdoors.

CONTENTS

JOIN THE ADVENTURE ix

CHAPTER 1
WHAT MAKES A TRAILMAN? 1

CHAPTER 2
TRAIL LIFE BASICS 23

CHAPTER 3
ADVANCEMENT STRUCTURE 37
Frontiers 37
Required Badges 41
Elective Badges 57
Ranks, Awards, and Worthy Life 59

CHAPTER 4
HOW A TRAILMAN ADVANCES 65
Navigator Ranks & Worthy Life Award Requirements 67
Adventurer Awards & Worthy Life Award Requirements 91
Trail Badge Requirements 117

CHAPTER 5
FIRST AID FOR THE TRAILMAN 199

SPECIAL SECTION
THE PATROL LEADERS' GUIDEBOOK 261
Welcome to a Life-Changing Opportunity! 263
What Is the Patrol Method? 265
Why Does Trail Life Use Boy-Led Patrols in the Outdoors? 267
What Does Patrol Life Look Like? 270
What Are the Patrol Roles and Responsibilities? 273

What Is the Officers' Conference?	277
How Can I Best Lead in My Troop or Patrol?	279
What Are the Activity and Project Essentials?	289

APPENDIX 304

PLANNING
Officer's Conference 3-month planning	305
Officer's Conference Annual Plan	306
Navigator/Adventurer Patrol Meeting Plan Pads	307
Checklist for Outdoor Adventures	308
Detailed Patrol Campout Schedule	310
Duty Roster Example	311

CAMPING
Low Impact Camping	312
Hiker's Responsibility Code	315
Backpacking Metrics	316

ADVANCEMENT
Advancement 101	318
Periodic Table of Advancements	320
Design Your Own Trail Badge	322
Band of Brothers	324
Uniform Insignia Placement	326

SAFETY
Woods Tools Safety Guidelines	327
Troop Safety 101 – How you can help	328
Swimming Competency Test	330
Safe Aquatics Method	333

SKILLS
Flag Folding	334

INDEX 336

FROM THE TEAM:

Why a new edition of the Trailman's Handbook for Navigators and Adventurers?

Although the Premier Edition was well received and has a special place in the hearts of many Trailmen, we took a careful look at the way Trailmen interacted with their handbooks, and thought we could improve it.

Rather than interrupt the content with bulleted lists and detailed field instruction, we aimed to create a flow of thought that will encourage you to turn to the next page, thriving in the culture of Trail Life USA and grasping a worldview built on the principles we hold dear as Christ-followers.

This book still contains all the essentials to track and earn the required Trail Badges as well as all the first aid information you'll need, but much of the detailed skills instruction has been moved to the Field Guides, which are built for the outdoors and are the perfect complements to the Trailman's Handbook.

So, enjoy your time in this handbook. Carry it with you to meetings and on the trail. Revisit the wise counsel in it, and share what you learn with others.

We've enjoyed preparing it for you.

THE VOLUNTEERS AND STAFF HANDBOOK TEAM

JOIN THE ADVENTURE!

Life is an adventure! With a can-do attitude and skills to back it up, you will take on new challenges and claim new rewards over each hill, through each valley, and around each bend in the river.

Explorers started the American adventure. Settlers carried it on. Defended by soldiers and tilled by farmers, America grew from an idea to a real and wonderful place stretching from the Atlantic to the Pacific, from Canada to Mexico. You should carry on the adventure with an enthusiasm worthy of our great nation.

The outdoor adventure will teach you important things about life. Nothing beats waking up in a tent you pitched yourself, then sitting down to a breakfast cooked in God's great outdoors. The wilderness will challenge you, and sometimes it will throw you a curve ball. At times, it will also feel like your home. When you learn how to live in it, you'll create unforgettable memories.

Whether you walk the misty pines of Maine, cross the open prairies of Kansas, or wade in the wild surf of Florida, this great country will be your heritage to enjoy and protect.

The spiritual adventure is the greatest one, the one that never ends. As a baby, you were the center of your own small universe. You soon learned that the faces around you were other people with thoughts and feelings just like yours. No longer were you alone!

The greatest discovery of all is to realize that you are never truly alone. As night falls on your campsite and you see the vast, starry sky above you, you will realize that the wise and loving God who made it also wants a relationship with you. He gave you a lifetime in this world of beauty and wonder. Make every day worthwhile and use your opportunities wisely. Seek to know and do His will.

What can be better than sharing the adventure with other like-minded boys who will help you each step of the way? In your Troop, you'll make friends who appreciate the blessings of God, the greatness of America, the boy you are today, and the man you will be tomorrow. Some of these boys will become lifelong friends, but all of them will be part of the happy memories you make.

CHAPTER

WHAT MAKES A TRAILMAN?

A TRAILMAN'S CHARACTER

A Trailman's body has a skeleton of bone. His soul has a skeleton of character. Both determine where and how far he will bend. Both cause pain when they are injured, and both need the right care to heal.

Character is a combination of strengths, weaknesses, and unique characteristics that make a Trailman who he is. A Trailman will strive to maximize his strengths and minimize his weaknesses. When he says the Trail Life motto, "Walk Worthy," it reminds him to build the best character he can and to use it to do the most good.

All of us build our character over time. Values, hardships, victories, education, and challenges build character. Character keeps its shape and form once it's built. It does not change easily.

Our society (culture) is unreliable in character as its values seem to change each day. We can't depend on society to help us build a strong character. But God's character does not change. He is the same yesterday, today, and forever; therefore, He can be trusted. His unchanging character helps us understand right from wrong. Morals and God's law are absolute and unchanging because God's nature and character are unchanging.

A Trailman is on a journey to be transformed by the renewing of his mind. He wants his character to be more like that of Jesus Christ, God's Son Who came not only to save us but also to model the character we should pursue and the way we should live. This process of being transformed into His image rather than conforming to the image of our society (culture) is most evident in your years as a Navigator and Adventurer when you are transitioning from the boy you are to the man you will become.

The Boy You Are

Sometimes you see the exciting things adults do and the wonderful places they go and you feel impatient. You want to have those same freedoms and experiences.

As you grow up, God and those who serve Him bring order into your life through their instruction, example, and care. God uses this process to transform and build your character so you will be more like Jesus Christ. God uses everything for His glory—even the hard things we don't understand. Maturing is a wonderful process. You should be glad you are going through it, and you should enjoy every opportunity God brings into your life.

The Man You Will Become

Manhood is not something you will suddenly experience when you awaken on the morning of your eighteenth birthday. In fact, manhood is something you achieve by degrees in areas such as leadership skills, wisdom, and emotional maturity. As you mature, you also will experience the freedom of new rights and responsibilities.

Areas of your life will develop at different rates and, at each phase, a Trailman will grow to meet increasingly greater challenges.

Because no two Trailmen are alike, there is no checklist of things that make you a man. However, faithful Christians know there are certain things a man is, and certain things he isn't.

Many people are confused and deceived about the differences between men and women. God, by His design, created men and women uniquely for His purposes and—at the same time—different from one another. He is clear about their uniqueness and the way they complement one another as members of the created world that perfectly reflects His nature.

Our society (culture) also has many false, shallow ideas about what it means to be a man. Being a man is definitely not about drinking alcohol, experimenting with sex, abusing drugs, or smoking. Being a man is not even about the good activities some men enjoy such as playing sports, lifting weights, hunting, and working on cars. God's design is for men to be leaders, protectors, and providers. To be both brave and kind. To be both hard working and fun loving. To be strong but also gentle. To be confident but also humble. Real men love God, love their families, and love their neighbors. They treat others with respect in the same way they wish to be treated.

WHAT MAKES A TRAILMAN? 3

Frontiers to Cross

There are Frontiers to cross on your journey in Trail Life USA. These Frontiers are designed to provide the adventurous type of living that makes a Trailman a Trailman. These Frontiers, which you may have known as "Branches" on the Woodlands Trail, are:

- Heritage
- Hobbies
- Life Skills
- Outdoor Skills
- Science and Technology
- Sports and Fitness
- Values

To guide you through these Frontiers, the Trail Life USA program uses Trail Badges, service opportunities, campouts, and leadership experiences. Exploring these Frontiers helps shape you into a courageous young man who will honor God, lead with integrity, serve others, and experience outdoor adventure.

A Trailman never stops exploring, even after he becomes a man. There will be other adventures and experiences on the trail of life such as college, career, marriage, and fatherhood. A Trailman will take his place in the vast parade of men, with the past as his heritage, the present as his opportunity, and the future as his vision.

You are about to inherit a great legacy of knowledge and wisdom that generations of men who came before you experienced. And as you walk this trail, you will gain a larger perspective of what it means to *Walk Worthy*.

The adventure you encounter, the character you develop, the leadership skills you learn, and the experience you gain will help you

grow mentally and spiritually to become the unique man God has designed you to be.

Congratulations! By committing to grow as a Trailman, you are on your way to maturing into a godly man.

A TRAILMAN AND OUTDOOR ADVENTURE

God could have brought you into the world fully grown with the knowledge and experience you need to survive in the outdoors. Instead, He created you as an infant and gave you a world to explore. As a Trailman, you will share many of its wonders with your Trail Life family, and you will make memories that remain vivid and fresh throughout your life.

> **Outdoor adventure is the purest adventure because it happens in the environment God created for you and me.**

When experiencing outdoor adventure, you will face challenges you are unlikely to face anywhere else. Outdoor adventure is the purest adventure because it happens in the environment God created for you and me.

You will hike the same trails that generations of men hiked. Those men grew through overcoming the challenge of the outdoors. As a Trailman, you will be aware of the footsteps you follow and the footsteps you leave for others. You have been given an opportunity to impact generations of future courageous young men who will also become godly and responsible husbands, fathers, and citizens, then influence others to follow their example.

A Trailman understands his place in outdoor adventure and welcomes the challenge.

A TRAILMAN AND LEADERSHIP

Leadership skills are important because God calls men to lead their families, in the church and in society. In the creation mandate given in Genesis 1:28, God made it clear that He expected us to lead by giving us dominion (the charge to rule or lead) over the earth and to be wise stewards of its many natural resources. Think about that ... to be in charge of the earth is such an important leadership role!

At first, you are a leader of yourself (something you learned back in Woodlands Trail). But as a Navigator, you will move into position to lead others.

A Trailman does his best to develop his leadership skills. He pays attention to leadership lessons and learns the secret of contentment through patiently following others in leadership while he looks and waits for opportunities to lead.

Your experience in Trail Life will give you many opportunities to lead and to see many examples of leadership, perhaps both good and bad. A Trailman can learn from every example he observes.

A TRAILMAN AND HIS RELATIONSHIPS

Your Relationship with God

Throughout life you will form many relationships. Some will be very important. Your relationship with your heavenly Father, God, is most important.

God is a living, eternal, personal being who wants to maintain a close, meaningful relationship with you. One of the ways you build that relationship is through prayer. The leaders in your Troop and church can help you improve your prayer life and deepen your relationship with God as you follow Jesus Christ, His only Son.

The Trail Life USA program has many symbols with great meaning. The name "Trail Life" is symbolic of the two types of life journeys. The Trail in nature represents the path you walk as you search for outdoor adventure and as you experience the blessings and challenges of life. The Trail of faith is the most important course you will set on your journey: following Jesus along the straight and narrow path that leads to eternal life.

If you have not yet decided to follow Jesus Christ with all your heart, there is an emptiness inside you that only God can satisfy. To learn more about this decision and how you can walk closer to God, talk with your pastor, your parents, or your Troop leaders.

If you are unable to talk with a pastor, a parent, or a Troop leader about God, then you can begin a relationship with God by praying like this:

> *"Dear Lord Jesus, I know I am a sinner because I've done many bad things. Please forgive me. I believe You died for my sins and rose from the dead, which proved that You are God. I trust and follow You as my Lord and Savior. Guide me and help me to do Your will. In Your name, amen."*

Relationships with Family

A family is a group of people related to each other by marriage, blood, or adoption. Families come in many shapes and sizes. You may have brothers or sisters, older siblings or younger ones, or you may be an only child. You may live with your birth parents or with one parent or with someone else who takes care of you. You may be adopted. Be grateful for the family God has given you, and try not to be envious of the family He gave to someone else.

> **Facing challenges with determination, patience, and a sense of humor is a good sign that you are becoming a man.**

Family relationships are often difficult. You may be upset if you must work harder around the house because of the loss of a parent or the presence of younger children. Your friends at school may have more free time because they have fewer chores, and you may feel this is unfair. You may be upset if you do not get the same privileges and freedom as an older brother or sister. You may think that your parents love a brother or sister more than they love you. These feelings are common, and you need to deal with them, but that does not mean they reflect reality. Facing challenges with determination, patience, and a sense of humor is a good sign that you are becoming a man.

Some people are very happy with their family, while others may be very angry. If you are like most people, you fall somewhere between those extremes. Where you stand depends a lot on your attitude. A Trailman chooses to have a good attitude and works at being content wherever God places him.

As you mature, your relationship with your parents will change. You will have new rights and new responsibilities. It is natural for you to feel pride in your newfound abilities, and it is natural that you will start questioning some decisions your parents make. At times, it will feel as if they are treating you like a younger child, and that can be frustrating. You may be tempted to forget your special relationship with your parents and to treat them like any other people. You may even become disrespectful. A Trailman should always respect authority, especially the authority of his parents. This is true even when your parents make mistakes and even if they have bad habits.

That said, unless they ask you to do something that violates the laws of God or man, you should respect and obey your parents. This is part of your duty to respect authority, which is stated in the Trailman Oath. That respect extends to people your parents delegate to have authority over you, such as teachers, doctors, clergy, and Troop leaders. Respecting parental authority does not mean you cannot express your opinion. If you raise objections in a respectful manner, especially if you explain your line of reasoning, you will find that they respect your thoughts and feelings even if they do not always agree with them. As you grow older, you'll realize that humility and forgiveness are two of

> **Humility and forgiveness are two of the great secrets to spiritual success as a follower of Jesus Christ. The Trailman who finds and uses these tools will go far in life.**

the best ways not only to honor your father and mother but also to maintain a successful Christian life. The Trailman who finds and uses these tools will go far in life.

Younger siblings can try your patience. Even so, you are more of a role model to them than you may think. They pick up your habits and imitate your manners. In the Trailman Oath, we repeat the words "treat others the way we would like to be treated." You should always treat your brothers and sisters the way you want your parents to treat you. You may find that the leadership skills you learn in your Troop also work quite well in your family—whether it is giving guidance with the right attitude or receiving it.

Relationships with Friends

Friends are some of your greatest treasures. And you will make some great friends in Trail Life.

Many people may recognize you and treat you well, but only some of them are true friends. So how do you know if you are truly a friend to someone or if that person is a real friend to you? Friends want what is best for each other—even if that means talking you out of making a bad decision. They are always willing to help, always willing to listen, and always willing to stick with you through good times and bad times.

> **If God has given you good friends, make sure you are a good friend too. The best way to have a good friend is to be one.**

A true friend stands with you and stands up for you—and you do the same for him. Friends rejoice with you in your successes and achievements. Friends like you for who you are. It has been said that a true friend is a person that knows *everything* about you ... and is still your friend.

Choose friends who truly like you and build you up; avoid people who use you and drag you down. Sometimes other people gain your trust just to get what they want. It may be something small and harmless, like borrowing a baseball bat or video game. We all have "friends" who only look for us when they want us to do them a favor. Some people may ask for bigger "favors"—things that can get you in serious trouble, steal your innocence, or threaten your safety. Not many people are like that, but even one in your life is too many. The Bible teaches that "bad company ruins good morals."[1]

If God has given you good friends, make sure you are a good friend too. When they need to talk or they are scared or upset, you should listen to them and offer encouragement or help. If you don't have friends like that yet, remember this time-tested advice: the best way to **have** a good friend is to **be** one.

Relationships with People who are Different

Our world is filled with all kinds of people. And, while each one is unique in some ways, every person is made in the image of God and has intrinsic value, worth, and dignity. We should be friendly and show Christian concern for all people, not just those who are like us or those who are family members and neighbors.

Some people will be very different from us. Some have different

[1] *1 Corinthians 15:33*

values, lifestyles, and faiths (or no faith at all). A Trailman recognizes that we can have differences—and even strongly disagree—but we should still respect one another.

A Trailman should show people who are different proper respect regardless of age, disability, economic status, ethnicity, race, sex, or sinful tendencies. While respecting people who live or believe differently can be a challenge, all Christians are called to be respectful and maintain firm Christian convictions. Proper respect is important because each person is made in the image of God.

Relationships with Strangers

The great American humorist Will Rogers once said that strangers are friends you have not met. While you may choose to limit the number of deep friendships you maintain, a Trailman will show all people the same consideration and courtesy he would show his family and friends, just as he would want them to show kindness to him and to those he loves. As Jesus said, "Just as I have loved you, you also are to love one another."[2]

We should be concerned with friends, neighbors, and even strangers. Some of these relationships can be risky, so always rely on your parent's advice and permission when talking with or doing any activity with people outside your family.

Dangerous Relationships

Ethan's Uncle Bob was smart and funny, and he always bought Ethan the best presents. Ethan's mother invited Bob over often because she was a widow and thought Bob was a good male role model. When Bob took Ethan to see football games or visit the zoo the way his father used to do, Ethan felt good inside. One day while they were boating alone on the lake, Bob took out his smartphone and showed Ethan some pictures of people with no clothes.

Ethan was shocked.

"I don't think I should be looking at those," Ethan said, because he had been told about inappropriate websites. So Bob put the

---

[2] *John 13:34*

phone away and did not mention it again. When Ethan got home, he wondered if he should tell his mother what happened, but he was afraid to say anything. After all, Uncle Bob was her brother and the experience was embarrassing.

But he couldn't forget what happened, so finally, he told his mother. She became upset, yet she knew her son would not lie to her. She reported the incident to the authorities. They discovered that the photos on the phone were of young girls who were being abused. Bob got the help he needed, and the pictures led the police to other people who were harming other kids.

> Any act that threatens to harm your physical, mental, emotional, or spiritual health is abuse and is wrong.

Speaking up was the right thing for Ethan to do.

Sometimes even people we trust do wrong things. They can misuse our trust and hurt us. Any act that threatens to harm your physical, mental, emotional, or spiritual health is considered abuse and is wrong. Unfortunately, some adults, and even other youth, sexually abuse children. Any sexual contact with a youth—regardless of who the other person is—is wrong and should be reported. The following Trail Life USA guidelines can help to reduce the possibility of that happening to you or other youth:

- Everyone should respect your privacy—especially when it comes to using the bathroom, changing clothes, showering, and sleeping arrangements.
- You should never be alone with only one adult (unless it is your parent).
- You should never participate in secret ceremonies, activities, or meetings.

- Appropriate clothing should always be worn—especially for swimming activities.
- There should be no humiliating activities, bullying, or physical hitting.
- Cameras, video, cell phones, and other electronics should never be used in bathrooms, showers, changing areas, or in any other way that violates someone's privacy or causes them harm.

If someone fails to follow these guidelines, you should report that person to your leaders and to your parents. It is the right thing to do, and it can help to protect you and others from harm.

You have certain rights over your mind and your body that other people should not take away from you. For example, a doctor may need to examine you in a personal, private way, but if the experience makes you feel uncomfortable, tell your parents or ask one of them to be with you during the examination.

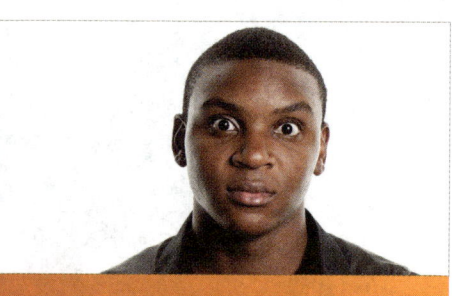

If someone asks you to see, read, or do something that makes you feel uncomfortable, you have the right to refuse.

People may talk about strange ideas you don't understand or with which you don't agree. If they go beyond what you think or have been taught is reasonable, or if someone asks you to see, read, or do something that make you feel uncomfortable—whether it's a physical act or a spiritual one—you have the right to refuse. And that is exactly what you should do. If they offer you alcohol or illegal drugs, or if they ask you to help them steal, or if they touch you or ask you to touch yourself or touch them in inappropriate ways, immediately find someone you trust and tell that person what happened. Tell that trusted person more than once if you must, or tell some other adult you trust. If you can't get through to them, find someone else—until you are believed.

How do you know if something is wrong? One way to find out is to ask a parent, pastor, or an official Trail Life adult leader. Adults should know better than to ask young people to perform sexual acts, disobey the law, or violate their religious principles. It is never your fault if someone asks you to do something wrong, even if they say it is. **Say NO, then GO, and TELL**.

Relationship Summary

Managing relationships is an art you can master. It can be hard, but it is worthwhile. Even good relationships have problems, and the best relationships take time and effort. With some help, you will regain confidence and reach out again.

A Trailman pays close attention to the health of his good relationships and is always aware of the possibility of bad relationships.

A TRAILMAN AND SERVICE

Part of the mission of Trail Life USA is to encourage Trailmen to "serve others." Many home schools and public schools require a certain number of volunteer service hours for each student.

Trail Life integrates service requirements into ranks and advancement because it's so critical to our mission. It's even in the Oath and Trail Life's mission statement!

"To serve God and my country…"

How do we serve God and why do we serve God?

First, we serve God by devoting our whole lives to following His purposes and His plans. We're not focused on doing what we want to do in life. Instead, in every decision, we serve God by asking, "Father, is this the direction You want me to go?" We serve God by submitting every part of our lives to Him. Many adults speak of being in the military as being in "the service." In a sense, when we decide to follow Christ, we are also in service to His kingdom and His purposes for us.

Second, we serve God by serving our families. Service is one of highest forms of love. Love is not merely a feeling; love is an act of our will and, in many cases, a decision to serve. We serve our family because we love our family. In a sense, we are called to love and serve *all* people as Christians, but our duty to serve our family is one of the most important ways we serve.

When you are older, you will need to find a career or job so you can provide for yourself at first and then eventually maybe a family. This may sound ordinary, but the commitment to earn a living is important both to God and to the family He may give you one day.

Many men who can work don't want to work. They have not  learned the value of hard work. They would rather have their wife, parents, or the government support them—and their family. The Bible says the man who does not take care of his own family is "worse than an unbeliever."[3] As a Trailman, you can learn to enjoy the satisfaction of hard work by doing chores without being asked, keeping your room clean, or looking for other ways to help around your house.

Third, we serve God by serving the church. After our families, serving our local church is the next most important way to serve God. God uses the people in churches to become the hands and feet of Jesus Christ. The church literally does what He would do if He were here. You can volunteer at church to serve as an usher, to move chairs, clean rooms, or go on a mission trip—these are acts of service to God and to God's people.

Finally, we serve God when we serve others in the Troop or community. Jesus said about Himself, "The Son of Man came not to be served but to serve."[4] When we are quick to meet a need, do a good

---

[3] 1 Timothy 5:8
[4] Matthew 20:28

deed, or volunteer for a task, we are also serving God. Jesus said, "as you did it to one of the least of these my brothers, you did it to me."[5] In other words, when we serve other people who are weak, poor, or disadvantaged in some way, Jesus says that is the same as serving Him directly. Wow, that's really something to think about!

How do we serve our country?

We can serve our country in many ways. Some of these forms of service will await you when you become an adult. Throughout American history, untold thousands of young men have served our country by enlisting in the US Army, Air Force, Navy, Marines, or Coast Guard. This is an option every young man should at least consider. Serving in the military offers the opportunity to live on your own, stretch and strengthen your physical abilities, learn discipline, and the possibility of earning special grants to pay for college after serving.

You can also help serve your country right now as a Trailman simply by advancing through the ranks and awards of Trail Life USA.

Learn the story of America. Read history books and study our founding fathers. Develop an appreciation for those who have paid the high price to establish and protect the country we live in and to provide the freedoms we enjoy.

Show appreciation for your country and for all veterans. One simple way you can show respect for a person who served in the military is to shake his or her hand and say, "Thank you for serving our country." Also, always respect the American flag by standing when it is raised, or during the pledge, or singing the national anthem, and use other proper flag protocol.

---

[5] Matthew 25:40

Learn about civics and politics, then prepare to vote and become an active citizen. Have conversations with your parents and leaders about the major political parties and what they stand for. Take a trip to your city hall, state capitol, or Washington, DC. Take an interest in and understand the different levels of city, county, state, and federal government. Think about whether you would like run for office one day as an elected public servant.

Make a commitment now, as a citizen, to fight for what is true, good, and beautiful in America. Many people show disrespect for America and don't think this country is special. Our country has made some mistakes, and we need to acknowledge them. But you can serve your country now by beginning to understand how uniquely religious, exceptional, and prosperous America is and why those qualities are so important. Decide now that throughout your life, you will respect and obey laws and be a good citizen. Decide that you will be a man of courage who will stand against what is evil, immoral, and corrupt.

It is God's design for men to be servants. Men should serve God, their families, their church, and their community. Men also are called in varying ways to serve their country. Trailmen should serve with a good attitude. When we do this, we honor God.

A TRAILMAN'S WORLDVIEW

The Bible teaches that there are three enemies of our soul. Those enemies are the world, the flesh, and the devil. The word "world" used in this way simply means the thinking, systems, or philosophies of this world. The "ways of the world" and the ways of God are usually very different. Many times, they are exact opposites. For instance, the world says to "love yourself," but God teaches us to "love others." The world says, "Live for today." God says, "Store up treasures in heaven and not on this earth." The world says there is no right or wrong. God says there is an absolute right and wrong that comes from Who He is.

A Trailman should desire to think clearly and to understand God's design and His truth about life and the world and how they were created to be.

Have you ever thought about deception? If someone is deceived, he usually has no idea that he has been deceived. He doesn't know that what he believes is wrong. Both the Old and New Testaments of the Bible use this phrase repeatedly: "Do not be deceived." Why? God wants us to be people of truth. He wants us to know the truth, believe the truth, and speak the truth. Truth is the only cure for the disease of deception.

The philosophies of this world lie to us about many important things. But as Trailmen, we don't want to be deceived. We want to walk in the truth.

That's why a Christian worldview is important. We don't want to be lied to, and we want to be able to recognize when we are hearing a lie and when we are hearing the truth.

Have you ever tried to assemble something that seemed simple at first but ended up being complicated? Have you ever tried to put something together, such as a toy or a piece of furniture, without reading the manufacturer's instructions or owner's manual?

> As Trailmen, we don't want to be deceived. We want to walk in the truth.

That's what the world tries to do. Worldly people try to understand human relationships, science, morality, art, politics, and many other areas of life without reading the product instructions or the owner's manual. The Bible is the ultimate owner's manual. And when we study the Bible, it helps us understand how the world we live in operates according to God's design. God is really like the ultimate manufacturer of the whole world! To know how the world was intended to work according to God's design is a big part of having a Christian worldview.

If our hearts and minds are influenced by the lies and darkness of this world, then it's as if our religion is polluted, defiled, and unclean.

James chapter 1, verse 27 is special because it is the only place in the Bible where God tells us what "pure religion" looks like. Think about these powerful words:

> "Religion that is pure and undefiled before God the Father is this: to visit orphans and widows in their affliction, and to keep oneself unstained from the world."

This verse may make you think about adoption or foster care or helping women whose husbands may have died. But the second part of this verse —*"to keep oneself unstained from the world"*—relates directly to the Christian worldview of a Trailman.

That kind of thought process, that whatever we do in life, big or small, God's Word has something to say about it, is living with a Christian worldview. As Trailmen, we don't want to be worldly in our thoughts and viewpoints. We want to be godly.

The challenge of being "in the world but not of the world"[6] is a lifelong journey. By studying God's Word, the Bible, and obeying His timeless principles that relate to each area of life, we can remain

---

[6] *John 17:11*

unstained by the world and think His thoughts about the way we ought to live.

Many Christians see their faith as something that is only applicable on Sunday inside a church building. But God's truth applies to all areas of life, not just matters of religion. The Bible teaches that "whether you eat or drink, or whatever you do, do all to the glory of God."[7]

So the worldview of the Trailman is to know, love, and walk in the truth. We never want to be known as people who are shallow or deceived. As Trailmen, we want to be wise and walk in the light of God's plan for our lives by committing to the Trail Life motto to "Walk Worthy" in every area of life.

Walking Worthy

The Trail Life USA motto, "Walk Worthy," sums up the worldview of a Trailman.

From Colossians 1:10, "so as to walk in a manner worthy of the Lord, fully pleasing to him: bearing fruit in every good work and increasing in the knowledge of God," it reveals the daily integration of an ideal lifestyle in a world that needs to see these principles in action.

Walking Worthy is a commission not only to do our best but also to get the most out of this life by living close to God, walking in a manner that honors Him. The pursuit of God and a commitment to a biblical worldview will not only help you become a better husband, father, and citizen but also it will enable you to enjoy the full, abundant life that Jesus Christ offers each of us.

And, for the same reason that your Trail Life Leaders expect you to cook your own meals on campouts, God desires that you investigate, gain insight, get involved, and integrate His truth in every part of your life.

God revealed truth to us through His Word. As we live by His character, lead by example, and serve others, we cultivate the image of God within us and know in the most intimate ways how much He truly loves us.

---

[7] *1 Corinthians. 10:31*

CHAPTER 2

TRAIL LIFE BASICS

PROGRAMS OF TRAIL LIFE USA

Trail Life USA's Christ-centered, boy-focused program is designed in levels that mirror natural development transitions you will experience as you mature.

WOODLANDS TRAIL

▶ The **Woodlands Trail** focuses on gaining *knowledge*. It is for boys in kindergarten through fifth grade who operate in patrols of Foxes (K–1st grade), Hawks (2nd–3rd grade), and Mountain Lions (4th–5th grade). Troops may decide to split these patrols into smaller patrols if they have a large number of boys.

NAVIGATORS

▶ The **Navigators Program** emphasizes *understanding*. It is an inspirational and richly rewarding program for sixth to eighth grade boys who seek to achieve mental, moral, emotional, and physical fitness exploring God's great outdoors. Trailmen begin to exercise the leadership skills they will need throughout their lives.

ADVENTURERS

▶ The **Adventurers Program** is designed to foster *wisdom*. It is a high-adventure, high-energy program for ninth to twelfth grade boys who want to take ownership of activities they plan and implement. The patrols are boy-led. Adult leaders are present but play a diminishing role as the boys mature in leadership skills.

GUIDON

▶ The **Guidon Program**, with a focus on *life,* is an outdoor adventure program for Christian men and women ages eighteen to twenty-five. Under charter organization adult mentors, young adults hold each other to a higher Christian standard and to purity in a challenging world.

WHERE TO START

If you're a boy of Navigator or Adventurer age, great! Go to a Troop in your area and introduce yourself to Trail Life USA leaders and boys. The Trailmen will help you learn about Trail Life and explain how you can advance through the Trail Life USA awards program and help build a successful patrol as you develop a relationship with God.

There are certain essentials that apply to all Trailmen that you will see through the activities of the Troop.

THE PLEDGE OF ALLEGIANCE

> I pledge allegiance to the Flag of the United States of America, and to the Republic for which it stands, one Nation under God, indivisible, with liberty and justice for all.

The flag of the United States is a symbol of the freedom and justice we enjoy as Americans. In 1892, Francis Bellamy wrote the Pledge of Allegiance to help citizens show respect for the flag. In 1954, the words "under God" were added to the pledge to thank God for the blessings we have as Americans.

We stand, salute, and observe proper flag protocol to show respect for the country the flag represents.

THE TRAILMAN SIGN, SALUTE, AND HANDSHAKE

Wolves howl to recognize their own. Foxes recognize familiar smells. Bears look for marks on trees, and whales have distinctive songs. As a Trailman, you can identify yourself to others using the Trailman sign, salute, and handshake. Along with your uniform, these actions identify you as a member of a great brotherhood of Trailmen throughout the country.

Trailman Sign

The Trailman sign is made by extending your upper right arm out to your side and parallel to the ground. Position your elbow at a right angle and your fingertips pointing up, the right hand held open, palm forward.

Trailman Salute

This is a traditional military salute. Bring the right hand up, palm down, until your forefinger touches the brim of your hat or the tip of your right eyebrow.

The Trailman salute is used to honor the flag. Your leaders will explain how your Troop uses the salute.

Trailman Handshake

The Trailman handshake is similar to a regular right-handed handshake, except that you reach further forward and grasp the other person's wrist.

TRAIL LIFE BASICS

THE TRAILMAN OATH

The Trailman Oath is unique to Trailmen in Trail Life USA and connects us in our shared commitment to live by it.

> *On my honor I will do my best*
> *to serve God and my country,*
> *to respect authority,*
> *to be a good steward of creation,*
> *and to treat others as I want to be treated.*

Your honor is similar to the wind. You can't see the wind directly, but you see the trees move, and the clouds go by. Likewise, you can't see honor, but you can see what it does. Honor is that quality that helps you keep promises and to make the right choices.

Because you are created in the image of God, you have unquestionable value, worth, and dignity. You are capable of being a person of honor and living up to the ideals expressed in the Oath.

When we say "On my honor," it's like saying to the world, "Listen up! This is important! Hold me accountable to my own personal integrity in these words." It's a pretty big deal to say, "On my honor," and then what comes after is also really important.

Doing your best does not end at the edge of your comfort zone. Most people never discover their best because they are fine with good or better. You discover your best by pushing yourself to take on new challenges and by watching how you achieve a higher level of best with study and practice.

You have certain gifts, skills, and abilities that were given to you by God. Consider them resources that help you do your best and bring glory to God by using them wisely.

Serving God and your country is more than a duty. It is a privilege. Knowing that God wants (and America needs) your help gives you a satisfying sense of belonging.

Your service may even include service to people who don't believe what you believe or live like you live. Nevertheless, a Trailman is called to serve.

Respecting authority is both a responsibility and a skill. Authorities include parents, teachers, police, judges, military officials, and elected political leaders. You have a responsibility to obey righteous laws and to use discernment within the framework of your Christian faith.

A good steward of creation does not waste or destroy the blessings God gives. That includes taking care of your own health and the upkeep of your house and yard. In the great outdoors, responsible stewardship includes preventing forest fires, keeping the air and water pure, and leaving a campsite like you found it. Each human being must be a good steward of the resources God provides and responsibly cultivate and conserve them for His glory.

Treating other people as you want to be treated is the Golden Rule taught by Jesus Christ. It is one of many absolute, unchanging truths God gives us about how to live. Although we may be tempted to lash out or respond to an offense in anger or disrespect, we should try to do what Jesus said. It is right because He said it's right.

THE TRAILMAN MOTTO

"Walk Worthy!"

Your journey in life is similar to your journey through Trail Life. The intentional symbolism in the Trail reminds us there will be challenging inclines and glorious vistas, rainy days and blue skies. But a Trailman walks worthy, no matter the terrain or the climate.

> *"... That you may walk worthy of the Lord, fully pleasing Him, being fruitful in every good work and increasing in the knowledge of God..."*
> Colossians 1:10 (NKJV)

TRAIL LIFE BASICS

YOUR UNIFORM

The Trailman Troop uniform (formal) is designed for adventure. It is durable and attractive, but it will last longer and look better if you take proper care of it.

The uniform shows others that you care about God, America, and adventurous living. It also connects your reputation and identity to every other Trailman. As a symbol of the goodwill and ideals of Trail Life USA, it should be worn at Troop events, but it should not be worn at political events, non-troop fundraisers, or any place or activity that does not reflect well on the principles and goals of the Trail Life program or your fellow Trailmen. This uniform should only be worn by members in good standing.

> The uniform shows others that you care about God, America, and adventurous living.

When you are wearing your uniform, everyone in public will be watching you. You are representing Trail Life USA, your local Troop and, most importantly, you are seen as an ambassador of God's Kingdom. Don't wear your uniform sloppily, incomplete, or untucked. Wear it clean, sharp, and properly. Wear it with confidence and pride.

Trail Life uses three terms in relation to uniforms: Troop, Travel, and Trail.

Troop

Travel

Trail

Your formal **Troop** uniform shirt will display the Woodlands Timberline Award, Navigator rank patches, Adventurer award patches, Worthy Life Award, and epaulettes of office. ***Your Troop uniform shirt should be neatly tucked at all times.***

Your Troop may also use the Trailman **Travel** shirt. This collared polo-style shirt is less formal than the Troop uniform but still looks nice.

Sometimes a Trailman will wear a **Trail** t-shirt with the uniform pants, shorts, or even jeans, especially when hiking or camping or if your leaders are concerned about messy conditions.

Your leaders will let you know what uniform is appropriate for each activity.

THE TRAILMAN'S STANDARD

The Trailman's Standard is the official uniform staff used by a Trailman. On it you will display your earned Trail Badges, service stars, Elective Badge awards and, if you reach the peaks of the Trail, your Freedom Award topper. Like you, the wood of the Standard started out small and helpless, then grew tall and sturdy, capable of supporting itself and others. The Trailman Standard is your partner, and it comes to you unadorned, awaiting the unique achievements you will fasten to it as you learn, grow, and make lifelong memories with Trail Life USA.

Some Troops may choose to create walking standards for use in the field, but your formal Troop Standard, which will display your awards, should be the official-issue Standard. It will not crack over time, and it is uniquely designed to accommodate your Freedom Topper, the highest award element in Trail Life USA.

YOUR TROOP

Your Troop is made up of patrols. Boys holding elected offices include the First Officer, Second Officer, and Quartermaster. The adult leaders are the Trailmaster (for Navigators), the Advisor (for Adventurers), and Trail Guides. (This is illustrated for you on page 274.) These may be people you already know from church or school, or they might be new to you. They share your love of adventure—a great thing to have in common.

The Troop is like a Trail Life USA family. It usually meets once a week and has an outdoor activity once a month. It is large enough to tackle big tasks and to plan exciting outings.

The Navigators Trailmaster signs paperwork, provides leadership and guidance, and runs the Navigators meetings, encouraging Navigators to embrace the leadership opportunities in the Trail Life USA boy-led model.

Adventurers are led by the First Officer, a youth who runs the meetings. Together with his Second Officer, Patrol Leaders, and Navigator Junior Patrol Leaders, the First Officer conducts the Officers' Conference to plan outings and discuss what went right or wrong with activities. The Adventurers Advisor is the adult who oversees the Adventurers, providing support when needed while allowing the Trailmen to lead themselves.

> **The Troop is made up of all the patrols.**

YOUR PATROL

A patrol is a group of six to eight boys who function as a small family inside the big family of your Troop. An elected Patrol Leader and a Junior Patrol Leader keep things moving. You will have fun in friendly competition with other patrols in your Troop.

Patrol members camp together, play together, and learn together. You can also work to be the best patrol in your Troop. This small community of youth Trailmen helps you begin to understand how God places people alongside one another for His glory. Young men grow strong and wise when they are committed to working and staying together, even through difficult challenges.

> **A patrol is a group of six to eight boys inside your Troop.**

A portion of each Troop meeting may be set aside for patrols to meet separately. During those times, you can work on patrol flags, plan menus, or plan patrol outings.

One patrol in your Troop may be reserved for new boys. An experienced Patrol Leader or an adult Trail Guide will help teach them the important first skills leading to the Ready Trailman rank.

If you just joined as a Navigator, you will have a lot of fun in your first days as a Trailman, but you will also want to reach Ready Trailman soon.

LEADER CONFERENCES

As part of the joining requirements, your Leader will talk with you about Troop safety and what lies ahead on the advancement trail. He will help you understand where you are and where you are going. Your feedback will give the Leader some idea of how well you are enjoying the program and what can be done to improve it for everyone.

For each new rank or award you complete, you'll have an Advancement Conference. That's because you are not just growing on the outside, you're also growing on the inside—in your heart and mind. Your Leader watches your progress and listens to your opinions to make sure you are getting the most out of the program.

NAVIGATOR RANKS

▶ **Recruit Trailman**—The Recruit understands and agrees with the ideals of the Trail Life. He takes advantage of the training and fellowship to learn and grow.

▶ **Able Trailman**—The Able Trailman is truly an able man. He knows how to hike safely and comfortably and handle many situations. These skills are the foundation for the Ready Trailman.

▶ **Ready Trailman**—The Ready Trailman is ready for whatever happens. He has a full set of camping skills and does his fair share of the work along with enjoying the fun. After you have earned this highest rank in Navigators, you have the confidence and experience to teach skills to newer members and give back to the Troop some of the help you received when you were starting out. As Christ teaches, those who would be great must serve others.

ADVENTURER AWARDS

▶ **Journey**—A Journey Trailman is at the beginning of a high adventure trail, which is designed to develop your character and leadership skills. As you hike the journey on this Trail, Christ should be your Guide. He is the Way, the Truth, and the Life. The Bible tells us He is a lamp for our feet and a light for our path, which allows us to walk in the light He provides.

▶ **Horizon**—A Horizon Trailman helps younger boys with their skills, but he also seeks to help the Troop succeed by assisting Freedom candidates with their servant leadership projects. You'll not only be useful to the Troop, you'll also be learning valuable life lessons that will pay off time and again when you are a man. This award symbolizes your ability to see the Horizon and the final place of Freedom at the end of the trail.

▶ **Freedom**—After earning the Freedom Award, a Trailman is referred to as a "Freedom Rangeman." The Freedom Award is symbolic of both natural and spiritual freedom. As a young man who will soon turn eighteen and leave your home to start a full-time job or go to college, the clear trail that was set for you by your parents is now an open range. You are free to set a new course and create a trail for the next chapter of your life. As a Christian young man, you are also mature enough to understand your freedom in Christ—that you are free from the penalty, curse, and the law of sin and death.

Attaining the highest award in Trail Life USA requires a special service project that demonstrates the skills and ideals you learned in your Troop. It will be challenging, but you can rise to that challenge and help freedom ring in your town, your country, and your world.

TRAIL LIFE BASICS 33

If you want to know more about these ranks and achievements, keep reading and access resources like the Periodic Table of Advancements (page 320).

GO FOR FREEDOM!

The Freedom Award is the highest award given in Trail Life USA. The path to Freedom is one that will stretch you as a young man as you hone necessary skills, gain experience in using those skills, and garner leadership and service. Your faith will be tested as you grow in "the knowledge of his will in all spiritual wisdom and understanding"[1] and learn to Walk Worthy. If you can attain and integrate these assets in becoming a godly man, they will serve you well as you chart your own course across the open rangelands of Freedom. The adventurous trail to the Freedom Award looks very long if you've only taken a few steps. Yet, before you know it, your Trailman Standard will tell an exciting story of progress and experience. Fix your sights on the Freedom Award today!

THE FREEDOM AWARD™

The Freedom Award™ is the highest award in Trail Life USA and recognizes traits found in a Freedom Rangeman. This award is a visible reminder of the freedom received only because of the life, death, and resurrection of Jesus Christ.

---

[1] *Colossian 1:9*

Here is some of the symbolism in the design of the award:

(1) The "Trinity Peaks" stand above all that we do on earth or in eternity. The Father, Son, and Holy Ghost exist as eternal authority *(Matthew 28:19, 2 Corinthians 13:14)*.

(2) The "Sword of The Spirit" is one part of the armor of Christ used in our battle against the spiritual forces of evil *(Ephesians 6:10-18)*. The hilt reminds us of the cross through which Jesus Christ provided the only way to eternal freedom *(John 3:16)*.

(3) The "Shield of Faith" represents God's protection *(Ephesians 6:16)*. Likewise a Freedom Rangeman should be a protector of liberty, faith, family, and the weak. The "Red Field" shows the debt paid through the blood of Jesus Christ *(Ephesians 2:13, Revelation 12:11)*.

Around the shield, a "Blue Sea" represents the fellowship of believers united through Jesus Christ *(1 John 1:7, Ephesians 4:13, Psalm 133:1)*.

(4) The "Mighty Stag" is a bold symbol of maturity and represents the ability to stand strong in faith *(2 Samuel 22:34)*. A Freedom Rangeman's desire is to follow Christ *(Psalm 42:1)*.

(5) The "Crossed Keys" represent citizenship in the Kingdom of Heaven and the eternal freedom which Jesus unlocked through the cross *(Matthew 16:19, Romans 6:23)*.

(6) The "TL Key Ward" on the blade of the key is a reminder of the knowledge, understanding, and wisdom that a Freedom Rangeman will have gained from his time in the program *(Proverbs 2:6, Proverbs 3:21-22)* and the themes of the Woodlands Trail, Navigators, and Adventurers units. The Guidon unit theme is "Life."

(7) "Freedom" is the banner we display to a broken and hurting human race. We hold this up as our highest award so that this world can see the true freedom that can only come through Christ Jesus *(Romans 8:2, Romans 8:21, 2 Corinthians 3:17, Psalm 119:45)*.

CHAPTER 3

STRUCTURE

The Trail Life USA advancement program is distinct for many reasons. First and foremost, it is designed to honor biblical values in everything we do.

Trail Life USA is not just an outdoor program having a Christian experience. It is, at its core, a Christ-centered program that utilizes the outdoors to draw boys and their families closer to Jesus.

A Christian worldview is integrated into every part of the program because it is critical to both our mission and vision as well as to the spiritual growth of every Trailman who commits himself to the values we uphold.

As a maturing Trailman, you see the Branches from your experience on the Woodlands Trail become Frontiers as you continue along the trail. There are both Required and Elective Trail Badges on these Frontiers, and your Freedom Experiences will require that you put into practice the knowledge and skills learned through these Badges. All of these elements help you become the well-rounded man you desire to be.

The seven Frontiers provide both structure for advancement and personal growth objectives that will make you a better man—more like Jesus, Who is our example.

THE SEVEN FRONTIERS

Heritage Frontier

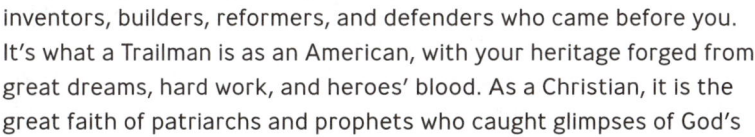

A Trailman's heritage can refer to practices or characteristics that are passed down from generation to generation. It's the head start you were given by the explorers, inventors, builders, reformers, and defenders who came before you. It's what a Trailman is as an American, with your heritage forged from great dreams, hard work, and heroes' blood. As a Christian, it is the great faith of patriarchs and prophets who caught glimpses of God's glory. In short, it is the combined influence of everything that came before you.

A study of your heritage should give you an appreciation of the opportunities your forefathers have given you, an awareness of how your heritage has shaped you, a commitment to remember its significance, and a resolve to avoid the mistakes others made.

Hobbies Frontier

Hobbies allow you to expand your horizons and put your main interests into perspective. Some hobbies have led people into careers that changed the world. Your hobbies may not become a career, but they can still play a significant role in who you are.

Hobbies can sharpen your mind, improve relationships, promote fitness, and relieve stress. They can send you on adventures, expand your knowledge of science and art, and teach you valuable skills.

As your experience grows, you may contribute part-time in a field that requires specialized knowledge, equipment, or preparation. These jobs may be as tame as helping with landscape maintenance at your church, as challenging as volunteer firefighting, or as technical as cinematography. Volunteerism is a great way to combine a hobby with service.

Life Skills Frontier

You will master at least four vital life skills on this Frontier.

First Aid training fosters a regard for the value of life and the reduction of suffering.

Emergency Preparedness equips you with rescue skills now because you won't have time to learn in the hour of greatest need.

Family Man emphasizes growth that prepares you to be a worthy husband and father who knows how to find fulfillment, maintain healthy relationships, and strengthen the image of your Creator God within you.

Personal Resources prepares you to be a good steward of your time, talents, presence, and finances.

Outdoor Skills Frontier

To place your feet on the crags and know their character of stone, to wade through the sea of prairie grass, or to find yourself lost in the murmur of a cold mountain stream are some of life's most memorable experiences. You can enjoy these adventures and share them with the friends you make in your Troop.

During your Frontier ventures, you may realize how the challenges and opportunities you face outdoors parallel your future life. A camp duty roster and an employee job description have much in common; so do feeding your patrol and providing for your family. As you master your outdoor skills and use them with the right attitude, you are preparing for success in your future roles of husband, father, and citizen.

Science and Technology Frontier

We travel, read, listen, and watch to learn. We also gather knowledge through scientific research. Some of what we learn allows us to do new things or to do old things better. We treat disease better, communicate better, calculate faster, and explore farther because of the dedicated work of scientists, inventors, and engineers.

Your Trail Life Troop Leaders understand that these changes shape the world you live in. They want you to understand these fields of study so you can be a part of that shaping process.

Science adds to mankind's knowledge through a carefully controlled process called the Scientific Method. Its strength is to build up a source of proven knowledge that can be relied upon. Its weakness is that it can only investigate what can be observed and tested by humanity. It cannot prove something does not exist; it can only prove something does exist if it can be directly or indirectly observed. The Scientific Method cannot make moral judgments or separate beauty from ugliness. It cannot tell you why things happen, only how they happen. In that sense, many of the greatest truths of our existence lie beyond its scope. We need both faith and science to gain even a rudimentary grasp of the wonders that exist around us and those that lie deep within us.

Technology is the use of knowledge to solve practical problems. Since it is built upon knowledge, great advances in technology usually follow great advances in science. Applied scientific knowledge is a powerful force, but it comes with great responsibility.

Sports and Fitness Frontier

The Sports and Fitness Frontier will expose you to opportunities to improve physical skills you possess as well as develop new ones.

Great confidence comes when we discover we can improve our personal fitness. We are spirit, soul, and body. Just as we can feed and strengthen our spirit through prayer and study of God's Word, and we can strengthen our mind through study, we can also strengthen our bodies through sports and fitness.

You'll be challenged to complete goals and to function as a team, to push yourself to do better, and to hone skills.

Values Frontier

Some would argue that the progress you'll make on the Values Frontier is the most important of all. And they may be right.

Your values shape you and give you the structural integrity both to stand strong in difficult times and to love people you may disagree with.

TRAIL LIFE
REQUIRED
TRAIL BADGES

NAVIGATOR REQUIRED TRAIL BADGES

AQUATICS
Outdoor Skills Frontier

Taking a swim on a hot summer day is one of life's great pleasures. Yet there is more to swimming than that—a lot more. Knowing how to stay afloat in water over your head and easily move from place to place makes you—and others around you—safer. It gives you the confidence to participate in water sports where you might end up "in the drink" before you realize what hit you. Think you might enjoy motor boating, water skiing, sailing, or rafting? Does canoeing, kayaking, or snorkeling appeal to you? Then make like an otter and learn to tread water.

Of course, you need to know what you're getting into. Is that water as deep as it looks? What dangerous obstacles may lurk beneath the surface? The difference between bravery and foolishness is avoiding unnecessary risks. A Trailman always follows the Safe Aquatics Method.

Being a swimmer opens the door to many exciting water sports such as rafting, canoeing, motor boating, water skiing, and kayaking.

Canoeing runs the gamut from a peaceful early-morning glide on the lake to a heart-racing trip through the rapids.

Sailing—especially if you sail far from shore—is not only exciting but also offers a historical link to many people who colonized America. Although your clothing and equipment may be modern, the feel of the sea beneath your boat and the unhurried rhythm of open water sailing is the same as that felt by traders, trappers, and pilgrims.

Some people enjoy the rush of a motorboat, whether they are sitting in a chair or standing on a pair of water skis. Like whitewater rafting or canoeing, raising a wake with a powerboat requires training and concentration.

ADVANCEMENT STRUCTURE

Trail Badges in these areas begin with passing the Trail Life USA Swimming Competency Test, so make up your mind to do so as soon as possible. Being comfortable in water over your head is one of the most important outdoor skills you can possess.

The Swimming Competency Test is located in the advancement tracking section (page 330).

CAMPING
Outdoor Skills Frontier

It's late. The call for lights out will come soon, so you move your folding camp chair from its place near the campfire and store it under the dining fly. The air turns chilly as the autumn stars come out. That's okay. You go into your tent, quickly shuck out of your uniform, get into your sleeping bag, and zip it up. The warmth returns, and all is comfortable again—like being in bed at home minus the traffic noises or the television downstairs. Instead, you hear the croaking of frogs, the preparations of your fellow campers,

> **Resolve to live simply and well by taking only the equipment and personal extras you actually need.**

and the soft rustle of grass beneath your tent floor as you roll onto your side. Life is good.

Camping is fun in general. It's a lot more fun when it's the result of proper equipment and good planning. The skills that helped you earn Ready Trailman rank are keeping you safe, happy, and comfortable.

FIRE RANGER
Outdoor Skills Frontier

The energy of the sun travels 93 million miles to earth. Trees take this light and store it chemically in the wood as they grow. In a sense, they bring the sun's flames to a fire ring, locked in the wood, waiting for a spark to help them give light and warmth again.

A campfire, properly prepared and supervised, will give you all the benefits fire provides without the destruction you want to avoid. You can use its warmth and light and prepare a hot meal, then retire its cool ashes to the soil for future use. There is one way a campfire can go right, and a dozen ways it can go wrong. As a responsible steward of God's creation, you want to enjoy fire without causing harm.

FIRST AID
Life Skills Frontier

You may give people presents on special occasions, such as birthdays or holidays. But the greatest gift you can give someone is life, and first-aid skills put that gift within your reach. First aid is not a substitute for professional medical care, but it can keep a victim alive, as comfortable as possible, and minimize permanent damage.

First aid is needed most at life's most unpleasant moments. The victim may be agitated and surrounded by upset people. It's easy to let your emotions run away with you too, but don't let that happen. Stay calm and encourage others to stay calm, then act decisively.

Remember that courage is not the absence of fear, it is putting fear on hold while you act. You can respond with courage and calmness. To ensure that you do, practice your first-aid skills often.

*See the First Aid section (page 199) for more detailed information.

OUR FLAG
Heritage Frontier

The United States flag is a symbol of our country, but it is also a uniquely beautiful picture of two ideals—things we value but cannot see or touch. It represents *liberty* and *justice*, which many people hoped for, worked for, sacrificed for, and even died for. Even as we struggle with how these ideals apply to us today, the sight of Old Glory streaming from the top of the flagpole reminds us that the struggle is worth winning.

The blue canon of the flag symbolizes a sky in which fifty stars shine in a constellation representing the fifty states (a constellation is a pattern of stars that seem to form a picture). The constellation on the American flag stands for a country where all states are equally important,

46 THE TRAILMAN'S HANDBOOK

so all the stars are the same size and are equally spaced.

By federal law, there is not one certain star that represents your state; the stars are to be viewed as a unit. Think of that the next time you recite the Pledge of Allegiance and say the words, "One nation under God, indivisible ..."

Even during the American Civil War when some states left the Union to form a separate Confederacy, the number of stars on the United States Flag was not reduced.

The thirteen stripes in red and white represent the thirteen original colonies whose residents fought Great Britain for their independence.

OUTDOOR COOKING
Outdoor Skills Frontier

Cooking is an important skill to master for long-term camping. A hot breakfast gives you a rousing start on a frosty winter morning. When you're tired after a long hike or a day of outdoor activity, you will have worked up a good appetite, and you need a good meal to satisfy it.

The ideal campsite meal may be quite different from the ideal backpack meal. If you are carting supplies a few yards from the van to your dining fly, you may enjoy a lot of extra gear. But when everything you eat and everything you use

to prepare it must be carried on your back, you'll develop a more sophisticated idea of what it means to "live simply and well." That's a lesson that has many more uses in life than planning a trail meal.

Also remember that this food, just like the glories of nature around you, was provided by our gracious heavenly Father. Always give thanks to God before you "dig in."

ROPEWORK
Outdoor Skills Frontier

Rope, properly used, is like a box of nails, a pot of glue, or a roll of tape—it can hold things together.

Unlike those other things, rope can be removed and reused many times. Rope is not merely a tool of sailors and campers. It is very versatile—suitable for everything from hanging a tire swing to rescuing stranded climbers. The better you learn to control it, the more indispensable it will become.

You exercise control over rope by learning knots and lashings.

Combine rope with wooden poles, and you unleash the ability to build everything from camp gadgets to towers, bridges, gateways, and rafts. The only limits are your imagination and, of course, common sense. Before you start stringing poles, learn how to brace structures and discover which lashings work best for each job.

TRAIL SKILLS
Outdoor Skills Frontier

There's a big difference between taking a walk and taking a trail. Walks tend to be informal activities. They don't require special clothing, equipment, or planning. Trails are more purposeful and benefit from proper equipment, attire, and preparation. So why take a trail instead of a walk? You'll see and hear things on a trail that you'll never experience on a leisurely stroll. You can reach a higher level of fitness so your body will be a suitable partner for your mind.

Several categories of trails are available in the Trail Life: Backpacking, Camping, Cycling, Paddling Craft, and Sailing.

WOODS TOOLS
Outdoor Skills Frontier

Some folks think food comes from a grocery store. These same folks think wood comes from a hardware store. Nothing could be further from the truth. Turning natural wood into fuel for a fire, camp gadgets, or even a worthwhile shelter gives you a broader perspective on our wonderful world and your place in it.

Of course, tools that can carve cured wood can easily carve people. Just as you want to control fire to avoid danger, you'll want to control woods tools for the same reason. That means knowing how to keep them in good working order and how to protect yourself and other people from injury.

Whether or Not to Use Tools

You *should* use woods tools to gain experience, practice safety, and participate in Troop activities. You may use woods tools to collect resources where permitted, such as cutting dead wood for fires or constructing an emergency shelter. You should not use woods tools to

deface public property, trees, or other natural objects; neither should you treat woods tools as toys, especially in reckless play with others.

Certain woods tools may only be used under proper supervision or in a special area, such as splitting firewood in a marked axe yard. Other tools, such as chainsaws, are restricted to adult use by the Trail Life USA Health and Safety Guide.

ADVENTURER
REQUIRED
TRAIL BADGES

CITIZENSHIP
Heritage Frontier

You belong to several different families. Just like your blood relatives, your community, national, and global families give you certain rights and expect you to fulfill certain responsibilities in return. The name for these rights and responsibilities is citizenship.

Past, Present, and Future

As a Trailman, you want to appreciate your rights and uphold your responsibilities. Citizenship is the art of living in the past, the present, and the future all at once. Yes, your past (heritage) is with you today and helps make you who and what you are. Your present (opportunity) is also close at hand as you make a difference for good using the options and resources you have today. Of course, as you pursue present opportunities, you also look to the future (vision) with your dreams and goals for yourself and the world around you.

The Highest Citizenship

While you seek to be a good citizen of your family, town, country, and world, you should also seek to be a child of God and a citizen of His Kingdom. We have earthly citizenship that relates to our nationality, but from there you must choose one of many paths that split off in different directions.

Some people believe all paths are equal, but only one leads to Jesus Christ and the joy and life He intends you to have. When you come face to face with God, it will not be as an American but as a man, and your record must speak for itself without any constitutional protections or Supreme Court rulings. Resolve today—this very minute—to walk worthy and live a life that speaks well of you as a man. If you do, you'll automatically be a great American.

> Resolve today—this very minute—to walk worthy and live a life that speaks well of you as a man.

Being a good citizen of God's Kingdom takes a lifetime to master, but that's exactly what you have—a lifetime. And you have your Troop and church friends encouraging you at every step.

CYCLING
Sports and Fitness Frontier

A bicycle opens new worlds of freedom, responsibility, and adventure. What begins as a ride around the corner to see a friend can turn into an enjoyable sport, a lifelong hobby, and a great form of exercise. Competitive cyclists can be found on BMX courses and mountain bike trails; they also race at breakneck speeds in pelotons around the world. (You may have seen a peloton—a pack of cyclists drafting off each other while cycling in tight formation on a road.) Even if you never go beyond jumping obstacles with your bike in the backyard or racing your friend to the end of your street, learning to ride a bike safely and efficiently is a lifelong skill that allows you to discover your surroundings, exercise almost every muscle in your body, improve balance, and develop friendships.

This is a Fitness badge. Fitness badges help you increase your fitness over time. They are progressive in nature, meaning they get more difficult as you improve. Only one of the four Fitness badges listed in this section is required (Cycling, Fitness, Hiking, or Swimming).

EMERGENCY PREPAREDNESS
Life Skills Frontier

Most of the time, emergencies are unexpected. Surviving and sustaining yourself and your family through various emergencies comes down to anticipating them and knowing what to do when they occur.

The time to prepare for emergencies is before they happen. Having access to supplies, training, and practice will equip you to effectively protect life and property. The work you do now will limit the damage of large disasters, and it may help prevent some disasters from occurring.

FAMILY MAN
Life Skills Frontier

Leading a family and being responsible for their safety, comfort, and happiness is challenging. Many of the skills you learn in your Troop, many of the chores you do around your home, many of the sermons you hear in church, and many of the facts you learn in school are designed to prepare you for future success as a man, a husband, and a father.

Achieving personal goals is admirable, yet the ability to extend your success to benefit people who love you and depend on you is even more rewarding.

FITNESS
Sports and Fitness Frontier

In a sense, every Trailman wears two uniforms. The one on the outside can be cleaned when it's soiled or replaced when it no longer serves you well. The one on the inside is the uniform God gave you (your body) to carry you through life. When this uniform gets damaged, it might heal, but it is far better to take good care of it in the first place so you can keep it attractive and get years of faithful service from it.

There are four types of fitness. *Physical fitness* is good stewardship of your body so you can do more things safely and comfortably and also enjoy a longer lifespan and more years of independence. *Moral fitness* is the ability to make decisions that may be difficult, when what you want and what you need conflict or when you run the risk of being unpopular. *Mental fitness* is about getting an education, developing your powers of reason, and learning from your mistakes. *Emotional fitness* does not mean being happy all the time. Rather, it is the ability to adapt to changing circumstances and to navigate the challenges of forming and maintaining relationships. All four types of fitness—mental, moral, physical, and emotional—benefit from a good diet, plenty of exercise, and getting enough rest.

This is a Fitness badge. Fitness badges help you increase your fitness over time. They are progressive in nature, meaning they get more difficult as you improve. Only one of the four Fitness badges listed in this section is required (Cycling, Fitness, Hiking, or Swimming).

HIKING
Sports and Fitness Frontier

Some forms of travel are nothing but moving from place to place. When you get out of a vehicle and put boots on the ground, you connect to your surroundings each step of the journey through a thousand sights, sounds, and smells. Unlike the motorist whizzing by, you are not just *on* the landscape; you are *in* it. You are a part of what is happening. If something catches your eye, you can pause to take a closer look. Hiking is most enjoyable when you have the right equipment, possess the right skills, and keep yourself in good shape.

Some people think they won't like hiking, and there is usually a story behind that. Perhaps you are one of those people. If you have had a bad experience hitting the trail, having a good experience will put it into perspective. Following the Hiker's Code (page 315) will help your next hiking experience be a good one.

This is a Fitness badge. Fitness badges help you increase your fitness over time. They are progressive in nature, meaning they get more difficult as you improve. Only one of the four Fitness badges listed in this section is required (Cycling, Fitness, Hiking, or Swimming).

OUTDOOR LIFE
Outdoor Skills Frontier

God made nature and said it was good. He ought to know. Humans made cities, and while they are fine in their own way, they simply can't match the level of artistry and skill you see in a simple forest glade or on a windswept prairie. Many lessons about yourself and the world can only be learned as you get back in touch with the order and pattern of nature.

As a Trailman, you will make some of your best memories in God's great outdoors. Nature is your birthright, but it is equally the birthright of your children and your children's children. Every tree, every flower, and every unspoiled view you enjoy exists because the person who came before you did not ruin it. Decide right now to keep it unspoiled for the person who comes along after you. Many people suggest that the only things that you "take with you" are pictures and memories and the only things you leave behind are footprints.

PERSONAL RESOURCES
Life Skills Frontier

Leading your life is a lot like leading a patrol. On payday you must be treasurer; at the store, you become quartermaster. When faced with temptation, you maintain discipline, and when you have things to learn you use the same skills you used to lead your patrol.

Economic Stewardship

Managing a budget is like fishing from a leaking canoe. The water coming in represents expenses. You also have a bucket, which represents income. By spending some time bailing out the canoe, you keep the water on the floorboards at an acceptable depth. Spend too much time fishing and not enough time bailing, and the water will get deeper until the canoe finally sinks.

Economic stewardship is the management of income and expenses to meet personal goals. Those goals should include payment of just debts, maintaining room and board, and keeping the tools you use to earn your living (equipment and education) in top shape. When you become a family man or buy a house, you will add more financial obligations that are equally important.

SWIMMING
Sports and Fitness Frontier

We speak of swimming skills, but what we really mean is the ability to breathe while we're in the water. To move safely and effectively through water without struggling for each breath turns lakes, rivers, and seas from obstacles into opportunities for fun and adventure. Fortunately, your body weighs a bit less than the same amount of water, which enables you to float. With a little practice, you can join the fun with confidence.

This is a Fitness badge. Fitness badges help you increase your fitness over time. They are progressive in nature, meaning they get more difficult as you improve. Only one of the four Fitness badges listed in this section is required (Cycling, Fitness, Hiking, or Swimming).

ELECTIVE BADGES

PUBLISHED ELECTIVES

While the required Trail Badges give you a foundation of knowledge and skills to help you navigate the frontiers of life, the Elective Badges strengthen your knowledge and skills, help round out your experience, and deepen your expertise with topics that have personal appeal.

Published Elective Trail Badges can be downloaded for personal use by the registered Trail Life USA member/owner of this Handbook, but they are copyrighted and may not be reproduced or shared outside of Trail Life USA.

The following list of Trail Badges is not exhaustive; rather, it is an example of the various types of offerings that are currently published.

- Backpacking
- Bible Basics
- Canoeing
- Computing
- Engineering Mechanics
- Fishing
- Genealogy
- Model Rocketry
- Martial Arts
- Respect Life
- Robotics
- Survival Skills
- Vehicle Care

DESIGN YOUR OWN BADGE

In addition to choosing published Elective Trail Badges you, as a Navigator or Adventurer Trailman, can choose an area of study that interests you and work with a Trail Badge Mentor and the Advancement Coordinator in your Troop to design and complete your own Elective Trail Badge.

Part of earning the badge is designing the steps to complete it, so this method is not intended as a way for Adult Leaders to introduce group badges of

ADVANCEMENT STRUCTURE 57

their own design; rather, it is an educational option for self-directed investigation in an area of individual interest to a youth Trailman. Trail Life USA has developed three methods a Trailman can use to design his own Elective Trail Badge. These methods are detailed on page 322.

T.E.A.M. METHOD (TROOP EXPERIENCE, ACTIVITY, AND MENTORING)

(For use by Troop Leaders only.)

Perhaps your patrol, unit, or any group of Trailmen will want to work together to earn a Trail Badge that does not currently exist.

Troop Experience, Activity, and Mentoring (TEAM) guidelines allow Navigator and Adventurer leaders to develop a badge for their Troop or Patrol for a group activity in which multiple Trailmen participate.

TEAM Elective Trail Badges align with the Mission, Vision, and Oath. They should include a group experience, activity, or mentoring by an adult leader and require a minimum of eight hours of effort. They should focus on hands-on experiences, and they should be fun and experimental. The full requirements and guidelines for your Troop Leaders can be found online and in the Navigators and Adventurers Leader's Guide.

RANKS, AWARDS, AND WORTHY LIFE

NAVIGATOR RANKS

Your first achievements as a Navigator Trailman will be earning the skill ranks of Recruit Trailman, Able Trailman, and Ready Trailman. These ranks recognize your growing ability to get along safely and comfortably in the outdoors and to contribute to the success of your fellow Trailmen, your Troop, and its activities.

Recruit Rank

This is the joining rank that concentrates on being safe and learning how to plug in to all the resources available to you in your Troop. You will attend your first hikes and campouts and make new friends in your Troop.

Able Trailman Rank

This rank concentrates on being comfortable in the outdoors and building on your knowledge and understanding of outdoor skills. You will learn about camping, nature, service, and working together in a patrol.

Ready Trailman Rank

This rank concentrates on helping you become a useful Trailman around camp. A Ready Trailman has mastered many outdoor skills. You'll continue to hone your skills and service as you focus on leadership and faith. A successful Trailman is expected to have a positive, can-do attitude. Working diligently as a Ready Trailman will help you develop that attitude.

ADVENTURER AWARDS

If you were involved as a Navigator, you've probably earned the rank of Ready Trailman and have proved yourself to be an all-around Trailman. Now you are ready to grow beyond the basics and tap into your wellspring of potential. You will do this as a member of an Adventurers Unit.

Adventurers is an advanced program that sets you apart as an older, more skilled member of the Troop. The program offers you more freedom to set and achieve your own goals and to chart your own adventures.

Adventurer Trailmen do not need to earn additional skill ranks because they have already demonstrated their ability as a Trailman. Now they earn awards for personal growth. The trail to the peak pauses briefly at the Journey Award and the Horizon Award, then leads to the highest achievement you can reach in Trail Life USA—the Freedom Award. The Freedom Award will follow you through life as a badge of honor.

The Journey Award

This is the joining award for the Adventurers Program. It is awarded to Navigators who bridge over to the Adventurers program or boys who join in high school. This is the beginning of the transition period to manhood, active citizenry, and mastering leadership.

The Horizon Award

The Horizon Trailman completes the required body of knowledge encompassed in the Trail Badge program as his focus changes from knowledge to higher-level understanding and the acquisition of wisdom as he reaches new horizons of adventure and personal growth.

> The trail to the peak pauses briefly at the *Journey Award* and the *Horizon Award* and leads to the highest achievement you can reach in Trail Life USA—the *Freedom Award*.

The Freedom Award

The Freedom Award is the highest recognition on the Adventurers Trail. The program's focus moves to Christian manhood with the Worthy Life Award, Freedom Experiences, and the Servant Leadership Project. It is our hope that Trailmen will grow in their Christian walk and experience eternal freedom in Jesus Christ along their Trail to the Freedom Award.

When you earn the award, you become a Freedom Rangeman—one who understands that God's plan for us includes certain freedoms but also entails great responsibility.

THE ADVENTURERS EXPERIENCE

Your Adventurers patrol is headed by an adult called the Advisor, who is assisted by one or more Trail Guides. Youth leaders occupy the offices of First Officer, Second Officer, Quartermaster, and Patrol Leader. You will have unprecedented control over the experience, and what you learn by participating in planning and carrying out your program will benefit you as you enter the job world. You will learn things about yourself as a leader that you might not have the opportunity to learn in many other settings.

Your Relationship to Navigators

As the most experienced youth in the Troop, the guidance and example of dedicated Adventurers is vital to the development of younger boys. Adults can be great role models, but you are the immediate model the younger Trailmen follow. You are not just working on your own advancement; you are indirectly working on theirs. Do the best job you can.

You will have a pivotal role in setting the monthly program of activities for the Troop. When the program comes together and everyone has a good time and learns something, you'll experience a first-rate feeling of accomplishment.

WORTHY LIFE

Adventure in Christ

Trail Life is an adventure from the start— deciding to go where few go in pursuit of something few attain. It is a life of discovery of all the amazing attributes of God as seen in creation through outdoor adventure. And it is experiencing personally the character of God as we pursue godliness in becoming true, noble Trailmen. Trail Life is not the easy, slowly winding, gently sloped downhill road that many travel. We aim for the peaks on "the narrow way that leads to life ... and few find it" *(Matthew 7:13–14)*.

Adventure in Christ and the pursuit of faith are blended into the Trail Life program in all facets, like sugar in sweet tea or carrot in carrot cake. Our purpose is to help Trailman learn by exposure, exploration, and experience to "walk in a manner worthy of our Lord" (Colossians 1:10). This integrated, experience-based, mentored godliness adventure training is what we call the Worthy Life.

Trail Life USA Spiritual Emphasis

Worthy Life is the Trail Life USA Faith Building Program. It focuses on the important spiritual ideals and truths identified in the Trail Life USA guiding principles including our Statement of Faith, Statement of Values, Vision, Mission, Motto, Oath, and Core Values. Pursuing these ideals develops godly character, spiritual leadership, and an appetite for the faith adventure. These principles and practices of duty and devotion provide age-appropriate challenges and responsibility that work alongside the core Trail Life program. What better way to grow integrity and manly Christian character than to learn and experience spiritual truths within the Trail Life experience-based patrol method? From Fox to Freedom Rangeman, the Worthy Life spiritual emphasis is aimed at training and guiding Trailmen to live as *godly husbands, fathers, and citizens* by first becoming *courageous young men who honor God, lead with integrity, serve others, and experience outdoor adventure.*

Worthy Life Award

Advancement along the path of Worthy Life can include Values Frontier Trail Badges that enforce the kind of values a Trailman needs, religious recognition opportunities, specialty partner ministry programs like Manhood Journey, boy-led discipleship like the Trail Life Band of Brothers program, and other opportunities your church provides.

The Worthy Life Award completes spiritual emphasis requirements for earning the Timberline, Ready Trailman rank, and the Freedom Award as a demonstration of the four marks of godly manhood: *to live responsibly, to live boldly and avoid being passive, to lead courageously, and to live for the greater rewards of God.*

The Worthy Life spiritual award can be earned at each level of the Trail Life program to symbolize that a Trailman is learning how to Walk Worthy!

CHAPTER 4

HOW A TRAILMAN ADVANCES

In the very design of you, God made you to be productive. You were built to achieve.

The Trail Life USA Program is designed to challenge you and award you for your achievements.

Advancement in the Trail Life USA Navigator and Adventurer programs is true progress. You won't find "participation trophies" here, only actual challenges and requirements that will help you grow.

As you progress along the Trail as a Navigator and Adventurer, this chapter will be the preferred place for recording your Advancement Records. While the adult Troop Leaders will walk with you as you advance through Badges, Ranks, and Awards, YOU are responsible for tracking and recording your achievements. It is also YOUR responsibility as a young man who is maturing to know and understand all of the requirements for each Rank and Award. Certain Ranks and Awards will require just an Advancement Conference with your Trailmaster or Advisor, Troopmaster, and Trail Guide while others will require both an Advancement Conference and/or a full Board of Review.

ADVANCEMENT CONFERENCES

Advancement Conferences are to be held with you (the Trailman) and at least one of the three following leaders: Trailmaster or Adventurer Advisor, Trail Guide, and Troopmaster. For accountability, a second leader is required for Advancement Conferences if one of the leaders is a realtive. The purpose of the Advancement Conference is to discuss with your Troop leader(s) your progress, morale, ambitions, questions, and suggestions about Trail Life USA as well as to review all of your work and service to ensure that each requirement has met the standards of Trail Life USA to the satisfaction of your Troop Leadership.

BOARDS OF REVIEW

Boards of Review are organized and staffed by at least three of your Troop's leadership. None of the Board of Review members should be a relative of yours. The purpose of the Board of Review is to allow the Troop leaders to interview you, examine your growth and character based on your achievements, and to perform a final evaluation for your Ranks and Awards.

Special Freedom Award Advancement Conference

Freedom Award Advancement Conference is the most crucial step along your trail to Freedom. This special conference is where your Adventurer Advisor and Troopmaster will examine in detail all of your work toward Freedom to ensure that all of the requirements were met in the correct order and timing. Note that one of the two leaders must be someone other than your relative. It is imperative that you are fully prepared and equipped to explain how and when you have completed the requirements for the Freedom Award.

Special Freedom Award Board of Review

The Freedom Award Board of Review is unique and different in that your Troop's Area Leadership will be involved in chairing this board. None of the Board of Review members should be a relative of yours. The purpose of this Board of Review is for the Area leadership along with your Troop's leadership to extensively interview you concerning your work throughout your time in Trail Life, thoroughly examine your spiritual and maturity growth, as well as recommend or not recommend you for the Final National Review for Freedom.

HOW TO TRACK YOUR PROGRESS USING THIS HANDBOOK:

In this chapter you will find the requirements for each Required Trail Badge and the Worthy Life Award. On each Rank, Award, and Badge requirement page, you can record and date your progress as you complete the various requirements for each. Directly behind the requirement pages, you will find the official Tracking charts where your Trail Badge Mentors and Troop Leaders will sign and date for pre-approvals, service hours, activities, Trail Badges, Advancement Conferences, Boards of Review, Ranks, and Awards.

NAVIGATOR RANKS & WORTHY LIFE AWARD REQUIREMENTS

RECRUIT TRAILMAN

Joining Requirements

Complete the following:

TRADITIONS:

- [ ] Memorize and agree to live by the Trailman Oath. (Page 26)
- [ ] Memorize the Trailman Motto. (Page 27)
- [ ] Demonstrate the Trailman sign and describe when to use it. (Page 25)
- [ ] Demonstrate the Trailman salute and describe when to use it. (Page 25)
- [ ] Demonstrate the Trailman handshake. (Page 25)
- [ ] Give your Patrol Leader's name, patrol name, and patrol yell.

CITIZENSHIP:

- [ ] Memorize the Pledge of Allegiance. (Page 24)
- [ ] Demonstrate properly folding the American flag. (Page 334)

ADVANCEMENT CONFERENCE:

- [ ] Discuss Troop safety. (See Troop Safety 101, on page 328 in the appendix)
- [ ] Discuss advancement program. (See Advancement 101, on page 318 in the appendix)

Have your Trailmaster, Trail Guide, or Troopmaster sign and date the Recruit Rank Advancement Conference Signature Page on page 69.

RECRUIT TRAILMAN RANK

Advancement Conference Signature Page

I (We) affirm that this Trailman has completed all of the requirements to earn the Rank of Recruit Trailman (page 68) and that at least one of the leaders listed below is someone other than the Trailman's relative.

DATE COMPLETED _____

Signature ☐ TRAIL GUIDE ☐ TRAILMASTER ☐ TROOPMASTER

Optional Signature ☐ TRAIL GUIDE ☐ TRAILMASTER ☐ TROOPMASTER

ABLE TRAILMAN RANK

Prerequisite: **Earn the Recruit Trailman Rank.**

TRAIL BADGE WORK:

☐ Complete any four of the nine Trail Badges required for the Ready Trailman Rank: Aquatics, Camping, Fire Ranger, First Aid, Our Flag, Outdoor Cooking, Ropework, Trail Skills, and Woods Tools.

☐ Earn an additional three Trail Badges of your choice. (Choose from the remaining required for Ready Trailman, published Elective Trail Badges, or Design Your Own Badges.) *(Note: The Horizon Required Trail Badges cannot be earned in the Navigators program)* Record these on the badge completion chart on page 71 and have each one signed by your mentor.

SERVANT SERVICE:

☐ Complete 15 hours of service for each year since joining Navigators. Record your hours on the service chart in this handbook (page 72) and have them verified by an adult.

TROOP INVOLVEMENT:

☐ Maintain a level of Troop meeting attendance acceptable to your Trailmaster (typically 60% or better).

☐ Participate in at least 8 Troop activities since becoming a Navigator, not including regular meetings. Record each activity (trips, camp, community outings, etc.) on the activity chart in this handbook (page 73) and have each one verified by an adult.

MARK YOUR PROGRESS:

☐ Successfully complete an Advancement Conference.

☐ Successfully complete a Board of Review.

Have your Trailmaster, Trail Guide, Troopmaster, and Board of Review Members sign and date the Able Trailman Rank Advancement Conference and Board of Review Signature Pages on pages 74 –75.

ABLE TRAILMAN RANK

Trail Badge Completion Chart

4 Required and 3 Electives needed for Able Trailman Rank

Required Badges	Date Completed	Trail Badge Mentor Signature
Aq (AQUATICS)		
Cp (CAMPING)		
Fr (FIRE RANGER)		
Fa (FIRST AID)		
Of (OUR FLAG)		
Oc (OUTDOOR COOKING)		
Rw (ROPEWORK)		
Ts (TRAIL SKILLS)		
Wt (WOODS TOOLS)		
Elective Badges (Write in name of Elective Badge selected)	Date Completed	Trail Badge Mentor Signature
El (ELECTIVE)		
El (ELECTIVE)		
El (ELECTIVE)		
El (ELECTIVE)		
El (ELECTIVE)		

ABLE TRAILMAN RANK

Servant Service Tracking Chart

15 Hours are needed each year for Able Trailman Rank

Service Type	Date	Hours	Running Total Hours	Year 1, Year 2, Year 3, (Circle corresponding year)	Verified by
				Y1 Y2 Y3	
				Y1 Y2 Y3	
				Y1 Y2 Y3	
				Y1 Y2 Y3	
				Y1 Y2 Y3	
				Y1 Y2 Y3	
				Y1 Y2 Y3	
				Y1 Y2 Y3	
				Y1 Y2 Y3	
				Y1 Y2 Y3	
				Y1 Y2 Y3	
				Y1 Y2 Y3	
				Y1 Y2 Y3	
				Y1 Y2 Y3	
				Y1 Y2 Y3	

ABLE TRAILMAN RANK

Troop Activities Tracking Chart

8 Activities are needed for Able Trailman Rank

Troop Activities	Date from	Date to	Camping Nights	Verified by

ABLE TRAILMAN RANK

Advancement Conference Signature Page

I (We) affirm that this Trailman has completed all of the requirements to earn the Rank of Able Trailman (pages 70 - 73) and that at least one of the two leaders listed below is someone other than the Trailman's relative.

DATE COMPLETED _____

Signature _____
☐ TRAIL GUIDE ☐ TRAILMASTER ☐ TROOPMASTER

Optional Signature _____
☐ TRAIL GUIDE ☐ TRAILMASTER ☐ TROOPMASTER

ABLE TRAILMAN RANK

Board of Review Signature Page

We affirm that this Trailman has completed all of the requirements to earn the Rank of Able Trailman and that none of the leaders listed below are the Trailman's relative.

DATE COMPLETED _____

Signature _____ POSITION

Signature _____ POSITION

Signature _____ POSITION

Optional Signature _____ POSITION

Optional Signature _____ POSITION

Optional Signature _____ POSITION

READY TRAILMAN RANK

Prerequisite: **Earn the Able Trailman Rank.**

TRAIL BADGE WORK:

☐ Complete the nine required Trail Badges: Aquatics, Camping, Fire Ranger, First Aid, Our Flag, Outdoor Cooking, Ropework, Trail Skills, and Woods Tools.

☐ Earn a total of at least five elective Trail Badges of your choice (published Elective Trail Badges or Design Your Own Badge) since joining as a Navigator. *(Note: The Horizon Required Trail Badges cannot be earned in the Navigators program)*
Record these on the badge completion chart on page 78 and have each one signed by your mentor.

SERVANT SERVICE:

☐ Complete 15 hours of service for each year as a Navigator. Record your hours on the service chart in this handbook (page 79) and have them verified by an adult.

TROOP INVOLVEMENT:

☐ Maintain a level of Troop meeting attendance acceptable to your Trailmaster (typically 60% or better).

☐ Participate in at least 16 Troop activities since becoming a Navigator, not including regular meetings. Record each activity (trips, camp, community outings, etc.) on the activity chart in this handbook (page 80) and have each one verified by an adult.

LEADERSHIP:

Since earning the Able Trailman Rank, complete one of the following leadership options:

☐ Serve as a Junior Patrol Leader for a minimum of six months. Record this on page 81 and have it verified by a leader.

☐ At five Troop meetings or outings, demonstrate your leadership ability by planning and instructing Recruit or Able Trailmen in significant Ready Trailmen required Trail Badge skills approved by your Trailmaster or Trail Guide. Record these on page 81 and have them verified by a leader.

☐ At five Troop meetings or outings, demonstrate your leadership ability by planning and instructing a Woodlands Trail group in significant skills approved by your Trailmaster or Trail Guide and the Woodlands Trail Ranger. Record these on page 81 and have them verified by a leader.

WORTHY LIFE AWARD:

☐ Complete the Navigators Worthy Life Award. (Requirements and Signature Pages on pages 84 through 90)

MARK YOUR PROGRESS:

☐ Successfully complete an Advancement Conference.

☐ Successfully complete a Board of Review.

Have your Trailmaster, Trail Guide, Troopmaster, and Board of Review Members sign and date the Ready Trailman Rank Advancement Conference and Board of Review Signature Page on pages 82 and 83.

READY TRAILMAN RANK

Trail Badge Completion Chart

9 Required and 5 Electives needed for Ready Trailman Rank

Required Badges	Check here if rolled over from Able Rank	Date Completed	Trail Badge Mentor Signature
Aq (AQUATICS)			
Cp (CAMPING)			
Fr (FIRE RANGER)			
Fa (FIRST AID)			
Of (OUR FLAG)			
Oc (OUTDOOR COOKING)			
Rw (ROPEWORK)			
Ts (TRAIL SKILLS)			
Wt (WOODS TOOLS)			
Elective Badges (Write in name of Elective Badge selected)	Check here if rolled over from Able Rank	Date Completed	Trail Badge Mentor Signature
El (ELECTIVE)			
El (ELECTIVE)			
El (ELECTIVE)			
El (ELECTIVE)			
El (ELECTIVE)			

READY TRAILMAN RANK

Servant Service Tracking Chart

15 Hours are needed each year for Ready Trailman Rank

Service Type	Date	Hours	Running Total Hours	Year 1, Year 2, Year 3, (Circle corresponding year)	Verified by
				Y1 Y2 Y3	
				Y1 Y2 Y3	
				Y1 Y2 Y3	
				Y1 Y2 Y3	
				Y1 Y2 Y3	
				Y1 Y2 Y3	
				Y1 Y2 Y3	
				Y1 Y2 Y3	
				Y1 Y2 Y3	
				Y1 Y2 Y3	
				Y1 Y2 Y3	
				Y1 Y2 Y3	
				Y1 Y2 Y3	
				Y1 Y2 Y3	
				Y1 Y2 Y3	

HOW A TRAILMAN ADVANCES

READY TRAILMAN RANK

Troop Activities Tracking Chart

16 Activities are needed for Ready Trailman Rank

Troop Activities	Date from	Date to	Camping Nights	Verified by
Eight Activities Rolled over from Able Rank	NA	NA	NA	

READY TRAILMAN RANK

Leadership Skills Demonstration Tracking Chart

Choose your Leadership option for the Ready Trailman Rank

Leadership Option	Date	Approved by	Verified by
Serve as a Junior Patrol Leader for six months	Date from Date to	NA	
Plan and instruct skills for ☐ Woodlands Trail or ☐ Recruit or Able Trailmen			
Event 1			
Event 2			
Event 3			
Event 4			
Event 5			

READY TRAILMAN RANK

Advancement Conference Signature Page

I (We) affirm that this Trailman has completed all of the requirements to earn the Rank of Ready Trailman and that at least one of the two leaders listed below is someone other than the Trailman's relative.

DATE COMPLETED _____

Signature ☐ TRAIL GUIDE ☐ TRAILMASTER ☐ TROOPMASTER

Optional Signature ☐ TRAIL GUIDE ☐ TRAILMASTER ☐ TROOPMASTER

READY TRAILMAN RANK

Board of Review Signature Page

We affirm that this Trailman has completed all of the requirements to earn the Rank of Ready Trailman and that none of the leaders listed below are the Trailman's relative.

DATE COMPLETED _____

Signature _____ POSITION

Signature _____ POSITION

Signature _____ POSITION

Optional Signature _____ POSITION

Optional Signature _____ POSITION

Optional Signature _____ POSITION

HOW A TRAILMAN ADVANCES

NAVIGATORS WORTHY LIFE AWARD

Before beginning any work on the Worthy Life Award, meet with your Trailmaster, Troop Chaplain, and mentor (approved by your parent or guardian) to create and document in your Handbook measurable goals, tasks, and reporting expectations before beginning any requirement (page 86). The Trailmaster, Troop Chaplain, and mentor must pre-approve, sign for completion, and date each activity. *No one-on-one, Two-deep,* and *Buddy System of Three* Youth Protection guidelines must be followed at all meetings with your mentor or leader(s) *(See page 328).*

Pre-Approval	REQUIREMENT	Completed
✓	**1 DEVOTIONAL ACTIVITY** *Complete one (1) of the following activities and discuss it with your mentor:*	✓
	☐ An age-appropriate Bible study program[1] consisting of at least ten (10) one-hour sessions.	
	☐ One Elective Trail Badge from the Values Frontier.	
	☐ At least three (3) modules of the Manhood Journey program[2] with your father or other male mentor.	
✓	**2 DISCIPLESHIP ACTIVITY** *Complete one (1) of the following activities and discuss it with your mentor:*	✓
	☐ Read a Christian book.[3]	
	☐ Participate in a Christian weekend retreat or mission trip.	

Pre-Approval		REQUIREMENT	Completed
	☐	Complete a service project using the Biblical principles or skills developed during your Devotional Activity.	
✓	**3**	**DISCIPLINES ACTIVITIES** *Complete three (3) of the following activities during your Devotional and Discipleship Activities:*	✓
	☐	Keep a Bible study journal of questions, principles, and thoughts.	
	☐	Memorize and recite scriptures, prayers, hymns, creeds, or catechisms.	
	☐	Keep a prayer journal.	
	☐	Regularly attend services/mass at your local church.	
	☐	Volunteer to serve with your local church/parish on an ongoing basis.	
✓	**4**	**DEMONSTRATION ACTIVITY**	✓
	☐	Complete a final conference with your Trailmaster, Troop Chaplain, and mentor, explaining what you have experienced and learned and how you have achieved your pre-determined goals, tasks, and expectations.	

[1] Any Bible Study Program should be in agreement with your Charter Organization's Faith Tradition. This may include Christian Religious Recognition Programs.
[2] Ask your leader for more information on the Manhood Journey program.
[3] Possible topics include: Biblical manhood, prayer, humility, grace, missions, fruits of the Spirit, true and false conversions, sacraments, biographies of important church leaders, etc.

NAVIGATORS WORTHY LIFE AWARD

Goals / Tasks / Reporting Expectations

Before you begin any work towards your Worthy Life Award, work with your Adventurer Advisor, Troop Chaplain, and Mentor to create and document here measurable goals, tasks, and reporting expectations for the Worthy Life Award.

Goals	Tasks	Reporting Expectations

DATE: _____

Signature **TRAILMAN** _____   *(Recorded before beginning)*

We have agreed upon, with this Trailman, the goals, tasks, and reporting expectations for his Worthy Life Award and that at least one of the leaders listed below is someone other than the Trailman's relative.

DATE *(Recorded before beginning)* _____

Signature **TROOP CHAPLAIN** _____

Signature **TRAILMASTER** _____

Signature **MENTOR** _____

NAVIGATORS WORTHY LIFE AWARD

Devotional Activity

We give our Pre-Approval to this Trailman for his selection of his Devotional Activity.

DATE PRE-APPROVED _____

Signature **TROOP CHAPLAIN** _____

Signature **TRAILMASTER** _____

Signature **MENTOR** _____

We give our Post-Completion approval to this Trailman for his completion of his Devotional Activity for the Worthy Life Award.

DATE COMPLETED _____

Signature **TROOP CHAPLAIN** _____

Signature **TRAILMASTER** _____

Signature **MENTOR** _____

NAVIGATORS WORTHY LIFE AWARD

Discipleship Activity

We give our Pre-Approval to this Trailman for his selection of his Discipleship Activity.

DATE PRE-APPROVED _____

Signature **TROOP CHAPLAIN** _____

Signature **TRAILMASTER** _____

Signature **MENTOR** _____

We give our Post-Completion approval to this Trailman for his completion of his Discipleship Activity for the Worthy Life Award.

DATE COMPLETED _____

Signature **TROOP CHAPLAIN** _____

Signature **TRAILMASTER** _____

Signature **MENTOR** _____

NAVIGATORS WORTHY LIFE AWARD

Disciplines Activities

We give our Pre-Approval to this Trailman for his selection of his Discipline Activities.

DATE PRE-APPROVED _____

Signature **TROOP CHAPLAIN** _____

Signature **TRAILMASTER** _____

Signature **MENTOR** _____

We give our Post-Completion approval to this Trailman for his completion of his Discipline Activities for the Worthy Life Award.

DATE COMPLETED _____

Signature **TROOP CHAPLAIN** _____

Signature **TRAILMASTER** _____

Signature **MENTOR** _____

NAVIGATORS WORTHY LIFE AWARD

Demonstration Activity

We have held a final conference with the Trailman and give our Final Post-Completion approval to this Trailman for his completion of all of the requirements for the Worthy Life Award.

DATE COMPLETED ____

FINAL COMPLETION SIGNATURES

Signature **TROOP CHAPLAIN**

Signature **TRAILMASTER**

Signature **MENTOR**

ADVENTURER AWARDS & WORTHY LIFE AWARD
REQUIREMENTS

JOURNEY AWARD

Joining Requirements

This is the joining award for the Adventurers program.

TRADITIONS:

- [ ] Memorize and agree to live by the Trailman Oath. (Page 26)
- [ ] Memorize the Trailman Motto. (Page 27)
- [ ] Demonstrate the Trailman sign and describe when to use it. (Page 25)
- [ ] Demonstrate the Trailman salute and describe when to use it. (Page 25)
- [ ] Demonstrate the Trailman handshake. (Page 25)
- [ ] Give your Patrol Leader's name, patrol name, and patrol yell.

CITIZENSHIP:

- [ ] Memorize the Pledge of Allegiance. (Page 24)
- [ ] Demonstrate properly folding the American flag. (Page 334)

LEADER CONFERENCE:

- [ ] Discuss Troop safety. (See Troop Safety 101 on page 328 in the appendix)
- [ ] Discuss advancement program. (See Advancement 101 on page 318 in the appendix)

Have your Adventurer Advisor, Trail Guide or Troopmaster sign and date the Advancement Conference Signature Page on page 93.

JOURNEY AWARD

Advancement Conference Signature Page

I (We) affirm that this Trailman has completed all of the requirements to earn the Journey Award and that at least one of the two leaders listed below is someone other than the Trailman's relative.

DATE COMPLETED _____

Signature _____

☐ TRAIL GUIDE ☐ ADVISOR ☐ TROOPMASTER

Optional Signature _____

☐ TRAIL GUIDE ☐ ADVISOR ☐ TROOPMASTER

HORIZON AWARD

Prerequisite: **Earn the Journey Award.**

TRAIL BADGE WORK:

☐ Earn the following nine badges: Aquatics, Camping, Fire Ranger, First Aid, Our Flag, Outdoor Cooking, Ropework, Trail Skills, and Woods Tools.

☐ Earn the following six Horizon Required Trail Badges as an Adventurer: Citizenship, Emergency Preparedness, Family Man, Outdoor Life, and Personal Resources, and any one Fitness Badge (Cycling, Fitness, Hiking, or Swimming).

☐ Earn a total of ten elective Trail Badges including Elective Trail Badges earned as a Navigator. Record these on the badges completion chart on page 96 and have each one signed by your mentor.

SERVANT SERVICE:

☐ Complete 20 hours of service for each year since joining the Adventurers level. Record your hours on the service chart in this handbook (page 98) and have them verified by an adult.

TROOP INVOLVEMENT:

☐ Maintain a level of Troop meeting attendance acceptable to your Advisor (typically 60% or better).

☐ Participate in at least eight Troop activities since becoming an Adventurer, not including regular meetings. Record each activity (trips, camp, community outings, etc.) on the activity chart in this handbook (page 100) and have them verified by an adult.

LEADERSHIP:

Since earning the Journey Award, complete one of the following leadership options. Record your chosen option on page 101 and have it verified by a leader.

- [ ] Serve as a First Officer, Second Officer, Quartermaster or Patrol Leader for a minimum of six months.
- [ ] Plan and implement program, food, and wilderness travel plans (biking, hiking, paddle craft, etc.) for a camping or high adventure trip approved by your Advisor.
- [ ] Plan and implement an Adventurers-only high adventure or extended travel experience including program, food, and travel plans approved by your Advisor.
- [ ] Plan and implement a unique Troop or patrol service project approved by your Advisor.
- [ ] At five Troop meetings, demonstrate your leadership ability by planning and instructing Navigators in significant Trail Badge skills approved by your Advisor or Trail Guide and the Trailmaster.
- [ ] At five Troop meetings, demonstrate your leadership ability by planning and instructing a Woodlands Trail group in significant skills approved by your Advisor or Trail Guide and the Woodlands Trail Ranger.

MARK YOUR PROGRESS

- [ ] Successfully complete an Advancement Conference with your Advisor.
- [ ] Successfully complete a Board of Review.

Have your Adventurer Advisor, Trail Guide, Troopmaster, and Board of Review members sign and date the Horizon Award Advancement Conference Board of Review Signature Pages on pages 103 and 104.

HORIZON AWARD

Trail Badge Completion Chart

15 Required and 10 Electives needed for the Horizon Award

Required Badges	Check here if rolled over from Navigators	Date Completed	Trail Badge Mentor Signature
Aq (AQUATICS)			
Cp (CAMPING)			
Fr (FIRE RANGER)			
Fa (FIRST AID)			
Of (OUR FLAG)			
Oc (OUTDOOR COOKING)			
Rw (ROPEWORK)			
Ts (TRAIL SKILLS)			
Wt (WOODS TOOLS)			
Cz (CITIZENSHIP)			
Ep (EMERGENCY PREPAREDNESS)			
Fm (FAMILY MAN)			
Ol (OUTDOOR LIFE))			
Pr (PERSONAL RESOURCES)			
Select at least one: Cy (CYCLING) Ft (FITNESS) Hk (HIKING) Sw (SWIMMING)			

Elective Badges - Write in name of Elective Badge selected.	Check here if rolled over from Navigators	Date Completed	Trail Badge Mentor Signature
EI (ELECTIVE)			
EI (ELECTIVE)			
EI (ELECTIVE)			
EI (ELECTIVE)			
EI (ELECTIVE)			
EI (ELECTIVE)			
EI (ELECTIVE)			
EI (ELECTIVE)			
EI (ELECTIVE)			
EI (ELECTIVE)			
EI (ELECTIVE, ADDITIONAL)			
EI ((ELECTIVE, ADDITIONAL)			

(Navigator Elective Trail Badges count toward the 10 needed for the Horizon Award.)

HORIZON AWARD
Servant Service Tracking Chart

20 Hours are needed each year for the Horizon Award

Service Type	Date	Hours	Running Total Hours	Year 1, Year 2, Year 3, Year 4 (Circle corresponding year)	Verified by
				Y1 Y2 Y3 Y4	
				Y1 Y2 Y3 Y4	
				Y1 Y2 Y3 Y4	
				Y1 Y2 Y3 Y4	
				Y1 Y2 Y3 Y4	
				Y1 Y2 Y3 Y4	
				Y1 Y2 Y3 Y4	
				Y1 Y2 Y3 Y4	
				Y1 Y2 Y3 Y4	
				Y1 Y2 Y3 Y4	
				Y1 Y2 Y3 Y4	
				Y1 Y2 Y3 Y4	
				Y1 Y2 Y3 Y4	
				Y1 Y2 Y3 Y4	
				Y1 Y2 Y3 Y4	

Service Type	Date	Hours	Running Total Hours	Year 1, Year 2, Year 3, Year 4 (Circle corresponding year)	Verified by
				Y1 Y2 Y3 Y4	
				Y1 Y2 Y3 Y4	
				Y1 Y2 Y3 Y4	
				Y1 Y2 Y3 Y4	
				Y1 Y2 Y3 Y4	
				Y1 Y2 Y3 Y4	
				Y1 Y2 Y3 Y4	
				Y1 Y2 Y3 Y4	
				Y1 Y2 Y3 Y4	
				Y1 Y2 Y3 Y4	
				Y1 Y2 Y3 Y4	
				Y1 Y2 Y3 Y4	
				Y1 Y2 Y3 Y4	
				Y1 Y2 Y3 Y4	
				Y1 Y2 Y3 Y4	
				Y1 Y2 Y3 Y4	

HORIZON AWARD

Troop Activities Tracking Chart

8 Activities are needed for the Horizon Award (more than 8 count towards the Freedom Award)

Troop Activities	Date from	Date to	Camping Nights	Verified by

HORIZON AWARD

Leadership Skills Demonstration Tracking Chart

Choose your Leadership option for the Horizon Award

Leadership Option	Date	Approved by	Verified by
Serve as a Patrol Leader, First or Second Officer or Quartermaster for six months	Date from Date to	NA	
Plan and Implement a camping or high-adventure trip	Date from Date to		
Plan and Implement an Adventurers-only high-adventure or extended travel experience	Date from Date to		
Plan and implement a troop or patrol service project	Date from Date to		

Plan and instruct skills for ☐ Woodlands Trail or ☐ Recruit or Able Trailmen

Event 1			
Event 2			

CONTINUED ON NEXT PAGE

Event 3			
Event 4			
Event 5			

HORIZON AWARD

Advancement Conference Signature Page

I (We) affirm that this Trailman has completed all of the requirements to earn the Horizon Award and that at least one of the two leaders listed below is someone other than the Trailman's relative.

DATE COMPLETED _____

Signature _____ ☐ TRAIL GUIDE ☐ ADVISOR ☐ TROOPMASTER

Optional Signature _____ ☐ TRAIL GUIDE ☐ ADVISOR ☐ TROOPMASTER

HORIZON AWARD

Board of Review Signature Page

We affirm that this Trailman has completed all of the requirements to earn the Horizon Award and that none of the leaders listed below are the Trailman's relative.

DATE COMPLETED _____

Signature _____ POSITION

Signature _____ POSITION

Signature _____ POSITION

Optional Signature _____ POSITION

Optional Signature _____ POSITION

Optional Signature _____ POSITION

ADVENTURERS WORTHY LIFE AWARD

Before beginning any work on the Worthy Life Award, meet with your Adventurer Advisor, Troop Chaplain, and mentor (approved by your parent or guardian) to create and document in your Handbook measurable goals, tasks, and reporting expectations before beginning any requirement (page 107). The Adventurer Advisor, Troop Chaplain, and mentor must pre-approve, sign for completion, and date each activity. *No one-on-one*, *Two-deep*, and *Buddy System of Three* Youth Protection guidelines must be followed at all meetings with your mentor or leader(s) *(See page 328).*

Pre-Approval		REQUIREMENT	Completed
✓	1	**DEVOTIONAL ACTIVITY** *Complete one (1) of the following activities and discuss it with your mentor:*	✓
	☐	An age-appropriate Bible study program[1] consisting of at least twelve (12) one-hour sessions.	
	☐	The Band of Brothers[2] Group Bible Study/Discipleship Program with a minimum duration of three (3) months.	
✓	2	**DISCIPLESHIP ACTIVITY** *Complete one (1) of the following activities and discuss it with your mentor:*	✓
	☐	Read a Christian book.[3]	
	☐	Participate in a Christian weekend retreat or mission trip.	
	☐	Complete a service project using the Biblical principles or skills developed during your Devotional Activity.	

Pre-Approval	REQUIREMENT	Completed
✓	**3 DISCIPLINES ACTIVITIES** *Complete three (3) of the following activities during your Devotional and Discipleship Activities:*	✓

- ☐ Keep a Bible study journal of questions, principles, and thoughts.
- ☐ Memorize and recite scriptures, prayers, hymns, creeds, or catechisms.
- ☐ Keep a prayer journal, including answers to prayers
- ☐ Regularly attend services/mass at your local church.
- ☐ Volunteer to serve with your local church/parish on an ongoing basis.
- ☐ Share/explain the Gospel to at least ten people individually.

Pre-Approval	REQUIREMENT	Completed
✓	**4 DEMONSTRATION ACTIVITIES** *Complete all three (3) of the following activities:*	✓

- ☐ Publicly share your personal testimony or Christian walk with your Troop or Bible study group.
- ☐ Make a significant presentation to your Troop or patrol including important concepts learned during your activities.
- ☐ Hold a final conference with your Adventurer Advisor, Troop Chaplain, and mentor, explaining what you have experienced and learned and how you have achieved your pre-determined goals, tasks, and expectations.

---

[1] Any Bible Study Program should be in agreement with your Charter Organization's Faith Tradition. This may include Christian Religious Recognition Programs.

[2] The Band of Brothers Group Bible Study/Discipleship Program guidelines and structure can be found on the Appendix on 324.

[3] Possible topics include: spiritual growth, spiritual disciplines, church history, missionaries, martyrs, biographies of important church figures, apologetics, etc.

ADVENTURERS WORTHY LIFE AWARD

Goals / Tasks / Reporting Expectations

Before you begin any work towards your Worthy Life Award, work with your Adventurer Advisor, Troop Chaplain, and Mentor to create and document here measurable goals, tasks, and reporting expectations for the Worthy Life Award.

Goals	Tasks	Reporting Expectations

DATE: _____
Signature **TRAILMAN**   *(Recorded before beginning)*

We have agreed upon, with this Trailman, the goals, tasks, and reporting expectations for his Worthy Life Award and that at least one of the leaders listed below is someone other than the Trailman's relative.

DATE *(Recorded before beginning)* _____

Signature **TROOP CHAPLAIN** _____

Signature **ADVENTURER ADVISOR** _____

Signature **MENTOR** _____

ADVENTURERS WORTHY LIFE AWARD
Devotional Activity

We give our Pre-Approval to this Trailman for his selection of his Devotional Activity.

DATE PRE-APPROVED _____

Signature **TROOP CHAPLAIN** _____

Signature **ADVENTURER ADVISOR** _____

Signature **MENTOR** _____

We give our Post-Completion approval to this Trailman for his completion of his Devotional Activity for the Worthy Life Award.

DATE COMPLETED _____

Signature **TROOP CHAPLAIN** _____

Signature **ADVENTURER ADVISOR** _____

Signature **MENTOR** _____

ADVENTURERS WORTHY LIFE AWARD

Discipleship Activity

We give our Pre-Approval to this Trailman for his selection of his Discipleship Activity.

DATE PRE-APPROVED _____

Signature **TROOP CHAPLAIN** _____

Signature **ADVENTURER ADVISOR** _____

Signature **MENTOR** _____

We give our Post-Completion approval to this Trailman for his completion of his Discipleship Activity for the Worthy Life Award.

DATE COMPLETED _____

Signature **TROOP CHAPLAIN** _____

Signature **ADVENTURER ADVISOR** _____

Signature **MENTOR** _____

ADVENTURERS WORTHY LIFE AWARD

Disciplines Activities

We give our Pre-Approval to this Trailman for his selection of his Discipline Activities.

DATE PRE-APPROVED _____

Signature **TROOP CHAPLAIN** _____

Signature **ADVENTURER ADVISOR** _____

Signature **MENTOR** _____

We give our Post-Completion approval to this Trailman for his completion of his Discipline Activities for the Worthy Life Award.

DATE COMPLETED _____

Signature **TROOP CHAPLAIN** _____

Signature **ADVENTURER ADVISOR** _____

Signature **MENTOR** _____

ADVENTURERS WORTHY LIFE AWARD

Demonstration Activities

We have held a final conference with the Trailman and give our Final Post-Completion approval to this Trailman for his completion of all three Demonstration Activities and all of the requirements for the Worthy Life Award.

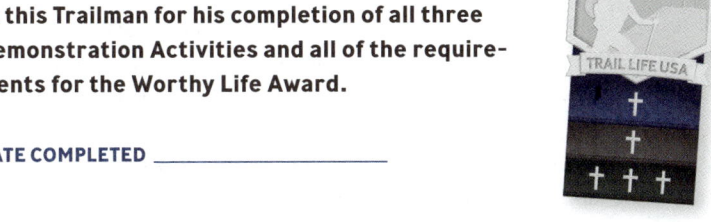

DATE COMPLETED _____

FINAL COMPLETION SIGNATURES

_____
Signature **TROOP CHAPLAIN**

_____
Signature **ADVENTURER ADVISOR**

_____
Signature **MENTOR**

HOW A TRAILMAN ADVANCES

FREEDOM AWARD

Prerequisite: **Earn the Horizon Award.**

Trail Life USA has created an extensive Freedom Award Procedure Guide for earning the Freedom Award. The Procedure Guide gives you more details regarding each requirement for the Freedom Award as well as checklists which must be used to walk you and your Troop/Area leaders step-by-step through earning the Freedom Award. Tracking for your Troop Involvement, the Freedom Experiences, and the Worthy Life Award are recorded in this handbook. (Pages 105, 114 and 115). The Servant Leadership Project Guide, Advancement Conference, and Board of Review signatures are all captured within the corresponding documents in the Freedom Award Procedure Guide available on Trail Life Connect.

TROOP INVOLVEMENT:

☐ Maintain a level of Troop meeting attendance acceptable to your Advisor (typically 60% or better).

☐ Participate in at least 16 Troop activities since becoming an Adventurer, not including regular meetings. Record each activity (trips, camp, community outings, etc.) on the activity chart in this handbook (page 114) and have them verified by an adult.

FREEDOM EXPERIENCES:

Complete at least four Trail Life USA approved Freedom Experiences of your choosing from the current Freedom Experience Course Catalog. Each Freedom Experience must be approved by your Advisor before you start. After completing each Freedom Experience, have a conference with your Advisor for final approval. Record your progress in the Freedom Experiences Tracking Chart in this handbook (page 115) along with your Advisor's approvals.

☐ Complete two Freedom Experiences in one field for your Major.

☐ Complete one Freedom Experience in a second field (this counts as a Minor).

☐ Complete one Freedom Experience in a third field (this counts as a Minor).

WORTHY LIFE AWARD:

☐ Complete the Adventurers Worthy Life Award *(Requirements and Signature Pages on pages 105 - 111).*

SERVANT LEADERSHIP PROJECT:

☐ Complete a Freedom Servant Leadership Project according to the standards in the Freedom Award Procedure Guide.

MARK YOUR PROGRESS:

☐ Successfully complete an Advancement Conference with your Advisor and Troopmaster.

☐ Successfully complete a Freedom Award Board of Review.

Note: The Horizon Award must be earned **before** *beginning work on any aspect of the Freedom Award except for Freedom Experiences and the Worthy Life Award, which can be earned by Adventurers before the Horizon Award.*

CONGRATULATIONS!

Upon a successful review by the National Freedom Award Review Committee, you will have earned the pinnacle accomplishment of Trail Life USA, the Freedom Award, and become a Freedom Rangeman. This is the rarest of "honor societies." You should be extremely proud. Through your effort and accomplishment, you will serve as a shining example to the thousands of Trailmen who are following you along the Freedom Trail.

FREEDOM AWARD
Troop Activities Tracking Chart

16 Activities are needed for the Freedom Award.

Troop Activities	Date from	Date to	Camping Nights	Verified by
Eight Activities Rolled over from Horizon Award	NA	NA	NA	

FREEDOM AWARD

Freedom Experiences Tracking Chart

At least 4 Freedom Experiences are needed for the Freedom Award.

Freedom Experience Course Number	Advisor Pre-Approval	Date from / Date to	Verified by

The Freedom Award Procedure Guide provides a helpful overview of the Freedom Award journey as well as step-by-step instructions and checklists. It can be found on Trail Life Connect.

TRAIL LIFE
REQUIRED
TRAIL BADGES

AQUATICS
Outdoor Skills Frontier

Do all of the following requirements (1-9)

1 Research what the Bible says about water. _____ COMPLETED

    a _____ Describe water in the creation process.

    b _____ How was it used as a curse and a blessing?

    c _____ Where did all the water in the world come from? If there ever was a time where nothing existed, how could all the water come from nothing?

    d _____ List the ways in which water sustains life on earth.

    e _____ List the ways that natural bodies of water (oceans, lakes, springs, & rivers) are a gift to man for food, travel, and recreation to enjoy God's creation.

2 Participate in a Safe Aquatics method orientation and fulfill the following requirements pursuant to the Safe Aquatics method. (Page 333) _____ COMPLETED

3 Complete the Swimming Competency Test at the Swimmer level. (Page 330) _____ COMPLETED

4 Demonstrate how to properly put on a personal flotation device (PFD) and while wearing the PFD do the following: _____ COMPLETED

    a _____ Jump feet first into deep water and swim 25 yards.

    b _____ Learn and demonstrate the Heat Escape Lessening Posture (HELP) cold water survival technique.

c _____ With a group, learn and demonstrate the Huddle cold-water survival technique.

5 **Demonstrate the following reach and throw rescues:** _____
COMPLETED

a _____ Several reach assists including arm, leg, and towel reaches without entering the water, and pole or shepherd's crook assists

b _____ Throwing a rescue tube or ring buoy to someone at least 25 feet out in the water

6 **After ensuring the safety of the swimming area, in deep water, do the following:** _____
COMPLETED

a _____ Tread water for 3 minutes.

b _____ Survival float on your stomach for 3 minutes.

c _____ Float on your back for 2 minutes.

d _____ Demonstrate a feet-first surface dive.

e _____ Demonstrate a head-first surface dive, and recover a diving ring or some other object from the pool bottom.

7 **While wearing shoes, long pants, and a long-sleeve shirt over your swimsuit, jump into deep water.** _____
COMPLETED

a _____ While treading water, remove the shoes and pants.

b _____ Inflate your shirt and float long enough to prepare your pants.

c _____ Inflate your pants and use them to float for one minute..

8 Demonstrate that you can continuously swim 200 yards without stopping to rest.

COMPLETED _____

a _____ Use at least three of the following five strokes: front crawl, backstroke, sidestroke, breaststroke, and elementary backstroke.

b _____ Swim each of the selected strokes for at least 50 yards.

9 Participate in a skill orientation and an open activity for three of the following aquatics activities:

☐ group water game, ☐ swim race, ☐ diving, ☐ snorkeling, ☐ Red Cross Junior Lifeguard, ☐ scuba, ☐ stand-up paddle boarding, ☐ boardsailing, ☐ canoeing, ☐ kayaking, ☐ rowing, ☐ sailing, ☐ peddle boats, ☐ water skiing, ☐ wake boarding, or ☐ an alternate water activity approved by your leader.

COMPLETED _____

A total of 9 requirements need to be fulfilled for this badge

120 THE TRAILMAN'S HANDBOOK

CAMPING
Outdoor Skills Frontier

Do all of the following requirements (1-8)

1 Explain how the low impact camping method (page 312) helps fulfill the Trailman Oath to "be a good steward of creation."
_____ COMPLETED

2 Research if people camped in the Bible.
_____ COMPLETED

    a _____ Did they use tents?

    b _____ Did they build fires?

3 Given the advancements in technology and housing, what makes camping so special, different, and fun for young people and families?
_____ COMPLETED

4 Explain what you experience when you camp in the outdoors that makes you think about God.
_____ COMPLETED

5 With your Troop, Patrol or another group of youth, complete the following activities:
_____ COMPLETED

    a _____ At a camping area, explain where the best place to pitch a tent would be and why.

    b _____ With a buddy or by yourself, correctly pitch a tent.

    c _____ Take the tent down, correctly fold it, and pack it away.

    d _____ Explain the proper care for tents.

    e _____ Correctly pitch a dining fly, tarp, or other type of covering.

HOW A TRAILMAN ADVANCES

6 **Camping equipment**

COMPLETED _____

a _____ Make a list of personal equipment you should pack on a weekend camping trip for hot, cold, and rainy weather.

b _____ Demonstrate on a camping trip that you have packed all your equipment from your list.

7 **Wilderness sanitation**

COMPLETED _____

a _____ Demonstrate digging and covering a proper cat hole for backwoods human excrement disposal using a small or backpacking shovel.

b _____ Explain proper disposal methods for toilet paper for your local wilderness area(s).

8 Spend at least 15 nights camping in a tent or under the stars and participate in assigned cooking, cleanup, and other camping related duties.

Log your camping trips on page 196.

COMPLETED _____

A total of 8 requirements need to be fulfilled for this badge

CITIZENSHIP
Heritage Frontier (Adventurers Only)

Because it is written with a mature preparation for manhood, this Trail Badge is to be earned only by registered Adventurer Trailmen.

Do all of the following requirements (1-9)

1 Research what the Bible says about God creating man and woman in his own image and likeness. Describe how this truth should affect the following: COMPLETED _____

  a _____ The sacredness of life itself and our view of human dignity

  b _____ How we should treat people in our society

  c _____ How the government makes laws

  d _____ Who you will or will not vote for in elections when you are an adult

2 Do one of the following activities: COMPLETED _____

  a _____ Participate in a discussion about the issues in requirement 1 above with your patrol, Troop, family, or another group.

  b _____ Write a paper or prepare a presentation about what you learned from your research and thinking about the issues addressed in requirement 1.

3 Political and economic systems: COMPLETED _____

  a _____ Define the following political systems: democracy, republic, autocracy, and oligarchy.

  b _____ Define the following economic systems: capitalism, socialism, and communism.

c _____ Name a country that practices each type of political system and a country that practices each type of economic system.

d _____ Select one of the above countries with a non-constitutional form of government and contrast the treatment of its citizens and non-citizens with the treatment of citizens and non-citizens in the United States (US).

4. Read the US Constitution and all its amendments and then do the following:

COMPLETED _____

a _____ Describe the three different branches of our federal government and explain their respective functions.

b _____ Find one federal program or service that is a constitutional function of the federal government and explain why it should be provided at the federal level.

c _____ Find one federal program or service that is not a constitutional function of the federal government and explain why it should be provided at the state or local level.

d _____ Explain how the Electoral College is used to elect the president and how that differs from the popular vote.

e _____ Explain the following constitutional principles: popular sovereignty, limited government, separation of powers, checks and balances, judicial review, and federalism.

f _____ Discuss the Bill of Rights, the rights we are guaranteed as citizens of the United States, and the circumstances under which a citizen can lose some of those rights.

5. Explain the responsibilities of US citizenship.

COMPLETED _____

6. **Investigate US citizenship and naturalization requirements using US Citizenship and Immigration Service publications or their web site and do the following:**   COMPLETED

   a _____ List the criteria for automatic US citizenship.

   b _____ List the qualifications to become a naturalized US citizen.

7. **Do the following requirements on international treaties:**   COMPLETED

   a _____ Explain how international treaties are negotiated, signed, and ratified.

   b _____ Describe the authority of ratified treaties in US law (US Constitution, Article VI).

   c _____ Investigate the issues involved in one controversial treaty that the US has signed, but has not ratified.[1]

   d _____ Present an argument either in favor or against ratification of your selected treaty.

[1] *Examples of such treaties include the United Nations (UN) Convention on the Rights of the Child, the UN Convention on the Rights of Persons with Disabilities, the UN Convention on the Elimination of All Forms of Discrimination against Women, and the UN Framework Convention on Climate Change.*

8 Do the following requirements on local, county, and state governments:

COMPLETED _____

a _____ Determine the types of local and county government used where you live.

b _____ List any major differences of your state government structure relative to the federal government structure. [2]

c _____ List at least five services or programs provided for citizens by each of your local, county, and state governments (at least five for each level of government). [3]

d _____ List the major taxes and fees collected by your local, county, and state governments to pay for the services they provide.

e _____ Explain jury duty, the county juror selection process, and the citizen's duty to serve.

f _____ List the residency, age, and registration requirements to vote where you live.

Complete three (3) options from those below for requirement 9

9 Do **three (3)** of the following citizenship activities:

COMPLETED 3 _____

9a _____ Examine the list of 100 Civics Questions from the US Citizenship and Immigration Services. Prepare for and pass the exam as given by USCIS (answer 6 out of 10 questions picked at random from the 100 questions).

9b _____ List the federal taxes that citizens may be required to pay and explain how each is assessed and collected. Compare federal government income with expenses for the last year reported.

---

[2] Examples include single-house legislature, direct election of judges, and periodic confirmation of judges by direct election, etc.

[3] Possible services include street repair, snow removal, trash collection and recycling, police and fire protection, parks and related facilities, educational programs, community swimming pools, tennis courts, skating rinks, stop signs and traffic lights, libraries and medical centers.

9c _____ Describe how a bill is written, passed in Congress or your state legislature, and signed into law.

9d _____ List your elected representatives in local, county, state and Federal governments. Select one representative and one issue you care about. Examine his voting record on that issue. Communicate with your representative by email, letter, fax, phone, or in person to express your support or disagreement with his position.

9e _____ List three important local, state, or national political issues for which Biblical moral principles directly apply. Name a bill currently in the local government, state legislature, or US Congress that addresses at least one of these issues. List at least three arguments supporting the bill and at least three arguments opposing the bill.

9f _____ Explain the differences between and the relationship of government debt and budget deficit. For your local, county, state, and federal governments, determine the amount of debt and budget deficit at the end of their last reported fiscal year.

9g _____ Attend a meeting of your local government, county government, school board, or park board. Discuss some of the agenda items that are discussed, voted on, or opened to the public for community comments.

9h _____ Participate in a debate of an issue of importance on a local, state, or national level.

9i _____ Visit your state capitol and sit in on a legislative session.

9j _____ Visit Washington D.C. and sit in on a legislative session.

more...

9k _____ Visit national landmarks in Washington D.C. such as the Capitol, Library of Congress, National Archives, Washington Monument or Jefferson Memorial, Lincoln Memorial, World War II Memorial, Korean War Memorial, or Vietnam War Memorial.

A total of 9 requirements need to be fulfilled for this badge

A visit to our Nation's Capitol could fulfill one of the requirements for your Citizenship badge.

128 THE TRAILMAN'S HANDBOOK

CYCLING (FITNESS BADGE)

Sports and Fitness Frontier (Adventurers Only)

Because it is written with a mature preparation for manhood, this Trail Badge is to be earned only by registered Adventurer Trailmen.

This is a Fitness badge. Fitness badges are designed to be used to increase your fitness over time and are progressive in nature, meaning they get more difficult as you improve.

A certified bicycle helmet is required and must be worn for each ride completed for this badge.

Do all of the following requirements (1-8)

1 Discuss why keeping your body healthy and strong is important to you and God and list examples of ways it is possible to spend too much time on exercise, sports, or physical training. _____ COMPLETED

2 Read I Timothy 4:8 and explain the value of "training the body" in relation to godliness. _____ COMPLETED

3 Complete the following about cycling basics: _____ COMPLETED

    a _____ Learn how to determine the proper seat height and bike height.

    b _____ Learn about different sizes and types of tires and when they might be used.

    c _____ Discuss the different types of bicycles.

    d _____ Compare the cost between different types of bikes.

    e _____ Discuss what type of clothing, shoes, or equipment should be worn while cycling.

    f _____ Discuss where it is proper and improper to go cycling.

HOW A TRAILMAN ADVANCES

g _____ Explain the traffic laws for bicycles in your state. Compare them with motor vehicle laws.

4 Discuss the types of foods and beverages that should be consumed before, during, and after a long bike ride.

_____
COMPLETED

5 Go on a ride with others including your leader and demonstrate the following:

_____
COMPLETED

a _____ Mounting, dismounting, steering, pedaling, stopping, and hand signals

b _____ Proper riding location on the side of the road and along parked cars

c _____ Gearing, pedaling on ascents and descents, and emergency stops

d _____ Turns, turn signals, left turn from the center of the street, and the alternate left turn (box) technique

e _____ Crossing of streets and railroad tracks and avoiding obstacles

6 Demonstrate how to perform basic bicycle repairs:

_____
COMPLETED

a _____ Inflating tires

b _____ Repairing and/or replacing a tire

c _____ Replacing a chain on the sprocket

d _____ Adjusting brakes

e _____ Raising and lowering the seat

7 Make a bicycle repair kit for your rides that includes those items necessary to make the repairs listed in the previous requirement.

_____
COMPLETED

8 Outline a training plan of at least three months but no longer than one year for improving your fitness *using one of the options below.* It should include progressive improvement goals and frequency schedule for practice. It must be based on your ability and take into account your current cycling fitness. It must be approved by your leader.

COMPLETED

Option 1: Road Biking: Using a map of your area, plan and take 10 rides with your leader's approval. Map out your course and plan for rest stops. Identify possible problem areas before riding and determine how you will minimize them. The first ride must be at least 5 miles and you must work up to a final ride of at least 50 miles. Each ride must take place on a separate day and must be complete*d in one day.*

Record the dates of your rides on the Cycling Log on page 132.

Option 2: Off-road Biking: Using trail maps, map your course and execute 10 off-road rides with your leader's approval. Identify possible problem areas before riding and determine how to minimize them. The first ride must be at least 2 miles and you must work up to a final ride of at least 20 miles. Each ride must take place on a separate day and must be completed in one day.

Record the dates of your rides on the Cycling Log on page 132.

Option 3: Track Cycling, Cyclo-cross, or Para-Cycling: Develop a goal for a cycling event or events based on your current average time and desired improvement, and then complete the event. It must be approved by your leader.

Goal & event approved

Ride completed

A total of 8 requirements need to be fulfilled for this badge

HOW A TRAILMAN ADVANCES   131

Cycling Log

Date(s)	Verified by	Description	Number of miles

Ep

EMERGENCY PREPAREDNESS
Life Skills Frontier (Adventurers Only)

Because it is written with a mature preparation for manhood, this Trail Badge is to be earned only by registered Adventurer Trailmen.

Do all of the following requirements (1-12)

1 Read Genesis Chapter 3.
_____ COMPLETED

    a _____ Explain how sin first entered the world.

    b _____ Why is this event referred to as the "Fall of Man?"

2 Read Psalm 24:1 and Genesis 1:28-31.
_____ COMPLETED

    a _____ Is the earth still good and owned by God even in its fallen state?

    b _____ Explain how the world's fallen and imperfect nature due to the entrance of sin into the world is connected to natural disasters (hurricanes, earthquakes, floods, wildfires) and major emergencies like war and terrorism.

3 Read Isaiah 55:9 and explain how we can we still trust in God even though bad things happen in our lives and in the world.
_____ COMPLETED

4 Do one of the following activities:
_____ COMPLETED

    a _____ Participate in a discussion about the issues in items 1-3 above with your patrol, Troop, family, or another group.

    b _____ Write a paper or prepare a presentation about what you learned from your research and thinking about the above issues.

5 Make a chart assessing your risk as high, medium, or low for the following emergencies and understand each one and the unique challenges each presents:

_____ COMPLETED

Natural
Flood
Tornado
Hurricane
Winter Storm
Extreme Heat
Earthquake
Volcano
Landslide
Tsunami
Wildfire
Pandemic

Technological
Blackout
Hazardous Materials
Nuclear Power Plants
Household Chemical

Terrorist
Explosions
Biological Attack
Chemical Attack
Cyber Attack
Nuclear Device
EMP

Person/Property
Home Fire
Vehicle Accident
Boating Accident
Gas Leak
Burglary
Carbon Monoxide Poisoning
Drowning
Wilderness/Backcountry Accident

6 Create an emergency plan for your family for the 10 highest risks that you discovered in your research for number 5 above. Include the following information:

_____ COMPLETED

a _____ Prevention and preparation necessary

b _____ Reaction during an emergency including alternate communication plans, meeting locations, and alternate methods for daily tasks of the home

c _____ Special needs to be considered for the elderly, infirm, infants, and small children and animals

d _____ What to do when the immediate danger is passed or in a prolonged evacuation

7	Create a list of necessary items and quantities for a Basic Disaster Supply Kit for three days and for two weeks. List additional items you may want for more serious long-term disasters. Check off the things you currently have on hand and circle those you don't have or need more of.	COMPLETED
8	Create a list of emergency items to keep in your car and at work.	COMPLETED
9	List local warning systems available in your area.	COMPLETED
10	Describe the emergency plans in place at your school, your church, your meeting location, and your workplace (if applicable).	COMPLETED
11	Explain the following emergency water treatment methods: chlorination, distillation, boiling, and filtering.	COMPLETED
12	Present the information you learned in this badge to your family.	COMPLETED

A total of 12 requirements need to be fulfilled for this badge

HOW A TRAILMAN ADVANCES

FAMILY MAN
Life Skills Frontier (Adventurers Only)

Because it is written with a mature preparation for manhood, this Trail Badge is to be earned only by registered Adventurer Trailmen.

Foundation Requirements: Do all of the Foundation Requirements (1-5)

1. Family
COMPLETED _____

a _____ A family is defined legally and seen in the Bible as a group of people related in one of three ways. What are the three ways?

b _____ Explain the difference between Immediate Family and Extended Family.

2. Marriage
COMPLETED _____

a _____ Read Genesis 2:18-24 and explain how the Bible defines marriage.

b _____ Explain how the unique relationship, marriage, reflects the triune nature of God.

c _____ Read Ephesians 5:22-33 and explain how the nature of marriage is created by God as a picture of His love for His people.

d _____ In Ephesians 5:25, how is the relationship between Christ and the Church similar to the relationship between a husband and his wife?

e _____ Having read Genesis 2:18-24, read Revelation 21:9 and explain how the Bible both begins and ends with a marriage.

3. Husbands & Fathers
COMPLETED _____

a _____ List some of the ways that God has designed men and women differently.

b _____ Explain how fathers and mothers bring different strengths that help raise children in a family.

c _____ Read 2 Thessalonians 3:6-12 and I Timothy 5:8. Explain the importance of hard work and the duty of being a provider as it applies to a man who is a husband or father.

4 Family, Society & Church

COMPLETED _____

a _____ Why are families important to a strong society?

b _____ What are some of the problems that come from families breaking down?

c _____ Explain how Christians and churches can help become a "father to the fatherless" for families that experience death, divorce, or abandonment involving a father.

5 Servant Leadership (Reference John 13:1-5, 12-17; Titus 1:6-9)

COMPLETED _____

a _____ Explain the concept of servant leadership.

b _____ Explain how servant leadership involves both demonstrating humility and strength.

c _____ Discuss several examples of servant leadership in the Troop.

d _____ Discuss several examples of servant leadership in your family.

e _____ Brainstorm implementations of servant leadership as future fathers.

Family Activities: Do one (l) Family Activity from each of the following four requirements (6-9)

6 Nutrition Using the Federal Food Guidelines

(Reference "My Plate," "Food Pyramid," or another equivalent balanced nutrition plan.)

Do one: ☐ 6a, ☐ 6b, or ☐ 6c

COMPLETED

6a Learn about the food guidelines.

_____ **i.** Determine the daily caloric needs for someone of your age and weight.

_____ **ii.** How much water should you be drinking each day and why?

_____ **iii.** Write down everything you eat and drink for one week.

_____ **iv.** Plan a menu of healthy meals for three days.

6b Learn the relationship between your diet and good health.

_____ **i.** Explain the food guidelines and causes of obesity in childhood and among teenagers.

_____ **ii.** List ways to avoid obesity, including diet and exercise.

_____ **iii.** Plan one week of healthy menus for your family.

_____ **iv.** Select one of your healthy meals and prepare it for your family. Clean up afterwards.

6c Learn about the food guidelines and plan balanced meals for your family for one day including breakfast, lunch, and dinner.

_____ **i.** Prepare a list of needed ingredients.

_____ **ii.** Show your menus and ingredients list to your Leader.

_____ **iii.** Prepare the planned breakfast, lunch, and dinner on one day.

_____ **iv.** Clean up after each meal.

7 Household Tasks

Do one: ☐ 7a or ☐ 7b

COMPLETED _____

7a Perform all of the following:

_____ **i.** Learn the proper way to do at least five household tasks and perform them for at least one month. *These are in addition to grocery shopping, laundry, and ironing task required for ii-iv below.* (See Sample Household Tasks on page 140 for ideas).

_____ **ii.** Help your family with the grocery shopping for one week, including bagging the groceries, carrying them in, and putting them away properly.

_____ **iii.** Learn how to do laundry and then do the laundry for yourself or your family for a week.

_____ **iv.** Learn how to use an iron and the appropriate temperatures for different fabrics. Press at least three items including something with sleeves.

7b With your parents, agree on at least five recurrent household tasks. Track your household tasks for three months on a tracking log sheet. (See sample household tasks on page 140 for ideas).

8 Family Projects

Do one: ☐ 8a, ☐ 8b, or ☐ 8c

COMPLETED _____

8a _____ **Help your family with a family project.** This could be a maintenance activity such as cleaning out the garage, spring landscaping, or spring-cleaning. Or it might be a new project such as painting a room or redecorating. List the role of each family member in the project completion.

8b _____ **Work with your family to clean out the basement or garage.** Sort items into three categories: things to keep, things to donate, and things for the trash. Reorganize as needed as you return items to the space. Take your donated items to a charity and the rest to the trash can.

8c _____ **Perform a community service project with your family.** Some examples are to: participate in a church service day project; help clean up your church or school; plant trees or flowers in a public area and care for them; plan, cook, and deliver a meal to someone in need; do yard work for someone in need; visit the elderly or disabled; or set-up a recycling drive and donate the proceeds to charity.

Sample Household Tasks

Make the bed	Wash the dishes	Wash the car
Change bed sheets	Dry and put away the dishes	Wax the car
Dust furniture	Load and unload a dishwasher	Clean inside your car
Polish furniture	Clean out the refrigerator	Cut the grass
Clean light fixtures	Defrost a freezer	Weed a garden
Clean blinds	Carry in and put away groceries	Water the grass or garden
Vacuum upholstery	Clean an oven	Take out trash
Vacuum floor	Sort or fold laundry	Do the family recycling
Sweep floor	Launder curtains if washable	Wash windows
Mop a floor		Shampoo a carpet
Clean the bathroom		Water house plants
Set the table		
Pack lunches		

9 Family Communication

Do one: ☐ 9a, ☐ 9b, ☐ 9c, or ☐ 9d.

COMPLETED

9a _____ Plan a celebration, holiday party or special outing for your family and help to implement it. Include in the plan any costs involved for supplies, invitations, food, preparations, cleaning, transportation, lodging, or needed equipment. Discuss with your family any changes you would make if you were to do it again.

9b _____ Plan and participate in a family meeting. Set ground rules, such as to respect all opinions and to have everyone attend and be allowed to share input. Discuss issues important to your family. For example, decide how chores will be completed, discuss vacation ideas and options, plan a family night or find solutions to a problem.

9c Help a sibling or younger child with homework for a week.

9d Read to a sibling or younger child each day for a week.

A total of 9 requirements need to be fulfilled for this badge

FIRE RANGER
Outdoor Skills Frontier

Do all of the following requirements (1-6)

1 Explain how the low impact camping method (page 312) relates to fires and helps fulfill the Trailman Oath to "be a good steward of creation." _COMPLETED_

2 Research what the Bible says about fire. _COMPLETED_

    a _____ List at least three instances of fire in the Bible.

    b _____ How is fire a curse and a blessing to mankind?

    c _____ Read Exodus 3:2, Judges 13:20, Hebrews 12:29, Acts 2:3-4. How does God use fire to describe His presence, passion, and purity in the Bible?

3 How did man's ability to start, sustain, and control fire change the world? _COMPLETED_

4 Fire Safety _COMPLETED_

    a _____ Explain the use of buckets, rakes, and shovels in containing a campfire in a certain location.

    b _____ Describe safe places to have a campfire, how to learn local regulations, and how to set up a fire circle.

    c _____ Describe safe vs. unsafe clothing near campfires and open flames.

    d _____ Describe safe vs. unsafe behavior around a campfire.

e _____ Demonstrate how to put out fire on your clothing, hair, or body.

f _____ Demonstrate safe striking of stick and book matches and safe use of a lighter.

5 **Fire materials**

COMPLETED

a _____ Explain the use and purpose of tinder, kindling, and fuel firewood.

b _____ Explain why wet, green, and ant/vine-covered wood is unsafe and not good for fires.

c _____ Describe several types of fire starters that can be made or purchased.

6 **Fire building**

COMPLETED

a _____ Demonstrate building at least three different fire-lays and explain when you would use each one.

b _____ Light one of the fire-lays, attend it, and keep it burning.

c _____ When finished with the fire, demonstrate the proper way to extinguish it to dead out.

A total of 6 requirements need to be fulfilled for this badge

HOW A TRAILMAN ADVANCES 143

FIRST AID
Life Skills Frontier

Do requirement 1

1 **Participate in a discussion with your patrol, Troop, family, or another group about the following:**

COMPLETED _____

a _____ Read Genesis 1:26-27. What do these scriptures tell us about why we as a society spend so many resources (time, effort, and money) to protect people's health and safety using first aid and other emergency care?

b _____ Do we expend the same amount of resources on similar animal care?

c _____ What biblical truth explains those answers?

For requirement 2, choose option 2a or 2b

2 **Cardiopulmonary Resuscitation (CPR), Automated External Defibrillator (AED) Use, and Choking First Aid**

Do one: ☐ 2a or ☐ 2b

COMPLETED _____

2a _____ **CERTIFICATION OPTION**

_____ **i.** Complete a CPR-AED certification class taught by the American Heart Association or American Red Cross, or Emergency Care and Safety institute that includes skill practice with CPR dummies and a teaching AED and teaches these three skill sets:
- Adult CPR, AED, and choking,
- Child CPR, AED, and choking, and
- Infant CPR and choking.

_____ **ii.** Find out if your meeting location has an AED and be aware of where it is located.

2b _____ **SELF-STUDY OPTION**

_____ **i.** Explain hands-only CPR

_____ **ii.** Stopped breathing

_____ **iii.** Explain the use of an AED.

_____ **iv.** Find out if your meeting location has an AED and be aware of where it is located.

_____ **v.** Describe and show how to tell if someone is choking and when intervention is required.

_____ **vi.** Describe and show the positions for treating choking in an adult, pregnant woman, child, and infant.

Do either requirement 3 or 4

3 **CERTIFICATION OPTION: Basic First Aid**
Complete a Basic First Aid certification class taught by the American Heart Association, American Red Cross, or Emergency Care and Safety Institute that includes a hands-on skills section.

_____ COMPLETED

4 **SELF-STUDY OPTION: Basic First Aid**

_____ COMPLETED

a _____ Demonstrate the following first aid action plan basics:

_____ **i.** Checking the scene

_____ **ii.** Calling for help (911 or Poison Control)

_____ **iii.** Approaching safely

_____ **iv.** Providing urgent treatment

_____ **v.** Treating for shock

_____ **vi.** Deciding the next steps

b _____ Demonstrate the following rescuer safety precautions:

_____ **i.** Wearing of eye protection, breathing mask, and vinyl gloves

_____ **ii.** Proper glove removal

_____ **iii.** Proper handwashing

c _____ Explain the symptoms and first aid for the following sudden illness emergencies:

_____ **i.** Heart Attack

_____ **ii.** Fainting

_____ **iii.** Low blood sugar

_____ **iv.** Stroke

_____ **v.** Seizure

_____ **vi.** Shock

_____ **vii.** Poisoning

d _____ Explain and demonstrate the first aid response for the following:

_____ **i.** Severe bleeding on a leg and arm

_____ **ii.** Nosebleed

_____ **iii.** Head, neck, and spine injuries

_____ **iv.** Broken bones, including splinting

e _____ **Explain the first aid response for the following injuries:**

_____ **i.** Severe bleeding you cannot stop with direct pressure

_____ **ii.** Bleeding from mouth

_____ **iii.** Tooth injuries

_____ **iv.** Eye injuries

_____ **v.** Penetrating and puncturing objects

_____ **vi.** Internal bleeding

_____ **vii.** Burns (first, second, and third degree)

_____ **viii.** Electric shock injuries

f _____ Explain the first aid for the following bites and stings:

_____ **i.** Animal and human bites

_____ **ii.** Snakebites

_____ **iii.** Insect, bee, and spider bites and stings

_____ **iv.** Poisonous spider, and scorpion bites and stings

_____ **v.** Ticks

g _____ Explain the first aid for the following temperature-related emergencies:

_____ **i.** Heat cramps

_____ **ii.** Heat exhaustion

_____ **iii.** Heatstroke

_____ **iv.** Frostbite

_____ **v.** Hypothermia

Trail Life USA First Aid Addendum:

Do requirements 5-12.

5 Explain and demonstrate first aid for the common outdoor injuries listed below:

COMPLETED

a _____ Cuts and scrapes

b _____ Splinters

HOW A TRAILMAN ADVANCES 147

    c _____ Blisters

    d _____ Something in your eye

    e _____ Sunburn

    f _____ Poisonous plants

    g _____ Dehydration

6 Explain how the following methods help prevent common outdoor injuries and emergencies: _____ COMPLETED

    a _____ Work gloves, mole skin, adhesive tape (splinters and blisters)

    b _____ Sunscreen, sunglasses, broad-brimmed hats

    c _____ Long pants and long-sleeved shirts

    d _____ Insect repellent

    e _____ Plenty of water and a water filter

    f _____ Synthetic insulating layers and nylon/Gore-Tex outer wear

    g _____ Sturdy, well-fitting hiking boots/shoes

7 Explain why sun protection is especially important while on the water, in the snow, or at high altitude. _____ COMPLETED

8 Make first aid kits yourself: _____ COMPLETED

    a _____ Make a personal first aid kit for hiking and other wilderness trips.

    b _____ Make a home first aid kit for your family

9 Explain how to get medical assistance while on a wilderness camping trip, river trip, and on open water. _____ COMPLETED

10 Demonstrate splinting, slings, and bandaging for the following injuries to permit transport of victims: _____ COMPLETED

a _____ Twisted ankle (sprain or strain)

    b _____ Broken ankle

    c _____ Broken lower arm

    d _____ Broken upper arm

    e _____ Broken collarbone

    f _____ Broken lower leg

    g _____ Broken upper leg

11 **Demonstrate the following methods of transporting victims:** _____ COMPLETED

    a _____ Walking assists: one and two rescuers

    b _____ Drags: Blanket, Shoulder, and Ankle (conduct these with great care)

    c _____ Two-rescuer Carries: two-hand seat, four-hand seats, and chair carry

    d _____ Human stretcher carry for 3-6 Trailmen

    e _____ Improvised stretchers: blanket and shirt/coat (2)

12 **Demonstrate the emergency procedures for the following clothing fire emergencies:** _____ COMPLETED

    a _____ Stop, Drop, and Roll response to your own clothes catching fire

    b _____ Response to another person who panics and runs

A total of 11 requirements are necessary for this badge because of your choice of either #3 or #4.

FITNESS (FITNESS BADGE)

Sports and Fitness Frontier (Adventurers Only)

Because it is written with a mature preparation for manhood, this Trail Badge is to be earned only by registered Adventurer Trailmen.

This is a Fitness badge. Fitness badges are designed to be used to increase your fitness over time and are progressive in nature, meaning they get more difficult as you improve.

Do all of the following requirements (1-6)

1 Discuss why keeping your body healthy and strong is important to you and God and list examples of ways it is possible to spend too much time on exercise, sports, or physical training.
COMPLETED

2 Read I Timothy 4:8 and explain the value of "training the body" in relation to godliness.
COMPLETED

3 Research exercises to improve your physical fitness including stretches, strength training and cardiovascular activities. Know the safety guidelines for each activity and at what age it is safe to start them. Make note of each of the exercises, and what muscle or muscle group is being targeted.
COMPLETED

4 Discuss what types of foods and beverages should be consumed before and after a hard workout.
COMPLETED

5 Know how to check and figure your heart rate and know why it is important.
COMPLETED

| 6 | Outline a training plan of at least three months but no longer than one year for improving your fitness based on your research. It should include progressive improvement goals and frequency schedule for exercise. It must be based on your ability and take into account your current fitness level. It must include strength training goals, cardiovascular training goals, and warm-up and cool-down activities and cover all major muscle groups. Once it has been approved by your leader and your parents, implement your training plan. |

COMPLETED

_____ Outline and approve your plan

_____ Plan implemented ___|___|___ to ___|___|___

A total of 6 requirements need to be fulfilled for this badge

HOW A TRAILMAN ADVANCES |5|

HIKING (FITNESS BADGE)
Sports and Fitness Frontier (Adventurers Only)

Because it is written with a mature preparation for manhood, this Trail Badge is to be earned only by registered Adventurer Trailmen.

This is a Fitness badge. Fitness badges are designed to be used to increase your fitness over time and are progressive in nature, meaning they get more difficult as you improve.

Do all of the following requirements (1-8)

1. Discuss why keeping your body healthy and strong is important to you and God and list examples of ways it is possible to spend too much time on exercise, sports, or physical training.
COMPLETED

2. Read I Timothy 4:8 and explain the value of "training the body" in relation to godliness.
COMPLETED

3. Review the Hikers Code. (Page 315)
COMPLETED

4. Research the proper food for extended hiking outings. Research the amount of food and water necessary for extended hiking outings.
COMPLETED

5. Review other items needed in your pack for an all day hike.
COMPLETED

6. Research exercises, stretches, and aerobic activities designed specifically for hiking conditioning.
COMPLETED

7. Prepare a hiking fitness and training plan of at least three months to prepare you for increasing hike lengths based on your research and review it with your leader. Include a training schedule and plans for warm-up, stretching, hiking, or other conditioning and a cool down
COMPLETED

8 Complete a progressive hiking program consisting of at least 10 hikes beginning at 5 miles for the first hike and increasing to at least a 20 mile hike. Prepare a hiking plan for each hike using the Hikers Code (page 315) including a trail map or route. Provide it to your leader before each trip.

Record your trips on the Hiking Log on page 154.

COMPLETED

A total of 8 requirements need to be fulfilled for this badge

Hiking Log

Date(s)	Hiking Plan Verified by	Location	Number of miles

Elevation Adjustment: 1,000 foot elevation gain = add 1.5 miles
Example: 7 miles with a 2,000 foot gain (1.5*2) = 10 miles.

OUR FLAG
Heritage Frontier

Do all of the following requirements (1-9)

1 Describe how and why we respect the American flag.
COMPLETED

2 How is respecting the flag related to "respect authority" in the Trailman Oath?
COMPLETED

3 Basic flag ceremonies:
COMPLETED

    a _____ Demonstrate folding the American flag. (see page 334)

    b _____ Demonstrate the proper placement of hands (and hats) while reciting the Pledge of Allegiance.

    c _____ Demonstrate displaying the colors for an outdoor flag ceremony.

    d _____ Demonstrate raising and lowering the American flag for an outdoor flag ceremony.

    e _____ Participate in a flag ceremony for your Troop meeting, award ceremony, or other indoor ceremony.

4 Know the Flag Code and its history. Diagram the proper way to display the American Flag in the following circumstances.
COMPLETED

    a _____ When carried in a procession with another flag or flag

    b _____ When displayed with another flag against a wall with crossed staffs

    c _____ When a number of flags on staffs are displayed with the American Flag

d _____ When state flags or other pennants are flown from the same halyard with the American flag

e _____ When flags of two or more nations are displayed

f _____ When a flag is displayed on a staff projecting horizontally from a windowsill or building

g _____ When the flag is not on a staff and is displayed flat against a wall horizontally and vertically

h _____ When used on a speaker's platform

i _____ When flown at half-staff

j _____ When used to cover a casket

5 Make a diagram of the American flag and flagpole, labeling all its parts. Include and be able to define the hoist, peak, fly, staff, halyard, and union.
COMPLETED

6 Learn the history of the Pledge of Allegiance.
COMPLETED

7 Learn the date, the conflict, the American flag's design, its physical condition, and the situation that prompted Francis Scott Key to write the Star Spangled Banner.
COMPLETED

8 Read through the words of the National Anthem written by Francis Scott Key. Explain line by line in your own words what was going on and his views on it.
COMPLETED

Complete three (3) options from those below for requirement 9

9 Do **three (3)** of the following activities:

COMPLETED 3

9a _____ Participate in the color guard for a flag ceremony for a community event.

9b _____ Participate in the color guard for an outdoor flag ceremony.

9c _____ Find a script giving a meaning or symbolism to each of the 13 folds required to properly fold an American Flag and use it in a flag ceremony.

9d _____ Find or write a special flag ceremony and perform it in front of an audience.

9e _____ Teach a Woodlands patrol a flag ceremony and help them perform it at a Troop function.

9f _____ Find or write a respectful American flag retirement ceremony and perform it at a campfire program.

9g _____ Participate in a flag planting service project at a cemetery for a Memorial Day service honoring veterans.

9h _____ Learn the history and usage of the 21 Gun Salute.

9i _____ Research the origins of Flag Day and plan a special event celebrating the day for your Troop or community.

A total of 9 requirements need to be fulfilled for this badge

OUTDOOR COOKING
Outdoor Skills Frontier

Do all of the following requirements (1-9)

1 Explain how the low impact camping method (page 312) relates to outdoor cooking and helps fulfill the Trailman Oath to "be a good steward of creation."
_____ COMPLETED

2 Demonstrate the following:
_____ COMPLETED

    a _____ Sanitation practices

    b _____ Washing dishes

    c _____ Personal hygiene

    d _____ Food storage

    e _____ Protecting your food from animals

3 Explain the advantages, disadvantages, and safety issues involved in using propane/butane camp stoves, liquid fuel stoves, lightweight stoves, wood fires, and charcoal.
_____ COMPLETED

4 Set-up, light, and use a lightweight camp stove.
_____ COMPLETED

5 Cook a one-pot meal over the fire or camp stove.
_____ COMPLETED

6 Cook a foil meal on charcoal.
_____ COMPLETED

7 Plan or help plan a balanced nutritious menu for a weekend camping trip.
_____ COMPLETED

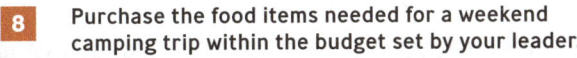

| 8 | Purchase the food items needed for a weekend camping trip within the budget set by your leader. | COMPLETED |

| 9 | With a buddy or by yourself, prepare, cook, and clean up the planned meals using any of the following means: campfire, propane stove, liquid fuel stove, charcoal, Dutch oven, sandwich irons, box oven, or solar cooker/oven. | COMPLETED |

A total of 9 requirements need to be fulfilled for this badge

OUTDOOR LIFE
Outdoor Skills Frontier (Adventurers Only)

Because it is written with a mature preparation for manhood, this Trail Badge is to be earned only by registered Adventurer Trailmen.

Select an Outdoor Life Trail you will use to complete the requirements for this Trail Badge: **Backpacking, Camping, Cycling, Paddle Craft,** or **Sailing.**

Then do requirements 1-3 in Part A; and all the requirements listed for your selected Trail—Part B; and the required number of Optional Activities in Part C.

PART A—Do all of the following requirements (1-3)

1 Consider what we can learn about God and his creation from working, playing, and doing activities outdoors as opposed to doing the same activities indoors.

Do one of the following: _____ COMPLETED

1a _____ Participate in a discussion about this topic with your patrol, Troop, family, or another group.

1b _____ Write a paper or prepare a presentation about what you learned from your research and thinking about the above issue.

2 For your selected Trail, explain or write out your plans for the following: _____ COMPLETED

a _____ Inclement and severe weather

b _____ Sleeping and shelter

c _____ Transporting equipment (individual and group)

d _____ Sanitation: safe drinking water, washing (self, dishes, etc.), and human waste disposal

e _____ Food supply, preparation, and protection from wild animals, bad weather, and spoilage

3 Construct a shelter or lean-to using only a tarp, rope, and any natural items at the location such as rocks, logs, or sticks or equipment associated with your selected Trail. Construct (if permitted) or describe how to make your own bedding using natural items and a ground cloth.

COMPLETED

PART B—Select a Trail and do all of the requirements listed for that Trail on the following pages.

HOW A TRAILMAN ADVANCES | 161

■ **Backpacking Trail**

4 On a patrol or Troop backpack trip, serve as the trip quartermaster and do the following:

COMPLETED

a _____ Plan the menu for the trip and purchase the food.

b _____ Check the weather report and update your individual and group equipment lists.

c _____ Demonstrate correctly packing your backpack for the group.

d _____ Lead a shake-down session to eliminate unnecessary weight, and do the following:

_____ **i.** Check the packs of your group for compliance with the individual equipment list for the trip.

_____ **ii.** Distribute the group equipment and food to each participant in a way that balances group needs with individual weight-carrying capacity.

_____ **iii.** Verify that each backpacker has an acceptable pack weight (no more than ¼ body weight).

5 On a patrol or Troop backpack trip, serve as the trip planner and do the following:

COMPLETED

a _____ Present a trail safety orientation to the group and explain why going downhill is where most injuries occur and why we do not short-cut switchbacks.

b _____ Using a map of the area where you will be hiking, plan your route and camp site(s) using one of the backpacking metrics to balance the difficulties of each of the days. See the Backpacking Metrics section in the Appendix for the metric definitions. (Page 316)

c _____ Give a copy of your route, camp site(s), departure time, and return time to your leaders and parents who are not hiking with you.

d _____ Check the weather report and update your trip plan as needed.

e _____ Review the navigation skills from the Trail Skills Trail badge. Lead the hiking and perform all trail navigation, including demonstrating orienting a map, correcting for magnetic declination, and finding your location on the map using bearings to landmarks.

6 **Participate in backpack trips as an Adventurer that include the following:**

COMPLETED

a _____ At least 10 nights backcountry camping as an Adventurer on backpack trips in addition to the 15 nights camping required for Camping Trail Badge. Includes nights in tent, improvised shelter, permanent trail shelter open on one side, or under the stars while in the backcountry on a backpack trip.

Log your backpack trips in the Backpacking Trips Log on page 164.

b _____ At least 7 days of backpacking with a BTM* of at least 4 hours per day (8 miles per day on level ground)

Log your backpack trips in the Backpacking Trips Log on page 164.

To compute your BTM, use the formula on page 316.

c _____ A total BTM* experience total of at least 40 hours (80 miles on level ground).

Record your BTM on the Backpacking Trips Log on page 164.

To compute your BTM, use the formula on page 316.

In addition to the above requirements, do any one (1) Outdoor Life Optional Activity (found in PART C at the end of this Badge).

7 **Your PART C Activity Category and Number:**

_____

COMPLETED

A total of 7 requirements need to be fulfilled for this Backpacking Outdoor Life Trail Badge

HOW A TRAILMAN ADVANCES

Backpacking Trips Log

Date(s)	Total Days	Description or location	BTM ≥ 4 Hours	Miles per day	Total Miles

■ Camping Trail

4 Plan a campout for your patrol or Troop with an individual equipment list, a group equipment list, duty roster, and activity/program plan.

COMPLETED

5 Spend at least 40 nights camping in a tent, in an improvised shelter, in a permanent trail shelter open on one side, or under the stars, and participate in assigned cooking, clean-up and other camping related duties. This includes all nights camping while a Navigator or Adventurer whether with your Troop or another group and includes the nights camping for Camping Trail Badge.

Record your camping nights in the Camping Log on page 194.

COMPLETED

In addition to the above requirements, do any five (5) Outdoor Life Optional Activities (found in PART C at the end of this Badge).

6 Your five PART C Activities Categories and Numbers:

_____
_____
_____
_____
_____

COMPLETED

A total of 6 requirements need to be fulfilled for this Camping Outdoor Life Trail Badge

HOW A TRAILMAN ADVANCES 165

■ Cycling Trail

4 On a patrol or Troop bicycle trip, serve as the trip quartermaster and do the following:

_____
COMPLETED

a _____ Plan the menu for the trip and purchase the food.

b _____ Check the weather report and update your individual and group equipment lists.

c _____ Demonstrate correctly packing your gear for the group.

d _____ Lead a shake-down session to eliminate unnecessary weight and do the following:

_____ **i.** Check the bike packs of your group for compliance with the individual equipment list for the trip.

_____ **ii.** Distribute the group equipment and food to each participant in a way that balances group needs with weight-carrying capacity.

5 On a Patrol, or Troop bicycle trip, serve as the trip planner and do the following:

_____
COMPLETED

a _____ Present a trip safety orientation to the group covering bicycle safety and traffic laws.

b _____ Using a map of the area where you will be bicycling, plan your route and camp site(s).

c _____ Give a copy of your route, camp site(s), departure time, and return time to your leaders and parents who are not traveling with you.

d _____ Check the weather report and update your trip plan as needed.

e _____ Review the navigation skills needed for bicycle touring. Lead the trip and perform all navigation.

6 Participate in bicycle trips as an Adventurer that include the following:

COMPLETED _____

a _____ At least 10 nights camping as an Adventurer on bicycle trips in addition to the 15 nights camping required for Camping Trail Badge.

Record your camping nights in the Camping Log on page 194.

b _____ At least 7 days of bicycling at least 40 miles per day.

Record your bicycling days in the Cycling Trips Log on page 168.

c _____ A total bicycling mileage of at least 400 miles

Record your bicycling mileage in the in the Cycling Trips Log on page 168.

In addition to the above requirements, do any one (1) Outdoor Life Optional Activity (found in PART C at the end of this Badge).

7 Your PART C Activity Category and Number: _____

COMPLETED _____

A total of 7 requirements need to be fulfilled for this Cycling Outdoor Life Trail Badge

Cycling Trips Log

Date(s)	Verified by	Location	Miles per day	Total Miles

Paddlecraft Trail

4 On a patrol or Troop wilderness paddle craft trip, serve as the trip quartermaster and do the following:

COMPLETED

a _____ Plan the menu for the trip and purchase the food.

b _____ Check the weather report and update your individual and group equipment lists.

c _____ Demonstrate correctly packing your gear for the group.

d _____ Lead a shake-down session to eliminate unnecessary weight and do the following:
   _____ **i.** Check the packs of your group for compliance with the individual equipment list for the trip.
   _____ **ii.** Distribute the group equipment and food to each participant in a way that balances group needs with boat and individual portaging weight-carrying capacity (if any portaging is part of the trip).

5 On a patrol or Troop wilderness paddle craft trip, serve as the trip planner and do the following:

COMPLETED

a _____ Present a trip safety orientation to the group covering water safety and portaging safety (if any portaging is part of the trip).

b _____ Using a map of the area where you will be paddling, plan your route and camp site(s).

c _____ Give a copy of your route, camp site(s), departure time, and return time to your leaders and parents who are not traveling with you.

d _____ Check the weather report and update your trip plan as needed.

e _____ Review the navigation skills from Trail Skills Trail Badge. Lead the trip and perform all on-water and portaging navigation including demonstrating orienting a map, correcting for magnetic declination, and finding your location on the map using bearings to landmarks.

HOW A TRAILMAN ADVANCES

6 Participate in wilderness paddle craft trips as an Adventurer that include the following:

COMPLETED _____

	Date(s)	Miles
a _____ At least 10 nights backcountry camping as an Adventurer on paddle craft trips in addition to the 15 nights camping required for Camping Trail Badge. Includes nights in tent, improvised shelter, permanent trail shelter open on one side, or under the stars while in the backcountry on a paddle craft trip. **Record your camping nights in the Camping Log on page 194.**		
b _____ At least 7 days of paddling with at least 10 miles per day (flat water)		
c _____ A total paddling mileage of at least 100 miles (flat water) *Note: Your Advisor may make adjustments in daily and total mileage based on number and length of portages, current, and headwinds. The values are based on an average of 3 mph for a two-person canoe with gear, no current, and no portages.*		

In addition to the above requirements, do any one (1) Outdoor Life Optional Activity (found in PART C at the end of this Badge).

7 Your PART C Activity Category and Number:

_____

COMPLETED _____

A total of 7 requirements need to be fulfilled for this Paddlecraft Outdoor Life Trail Badge ✓

Sailing Trail

4 On a patrol or Troop ocean or great lakes sailing trip, serve as the trip quartermaster and do the following:

COMPLETED _____

a _____ Plan the menu for the trip and purchase the food.

b _____ Check the weather report and update your individual and group equipment lists.

c _____ Demonstrate correctly packing your gear for the group.

d _____ Lead a shake-down session to eliminate unnecessary weight: Check the packs of your group for compliance with the individual equipment list for the trip.

5 On a patrol or Troop ocean or great lakes sailing trip, serve as the trip planner and do the following:

COMPLETED _____

a _____ Present a trip safety orientation to the group covering water safety and boat safety.

b _____ Using a map of the area where you will be sailing, plan your route and camp site(s).

c _____ Give a copy of your route, camp site(s) or mooring locations, departure time, and return time to your leaders and parents who are not traveling with you.

d _____ Check the weather report and update your trip plan as needed.

e _____ Review the navigation skills for sailing. Perform on-water navigation and man the helm.

6 **Participate in sailing trips as an Adventurer that include the following:**

_____
COMPLETED

a _____ At least 10 nights camping or sleeping aboard as an Adventurer on sailing trips in addition to the 15 nights camping required for Camping Trail Badge. Includes nights in tent, improvised shelter, permanent trail shelter open on one side, under the stars or on-board the sailboat while on a sailing trip.

Record your camping nights in the Camping Log on page 194.

_____
COMPLETED

b _____ At least 10 full days of sailing

Record the dates of your sailing days here.

COMPLETED

In addition to the above requirements, do any three (3) Outdoor Life Optional Activity (found in PART C at the end of this Badge).

7 **Your three PART C Activities Categories and Numbers:**

_____

_____

_____

COMPLETED

A total of 7 requirements need to be fulfilled for this Sailing Outdoor Life Trail Badge

PART C—Outdoor Life Optional Activities

	Adventure Activities	Date completed
1	Ascend a mountain to reach the summit requiring at least 10 equivalent miles and gaining at least 1,000 feet in elevation (for day hiking each 1,000 feet of elevation gain is equivalent to 1.5 additional miles).	
2	Backpack at least overnight covering a total of 10 equivalent miles (for backpacking each 1,000 feet of elevation gain is equivalent to 2 additional miles).	
3	Snow shoe or cross country ski at least 5 miles.	
4	Take a paddle craft day trip of at least 5 hours paddling and requiring the packing of one meal to eat en-route.	
5	Go on a road bike camping trip of at least 20 total miles and 1 night camping.	
6	Go on a mountain bike camping trip of at least 5 total miles and 1 night camping.	
7	Camp overnight in the snow (winter camping).	
8	Participate in a rock climbing day with at least 4 climbs, one rappel, with one climb of at least 5.6 on the Yosemite Decimal System (YDS) rating system.	
9	Go camping at least overnight and sleep under the stars (no tent).	
10	Lead a younger patrol on a backpacking trip.	

	Service Activities	Date completed
1	Participate in a trail conservation or service project with your Troop, patrol, or family.	

HOW A TRAILMAN ADVANCES 173

Outdoor Cooking Activities	Date completed
1 Demonstrate to a younger boy or patrol two things you can cook in either a box oven, Dutch oven, or can stove.	
2 Create an Outdoor Meal Cookbook for your Troop or add to an existing one, include a minimum of two breakfasts, two dinners, and two desserts. Try out each recipe first.	
3 Cook something in two of the following ways: a paper bag, paper cup, orange peel, or cardboard milk carton.	
4 Using a box oven, prepare and bake a meal and a dessert or bread.	
5 Learn how to use a Dutch oven. Use the Dutch oven to cook a dinner and bake either bread or a dessert.	
6 Plan two days' worth of meals for a backpacking trip. Keep in mind items that are lightweight and do not require refrigeration or a cooler. Go to the grocery and make a price list for the cost of the items you have planned. Discuss how "re-packaging" your ingredients can help use space more efficiently and divide the weight evenly among participants.	

Outdoor Information Activities	Date completed
1 Make a presentation to your patrol or Troop about one of the following: **a** _____ A scenic or historic trail (for examples, see National Park Service National Trails System) **b** _____ National, State, or other parks with camping areas and adventure activities **c** _____ National or state bike paths or routes **d** _____ Wilderness paddle craft areas (Boundary Waters, Channel Islands, etc.) **e** _____ An ocean or Great Lakes area for sailing adventures	

2	Have an experienced adult speak to your Troop or patrol about nearby wilderness destinations and safety. Speakers may be found at local outdoor clubs, local outdoor stores, the Department of Natural Resources, or other outdoor related agencies and companies.
3	Attend a free seminar at an outdoor equipment store on a topic related to backpacking, camping, cycling, paddle craft, or sailing.
4	Invite an experienced backpacker, camper, paddler, or sailor to give your Troop or patrol a talk about his travels.

Outdoor Gear Activities	Date completed
1 Research at least three different materials for sleeping bag filling. Explain the advantages and disadvantages of each, including weight, insulation, and performance when wet. Present your findings to a patrol in your Troop.	
2 Research warm and cool weather clothing for outdoor activities. Include information about layering, insulation, wicking materials, rain gear, head coverings, and footwear. Present your findings to a patrol in your Troop.	
3 Research types and options when buying a tent for camping and for backpacking. Include information about weight, price, space, weather, extras and other considerations. Present your findings to a patrol in your Troop.	
4 Make an item of gear from scratch (e.g. small drawstring bag).	
5 Make an item of gear from a kit (e.g. gaiters).	
6 Explain the advantages and disadvantages of internal and external frame backpacks. Visit a store and try out both. Find one that fits your back. Show the key elements for sizing the pack correctly for an individual, and demonstrate how to use the adjustment features on your backpack.	

HOW A TRAILMAN ADVANCES 175

PERSONAL RESOURCES
Life Skills Frontier (Adventurers Only)

Because it is written with a mature preparation for manhood, this Trail Badge is to be earned only by registered Adventurer Trailmen.

Do all Foundation Activities (1-5)

1 Where do all the physical things in the world we use and work with come from?
COMPLETED

2 Read Genesis 1:28-31.
COMPLETED

    a _____ What do these verses say about whether or not we should use the natural resources of the earth?

    b _____ What does it mean to "subdue the earth and have dominion over it"?

    c _____ In the Trail Life Oath, what does it mean "to be a good steward of creation"?

    d _____ How is money used as a tool to place a value upon, acquire, and help exchange wealth and natural resources?

3 Read 1 Timothy 6:9-10.
COMPLETED

    a _____ What does this verse say about money?

    b _____ How can this verse be easily misunderstood?

4 Read Mathew 19:23-26.
COMPLETED

    a _____ Discuss the need to acquire wealth and the dangers of becoming rich.

b _____ Research if there were godly men of great wealth in the Old and New Testaments of the Bible.

c _____ Discuss how much more effectively you can feed the poor, care for widows and orphans, support missionaries, and be generous with others when you have wealth.

5 Do one of the following activities: 5a or 5b

_____ COMPLETED

5a _____ Participate in a discussion about the issues in requirements 1-4 above with your patrol, Troop, family, or another group.

5b _____ Write a paper or prepare a presentation about what you learned from your research and thinking about the above issues in requirements 1-4 above.

Do all Time Management Activities (6-9) sequentially

6 Make a prioritized list of activities and tasks for a week.

_____ COMPLETED

7 Make a schedule for that same week showing, at a minimum, school, church, meal times, exercise, activities, and tasks.

_____ COMPLETED

8 Follow your schedule and check off items on your list as they are completed. Note which items went as planned and which, if any, were late or took longer than expected.

_____ COMPLETED

9 Tell your mentor what you learned from this exercise and discuss whether you are more schedule or task-oriented.

_____ COMPLETED

For the Money Management requirement, do either 10 or 11-14

10 **OPTION 1: Money Management Course**
Complete a biblically based money-management course for teens that covers the topics in this section such as *Dave Ramsey's Foundations in Personal Finance: High School Edition for Self Study or for Homeschool.*

_____
COMPLETED

OPTION 2: Money Management Forums
Complete the Money Management Forums and Activities requirements below in part or in full by independent study, school coursework, with your patrol, or in a group communicating via the Internet (e.g. videoconferencing).

In a forum, everyone studies beforehand and then they discuss the issues. Rotate the forum facilitator for each topic. **Do requirements 11-14.**

11 **Economic Stewardship Forum Topics**

_____
COMPLETED

a _____ Concept of stewardship

b _____ Difference between the things you want, the things you need and things you should share

c _____ Danger in finding your value or identity in material things instead of Christ [1]

d _____ Explain the importance of charitable giving [2]

12 **Insurance Forum Topics**

_____
COMPLETED

a _____ Insurance is meant to protect against what?

---

[1] Indentity in Christ – Genesis 1:26-27, Psalms 139:13-16 and Matthew 10:29-31
Materialism and contentment – Matthew 6:19-34 and Philippians 3:11-13

[2] Chritable giving – Leviticus 27:30-32, Psalms 24:1-6, Matthew 6:1-4, Mark 10:17-25, 2 Corinithians 9:6-8

b _____ Discuss which of the following types of insurance you need and under what circumstances:

    _____ **i.** Life and Health Insurance: life, health, disability, accidental death and dismemberment, and long term care.
    _____ **ii.** Personal Property and Casualty Insurance: homeowners, renters, auto, personal umbrella, recreational vehicle, boat owners, jewelry or other fine arts.
    _____ **iii.** Business Property and Casualty Insurance: general liability, professional liability, umbrella liability, workers compensation, property, and industry specific policies.

13 Debt Forum Topics

_____ COMPLETED

a _____ Consequences when expenses exceed income and the possible causes being in debt

b _____ Explain these types of debt, their advantages and disadvantages:
Mortgage, auto loan, home equity loan, credit card.

c _____ Why credit card debt is especially dangerous

d _____ Difference between a debit card and a credit card

e _____ Alternatives to going into debt for a purchase

f _____ What steps can be taken to get out of debt?

g _____ How a budget helps you to avoid debt

14 Investment Forum Topics

_____ COMPLETED

a _____ Discuss the advantages, disadvantages, and expected rates of return for:

    _____ **i.** Stocks
    _____ **ii.** Bonds
    _____ **iii.** Mutual funds
    _____ **iv.** Certificates of deposit

more...

HOW A TRAILMAN ADVANCES

_____ **v.** Money market accounts
_____ **vi.** Bank savings accounts
_____ **vii.** Annuities.

Do all Money Management Activities (15-17)

15 **Money Management Activities**
CATEGORY I: Budgeting

Do one: ☐ 15a, ☐ 15b, or ☐ 15c

_____
COMPLETED

15a _____ **Pick two jobs or businesses**

_____ **i.** Compute the cost to get into each job (school, training, tools, equipment, business start-up costs, etc.).

_____ **ii.** Determine pay or typical net income.

_____ **iii.** Ignoring interest, determine how long it takes to earn back your start-up costs using 25% of income.

_____ **iv.** Compare start-up costs and time to pay them back.

15b _____ **Develop a budget for you as a single 25 year old not living at home.**

_____ **i.** Pick a job.

_____ **ii.** Research average pay.

_____ **iii.** Make complete budget including:

Housing – rent or mortgage *(no more than 25% of gross income)*

Utilities *(electric, gas, phone, Internet, cable, etc.)*

Food, clothing, and hygiene supplies

Auto *(loan payment, gasoline, insurance, maintenance, licensing)*

Other transportation *(bus, train, etc.)*

Health *(insurance, doctor/dentist visits, drugs, etc.)*

Fun *(travel, movies, eating out, and other entertainment)*

Education and training

Charitable giving *(church, missions, and other charities)*

Taxes *(income, FICA, self-employment, property, miscellaneous state taxes)*

_____ **iv.** Compute the percentage of your gross income budgeted for each category and present in tabular or graphical form (e.g. a pie chart).

15c _____ **Develop a three-month budget and track your income and expense.**

_____ **i.** Create a three-month budget for all of your income and expenses, including spending, saving, and giving.

_____ **ii.** If you do not have one, set up a checking and a linked savings account to use for this activity.

_____ **iii.** Track your actual income and expenses for three months.

_____ **iv.** Deposit your saving amount in your savings account and some of your giving or spending amount in your checking account.

_____ **v.** During the three months, write several checks, make several deposits, keep a checkbook, and balance your checkbook with the monthly bank statement.

_____ **vi.** After one month, explain to your mentor any deviations from your original plan including unexpected expenses.

_____ **vii.** Adjust your budget based on what you learned from the first month.

_____ **viii.** At the end of three months, explain any deviations from your adjusted plan including unexpected expenses.

16 Money Management Activities
CATEGORY 2: Investments

Do one: ☐ *16a,* ☐ *16b,* ☐ *16c, or* ☐ *16d*

COMPLETED

16a _____ **Play an online virtual Stock Exchange game.**

_____ **i.** Play for at least three months to see some of the long-term effect of the market.

_____ **ii.** Have your mentor set up a game for all in your Unit working on this badge or include multiple units to have enough players.

_____ **iii.** Check at least weekly on your investments and make any adjustments you think will help your portfolio grow.

_____ **iv.** Discuss the results at the end, comparing how each person did with his strategy.

16b _____ **Play the Portfolio on Paper investment game for at least three months.**

_____ **i.** You have $5,000 in pretend money to invest in the stock market.

_____ **ii.** Investigate companies in which you would like to invest.

_____ **iii.** Create a portfolio on paper or on the computer and track your virtual investment.

_____ **iv.** You may sell and purchase new stocks as often as you wish but you must deduct $10 each time you do so.

_____ **v.** At the end of the game, evaluate the income and change in your investment value.

_____ **vi.** Compare your results with others in your patrol who also complete this exercise.

16c _____ Select a buy/sell rule and analyze five (5) stocks and a market index fund using one year of historical data to assess how well the rule worked over that year for the 5 stocks and the index fund vs. a buy and hold strategy.

16d _____ Assume that right now you are retiring at age 67 after having worked and paid into social security for 45 years. Do the following:

_____ **i.** Compute your approximate social security benefit and life expectancy. [Visit: https://www.ssa.gov/planners/benefitcalculators.html]. From those compute the present value of your expected social security payout.

_____ **ii.** Select two stock indexes or funds that have existed for at least 45 years and collect a value for each year (same date such as year-end). For each stock index or fund, compute the present value of annual investments of your total annual social security part of the FICA payroll tax. Use the sum of the employee and employer's share (the self-employment rate) of the social security part of FICA payroll tax. Use the current combined tax rate of 12.4% for all years and the income level(s) you assumed for the social security benefit calculation.

_____ **iii.** Compare the present values from i and ii above and discuss the results.

17 **Money Management Activities**
CATEGORY 3: Debt

Do one: ☐ 17a *or* ☐ 17b

_____
COMPLETED

17a _____ Student loan payback analysis

_____ **i.** Choose a field of study and associated business or career. Determine the current average annual pay for that career or business.

_____ **ii.** Pick two schools with significantly different annual costs.

_____ **iii.** Total up those costs and determine a reasonable amount per year you can pay for school.

_____ **iv.** Assume the remainder is funded with student loans and total the loan amount for each school.

_____ **v.** Look up the current student loan rate and compute how long it will take to pay each loan back at ten percent of your income.

17b _____ Compute the monthly payment and total interest paid for the following loans and explain what you learned from this exercise.

    _____ **i.** 15-year mortgage of $100,000 at 5% annual interest (180 monthly payments)

    _____ **ii.** 30-year mortgage of $100,000 at 5% annual interest (360 monthly payments)

    _____ **iii.** 15-year payoff of $20,000 credit card debt at 20% annual interest (180 monthly payments)

    _____ **iv.** 30-year payoff of $20,000 credit card debt at 20% annual interest (360 monthly payments)

Do all Communication Activities (18 and 19)

18 Document one money management activity in a short written report including graphics to communicate the results. — COMPLETED

19 Present the findings of either the same or a different money management activity in a short presentation to your mentor and patrol. — COMPLETED

A total of either 15 or 18 requirements need to be fulfilled for this badge, depending on your choices.

ROPEWORK

Outdoor Skills Frontier

Do all of the following requirements

1 Explain how the low-impact camping method (page 312) relates to ropework and helps fulfill the Trailman Oath to "be a good steward of creation."
_____ COMPLETED

2 Whipping and fusing
_____ COMPLETED

    a _____ Demonstrate whipping the ends of a natural fiber rope.

    b _____ Demonstrate fusing the ends of a synthetic rope.

3 Tie the following knots and describe their usefulness:
_____ COMPLETED

    a _____ square knot

    b _____ bowline

    c _____ two half-hitches

    d _____ taut line hitch

    e _____ clove hitch

    f _____ timber hitch

4 Lashing:
_____ COMPLETED

    a _____ Tie the following lashings and describe their function:

        _____ **i.** Square

        _____ **ii.** Diagonal

        _____ **iii.** Shear

_____ **iv.** Tripod

_____ **v.** Round

_____ **vi.** Floor

b _____ Lash the following trestles:

_____ **i.** X-Trestle

_____ **ii.** A-Trestle

_____ **iii.** H-Trestle

c _____ Make a useful structure for camp using at least three different types of lashings

A total of 4 requirements need to be fulfilled for this badge

SWIMMING (FITNESS BADGE)

Sports and Fitness Frontier (Adventurers Only)

Because it is written with a mature preparation for manhood, this Trail Badge is to be earned only by registered Adventurer Trailmen.

This is a Fitness badge. Fitness badges are designed to be used to increase your fitness over time and are progressive in nature, meaning they get more difficult as you improve.

Do all of the following requirements (1-6)

1 Discuss why keeping your body healthy and strong is important to you and God and list examples of ways it is possible to spend too much time on exercise, sports, or physical training. — COMPLETED

2 Read I Timothy 4:8 and explain the value of "training the body" in relation to godliness. — COMPLETED

3 Research exercises to improve your swimming fitness including stretches, strength training, and conditioning drills. — COMPLETED

4 Discuss what types of foods and beverages should be consumed before and after a swimming workout. How much should you eat and drink, and why? — COMPLETED

5 Learn and explain the different strokes used in competitive swimming. Learn how improvements to your stroke, kick, and turns can improve your fitness and speed. — COMPLETED

6 Outline a training plan for improving your fitness using one of the options below of at least three months but no more than one year. It should include progressive improvement goals and frequency schedule for practice. It must be based on your ability and take into account your current swimming fitness. It must be approved by your leader.

See options on the following page. — COMPLETED

HOW A TRAILMAN ADVANCES

☐ **Option 1:** Improve your USA Swimming Motivational Time Standard for your age for a specific stroke or strokes (e.g. BB to A).

☐ **Option 2:** Develop a goal for a swim event(s) based on your current average time and desired improvement (e.g. Go from 1:05 in the 100M Free to below 1 minute).

☐ **Option 3:** Build up endurance to be able to swim a specific distance in a time agreed upon by your leader (e.g. Swim a mile in under 30 minutes).

A total of 6 requirements need to be fulfilled for this badge

TRAIL SKILLS
Outdoor Skills Frontier

Do all of the following requirements (1-9)

1 Discuss and describe how our name "Trail Life" has both natural and spiritual meanings.
_____ COMPLETED

2 Explain what these scriptures teach us about the "spiritual trail" of Christian life.
_____ COMPLETED

    a _____ Matthew 7:13

    b _____ Psalms 119:105

    c _____ Psalms 16:11

    d _____ Proverbs 3:6

    e _____ John 16:4

3 Trail ethics
_____ COMPLETED

    a _____ Explain how the low impact camping method (page 312) relates to Trail Skills and helps fulfill the Trailman Oath to "be a good steward of creation."

    b _____ Participate in a Hiker's Code (page 315) orientation and learn the buddy system (page 328).

4 Trail safety
_____ COMPLETED

    a _____ Describe how to identify poisonous plants in your area, such as poison ivy, poison oak, poison sumac, stinging nettle, and Flowering Poodle Dog Brush (Sticky Nama).

    b _____ Describe how to identify venomous snakes in your area (such as rattlesnakes, coral snakes, or water moccasins).

c _____ Describe natural hazards you might encounter on a hike, including river crossings, and what to do if you are faced with them.

d _____ Describe the importance of safe, clean water, and explain how to identify safe or unsafe water. Demonstrate at least two methods of water purification.

5 Equipment

COMPLETED _____

a _____ Describe the clothing necessary for hiking, including proper footwear and socks.

b _____ Explain the limit on how much weight you should carry and how much water you should take.

c _____ Demonstrate proper packing and necessary items for a day pack for a day hike.

6 Navigation

COMPLETED _____

a _____ Explain how an orienteering compass works.

b _____ Explain what a topographic map is and what the contour lines and map symbols mean.

c _____ Demonstrate how to hold an orienteering compass and take a reading.

d _____ With an orienteering compass, orient a map to North.

e _____ With an orienteering compass and a topographical map, demonstrate one method of adjusting for magnetic declination.

f _____ With an orienteering compass and a topographical map, demonstrate finding your location using bearings to landmarks.

| 7 | **Measurements** | COMPLETED |

a _____ Measure the average length of your pace.

b _____ Using pacing and the felling method, measure the height of a building, tree, flagpole, or other feature.

c _____ Demonstrate course direction finding in daylight or moonlight without a compass or GPS receiver.

| 8 | **Skills practice** | COMPLETED |

Do ONE of the following options:

8a _____ Complete an orienteering course of at least 1 mile and 5 stations.

8b _____ Complete a compass course of at least one mile and 8 bearings.

| 9 | Using a map and compass together, take a five-mile hike with your patrol or Troop. | COMPLETED |

A total of 9 requirements need to be fulfilled for this badge

HOW A TRAILMAN ADVANCES

WOODS TOOLS

Outdoor Skills Frontier

Do all of the following requirements (1-8)

1 Explain how the low-impact method (page 312) relates to Woods Tools and helps fulfill the Trailman Oath to "be a good steward of creation."
COMPLETED _____

2 Describe how knives, swords, and axes were used in history as weapons and tools.
COMPLETED _____

3 Give at least 5 Biblical references to knives, swords, and axes.
COMPLETED _____

4 Describe the Woods Tools Safety Rules (page 327).
COMPLETED _____

5 Demonstrate how to clean and sharpen a pocketknife.
COMPLETED _____

6 Demonstrate how to clean, stow/cover, and change a saw blade for either a folding or bow saw.
COMPLETED _____

7 Demonstrate cleaning and sharpening an ax or hatchet.
COMPLETED _____

8 Following the Woods Tools Safety Rules (page 327), participate in skill instruction as needed and do three of the following using a knife, bow saw, folding saw, hatchet, or ax:
COMPLETED _____

  a _____ Whittle a cooking stick and cook a food item over a wood or charcoal fire.

  b _____ Whittle something out of soft wood.

  c _____ Make a fuzz stick.

  d _____ Prepare tinder, kindling, and fuel wood for a small fire.

e _____ Saw off a piece of a log at least 2-inches in diameter.

f _____ Chop through a log at least 2-inches in diameter on a chopping block.

g _____ Split a log.

h _____ Limb a log (stand on the opposite side of the log from where you are limbing).

i _____ Use an ax to cut a V-shaped notch at least two-inches (2") deep in a large log (bucking).

A total of 8 requirements need to be fulfilled for this badge

Camping Log

Date(s)	Hiking Plan Verified by	Location	Number of nights

Camping Log

Date(s)	Hiking Plan Verified by	Location	Number of nights

Camping Log

Date(s)	Hiking Plan Verified by	Location	Number of nights

NOTES

CHAPTER 5

FIRST AID

You may give birthday presents or Christmas presents, and that's great. Yet the greatest gift you can give someone is life, and first-aid skills put that gift within your reach. First aid is not a substitute for professional medical care, but it can keep a victim alive, as comfortable as possible, and avoid or minimize permanent damage.

First aid is needed most at life's most unpleasant moments. The victim may be upset and surrounded by other people who are upset. It's easy to let your emotions run away with you too, but don't let that happen. Stay calm. Encourage others to stay calm. And then act decisively.

Remember that courage is not the absence of fear; rather, it is putting fear on hold while you act. To ensure that this happens, practice your first aid skills often. There are three stages you'll go through: when you can't get it right, when you can get it right, and when you can't get it wrong. Aim for the last stage, and take a refresher course from time to time to stay there.

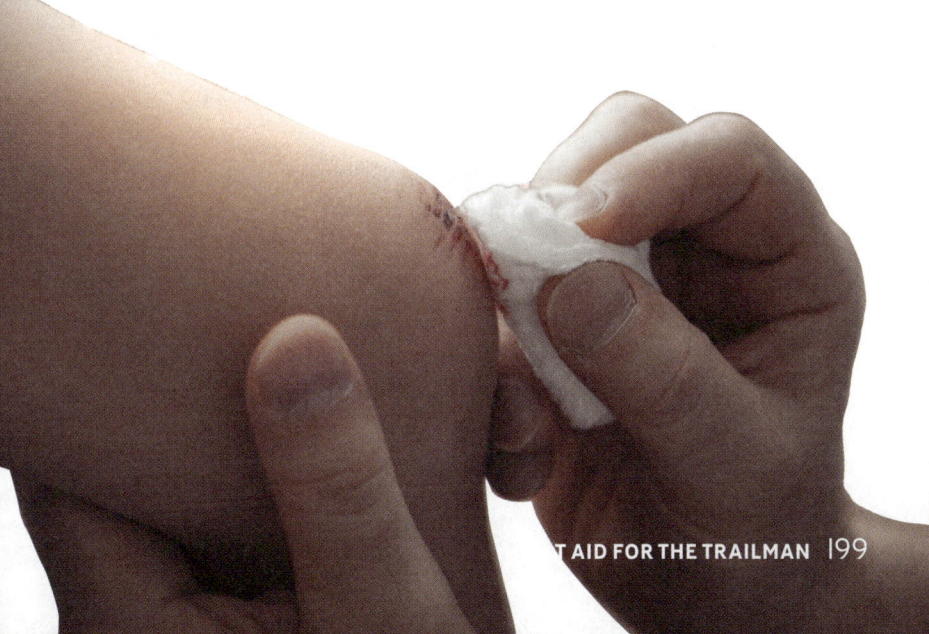

HANDS-ONLY CPR

Hands-only CPR (Cardiopulmonary Resuscitation) is taught by the American Red Cross. This technique is used to get air into the victim's chest and to get blood to carry that oxygen to the body's tissues.

1. If you see someone suddenly collapse, check the scene for safety. See if the victim responds to you by tapping him on the shoulder and saying, "Are you okay?"
2. Briefly look at the chest for signs of breathing.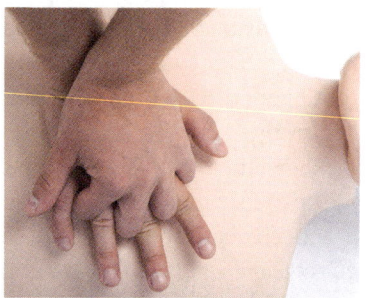
3. If the victim doesn't respond, call or send someone to call for help.
4. If the victim is not breathing or is gasping, prepare to give chest compressions. Kneel beside him and put the heel of one hand on the center of his chest. Place your other hand over that hand, lacing your fingers together. Position your shoulders directly over your hands, keeping your arms straight and your fingers off the chest.
5. Push hard and fast, at least 2 inches strokes, and a rate of 100 compressions per minute. Then let the chest rise completely before pressing down again. Don't take your hands off the chest, just your weight.
6. If the victim is a child (1–8 years of age), the technique remains the same, except you may only need one hand to give adequate chest compressions and your strokes should be shorter.
7. If the victim is an infant (less than 1 year of age), everything is the same except the chest compressions are done with 2 fingers in the middle of the chest just below the nipple line and your strokes should be shorter.
8. Keep going. Do not stop compressions until the victim shows an obvious sign of life (such as breathing), the scene becomes

unsafe, an Automatic External Defibrillator (AED) is ready, you are too exhausted to continue, or a trained responder takes over.

9. If there are other bystanders, teach them to do compressions and take turns with you. Switch places about every 2 minutes to avoid fatigue.

Hands-only CPR is a great first step, but it is somewhat limited. Learning full CPR that involves rescue breathing and chest compressions will enable you to give greater levels of assistance in a wider variety of circumstances.

RESCUE BREATHING

The next level in CPR is to breathe for the victim. You need to use a protective barrier device or mask when performing rescue breaths. This skill should be taught by a qualified instructor and practiced on a simulator CPR dummy.

Clear the airway

1. After you have performed 30 chest compressions, open the victim's airway using the head-tilt, chin-lift maneuver. Put your palm on the victim's forehead and gently tilt the head back. With the other hand, gently lift the chin forward to open the airway.
2. Check quickly for normal breathing, taking no more than 5 to 10 seconds.
3. Look for chest rise.
4. Gasping is not considered to be normal breathing.
5. If the victim isn't breathing normally and you are trained in CPR, begin mouth-to-mouth Rescue Breathing.

You need to use a protective barrier device or mask when performing rescue breaths.

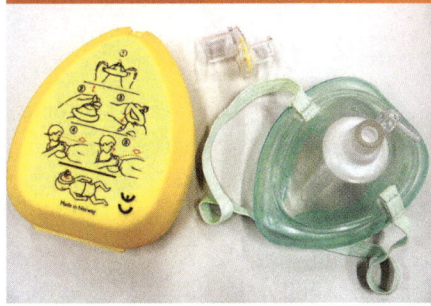

Breathe for the victim

Rescue Breathing can be mouth-to-mouth breathing or mouth-to-nose breathing if the mouth is seriously injured or can't be opened.

1. With the airway open (using the head-tilt, chin-lift maneuver), pinch the nostrils shut for mouth-to-mouth breathing and cover the victim's mouth with yours, making a seal.
2. Give the first of 2 rescue breaths, each over 1 second.
3. Deliver enough air to make the chest rise.
4. Watch to see if the chest rises.
5. If it does, then give another breath.
6. If not, then repeat the head-tilt, chin-lift maneuver and try again.
7. If still no chest rise, consider airway obstruction. *(See Choking)*
    1. Resume chest compressions to restore circulation. *(See Hands-Only CPR)*
    2. Do not stop chest compressions for more than 10 seconds at a time.
8. Thirty chest compressions followed by 2 rescue breaths is considered 1 cycle.
9. If the victim has not begun to move after 5 cycles (about 2 minutes) and an AED is available, apply it and follow the prompts. *(See AED)*
10. Administer one shock, then immediately resume chest compressions.
11. Continue for two more minutes before analyzing for a second shock.
12. The AED will prompt you.
13. Continue these cycles of 30:2 and then AED after each 5th cycle (about 2 minutes).
14. Continue CPR until there are signs of movement or until emergency medical personnel take over.

15. If there are other rescuers, take turns switching every 5 cycles (about 2 minutes).

Breathe for the young victim
Child (1-8 yrs of age)
- Deliver enough air to make the chest rise, not too much.
- Use the same technique.

Infant
- Deliver enough air to make the chest rise—just what is in your cheeks.
- Cover infant's mouth and nose with your mouth.

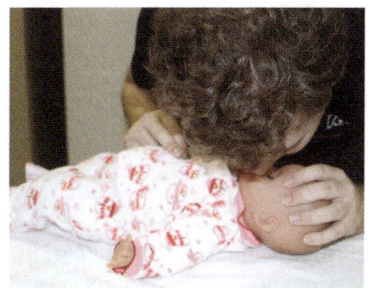

AED

An AED, or Automated External Defibrillator, is used to reset the heart when it is in a **deadly rhythm.**

Just like you see on TV, the AED will shock the victim. The AED will decide whether to shock or not, depending on if it would help the victim. The AED will guide you through the process; you only have to turn it on or open the lid.

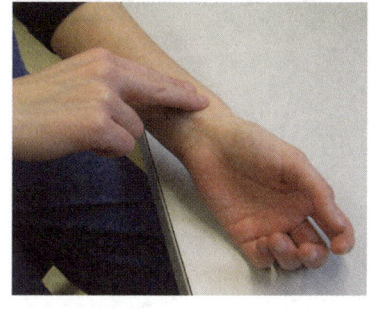

- Call 9-1-1 or have someone else call 9-1-1. If two rescuers are present, one can provide CPR while the other calls 9-1-1 and gets the AED.
- Check the victim's breathing and pulse. If breathing and pulse are absent or irregular, prepare to use the AED as soon as possible.
- If no one knows how long the victim has been unconscious, or if an AED isn't readily available, do 2 minutes of CPR. Then use the AED (if you have one).
- After you use the AED, or if you don't have an AED, give CPR until

emergency medical help arrives or until the victim begins to move. Try to limit pauses in CPR.
- After 2 minutes of CPR, you can use the AED again to check the victim's heart rhythm and give another shock, if needed. If a shock isn't needed, then continue CPR.

Using an Automated External Defibrillator (AED)

AEDs are user-friendly devices that untrained bystanders can use to save someone's life.
- **Before using an AED**, check for puddles or water near the victim who is unconscious. Move the victim to a dry area, and stay away from wetness when delivering shocks (water conducts electricity).
- **Turn on the AED's power.** The device will give you step-by-step instructions. You'll hear voice prompts and may see prompts on a screen.

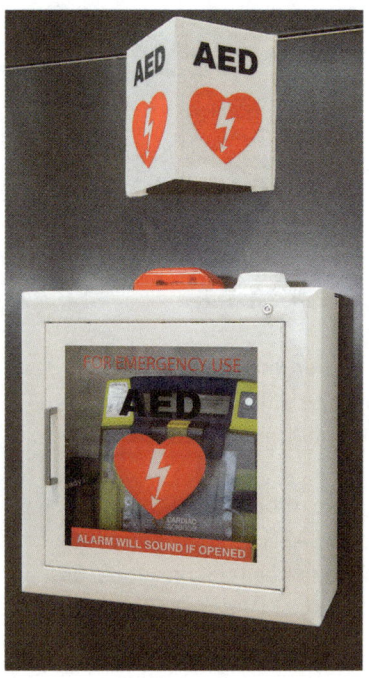

- **Expose the victim's chest.** If the victim's chest is wet, dry it. AEDs have sticky pads with sensors called electrodes. Apply the pads to the victim's chest as pictured on the AED's instructions.
- **Place one pad on the right center of the victim's chest above the nipple.**
- **Place the other pad slightly below the other nipple and to the left of the ribcage.** See photo here.
- Make sure the sticky pads have good connection with the skin. If not, the machine may repeat the phrase "check electrodes."
- There are usually different

pads for children than for adults—make sure you select the correct pads.
- If the victim has a lot of chest hair, you may have to trim it.
- If the victim is wearing a medication patch that's in the way, remove it and wipe the area clean.
- Remove metal necklaces and underwire bras. The metal may conduct electricity and cause burns.
- Check the victim for implanted medical devices, such as a pacemaker. Also check for body piercings.
- Move the defibrillator pads at least I inch away from implanted devices or piercings so the electric current can flow freely between the pads.

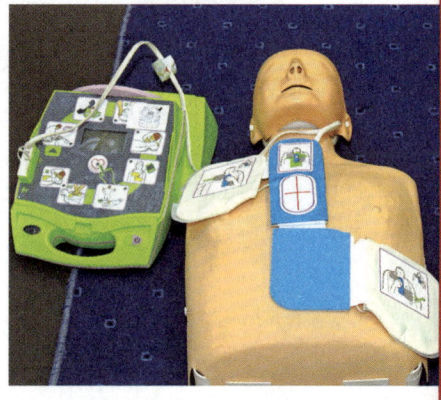

- Check that the wires from the electrodes are connected to the AED. Make sure no one is touching the victim, and then press the AED's "analyze" button. Stay clear while the machine checks the victim's heart rhythm.
- If a shock is needed, the AED will let you know when to deliver it. Stand clear of the victim and make sure others are clear before you push the AED's "shock" button.
- Start or resume CPR until emergency medical help arrives or until the victim begins to move. Stay with the victim until medical help arrives, and report all important information to them.

First Aid Kits

When you go on outings, you should always have a personal first aid kit to treat minor problems. Unlike your Troop first aid kit, the personal kit is lightweight and small, just right for your pack. Store yours in a re-sealable plastic bag. It should contain the following:

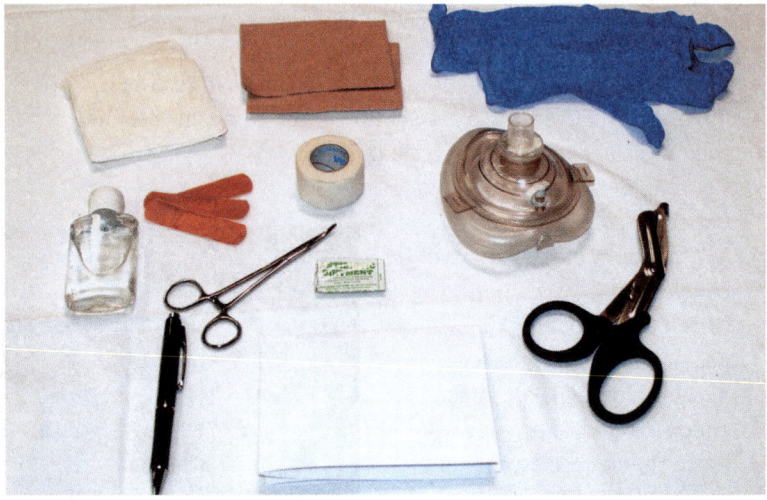

- 6 adhesive bandages
- 2 sterile 3 x 3 inch gauze pads
- Small roll of adhesive tape
- 3 x 6 inch piece of moleskin
- Small bottle of alcohol-based hand sanitizing gel
- Small tube of triple antibiotic ointment
- Scissors
- Tweezers
- Disposable non-latex gloves
- CPR breathing barrier
- Pencil and paper

Your Troop first aid kit will contain a larger variety of supplies to handle more serious emergencies. It should be kept in plain view under the dining fly, clearly marked with a red cross on a white background.

Both personal and Troop first aid kits should be checked at least once a year to make sure that the supplies are present and that nothing has expired.

ACTION PLAN

There is no need to rush to treat a skin rash or a scraped knee. For more serious injuries, use the first aid action plan to make sure proper procedures are carried out in the best order.

Check the scene. You may spot clues to what caused the accident, and you may spot dangers that pose further hazard to the victim, bystanders, or you.

Call for help. Look for a bystander who has more experience or for someone who can call for medical assistance. In the backcountry, send two or more people with as much of the following information as you can:
- Location of the victim
- Description of the illness or injuries
- Time the problem occurred
- Treatment the victim has received thus far
- Number of people with the victim and their level of training
- Approach safely.

You're not being helpful if you become a victim too. Introduce yourself to the victim and tell him that you know first aid. Ask if he needs help. If he's unconscious or too badly injured to respond, assume the answer is yes.

Provide urgent treatment. Begin by checking the victim's condition. Is he conscious and breathing? Is his heart beating? Is there severe bleeding? Do you see evidence of a cause such as allergies, a diabetic bracelet, or a container of poison?

Triage: What do you do if you come upon more than one victim? Triage involves quickly evaluating the severity of condition of each victim, prioritizing which victim needs immediate treatment, and determining how to best ration your resources: rescuers, supplies,

FIRST AID FOR THE TRAILMAN

and transportation options.

Treat every victim for shock. When a victim is badly injured, his heart and lungs may not be providing enough blood and oxygen to body tissues. Shock requires rapid treatment. Its onset can be sudden, and people can go from alert talking and moving to acting strangely or slipping out of consciousness before you know it.

Decide where to go from here. If medical help will arrive shortly, keep the victim comfortable where he is and monitor his condition.

On a wilderness camping trip

If in your best judgment the victim can travel and should hike to the nearest road, help him travel. If the injuries are serious, it is usually better to send two or more people to get medical help. At any rate, continue to monitor the victim closely and see if you need to take further action.

On the open water

Radio for help. GPS coordinates will be useful. Otherwise, you need another plan to get help.

On a canoe trip

A Personal Locator Beacon or satellite phone is the best way to get help. Otherwise, you need another plan to get help.

PROTECT YOURSELF

Always protect yourself from blood and bodily fluids
- Wear gloves when you may be exposed to blood or bodily fluids, mucous membranes, or non-intact skin of an injured victim. Also wear gloves if someone is infected with a germ or bacteria that might infect you.
- Wear eye protection when you may be exposed to splashing of blood or bodily fluids.
- Use a barrier device when giving mouth-to-mouth breaths—preferably a device with a one-way valve.

Proper way to remove gloves
- Grasp outside edge near wrist.
- Peel away from hand, turning glove inside out.
- Hold in opposite gloved hand.

- Slide ungloved finger under the wrist of the remaining glove; be careful not to touch the outside of the glove.
- Peel off from inside, creating a bag for both gloves.
- Discard properly.
- Wash hands thoroughly.

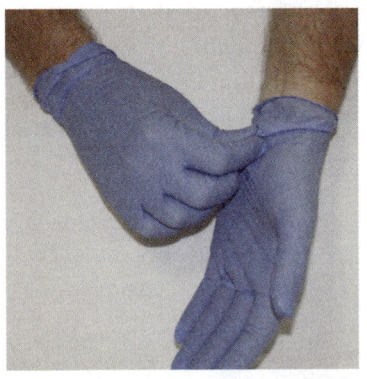
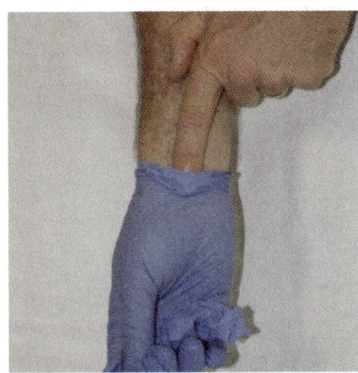
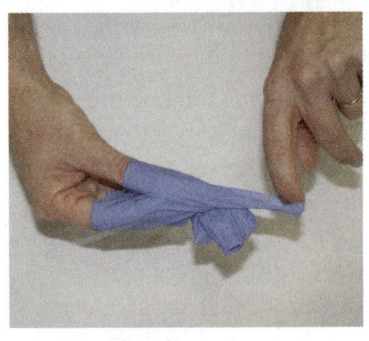
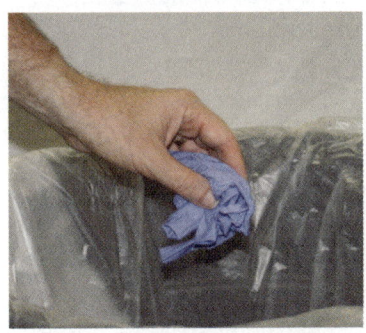

Hand washing
- When decontaminating hands with an alcohol-based hand gel, apply product to hands and rub until hands are dry.
- When washing hands with soap and water, wet hands first with water, apply an amount of product recommended by the manufacturer to hands, and rub hands together vigorously for at least 15 seconds. Cover all surfaces of the hands and fingers, including under the fingernails. Rinse hands with water and dry thoroughly with a disposable towel. Use the towel to turn off the faucet.

- Liquid, bar, leaflet, or powdered forms of plain soap are acceptable when washing hands with water and a non-antimicrobial soap.

SHOCK

When a victim has been injured or subjected to another stress, the circulatory system may not be able to provide enough blood to all parts of the body. **Shock is a life-threatening condition.**

Shock may have all, some, or none of these symptoms:

- Weakness
- Extreme thirst
- Restlessness or irritability
- Confusion, fear, and dizziness
- Skin that is moist, cool, clammy, and pale or gray
- A weak, quick pulse
- Blood pressure below normal
- Shallow, slow, rapid, deep, or irregular breathing
- Nausea and vomiting

Treat every accident victim for shock even if there are no symptoms. Victims almost always experience some degree of shock, although they might not be affected right away. Your quick response may prevent shock from setting in.

Treatment for shock includes sending for help, treating the immediate cause of the distress with first aid, helping the victim lie down, and—if you don't suspect back, neck, or head injuries or fractures of the leg or hip—raising the feet about a foot high to move blood from the legs to the vital organs. Keep the victim warm with blankets, sleeping bags, or coats. If you remain calm, you will increase the victim's ability to be calm.

> **Treat every accident victim for shock even if there are no symptoms.**

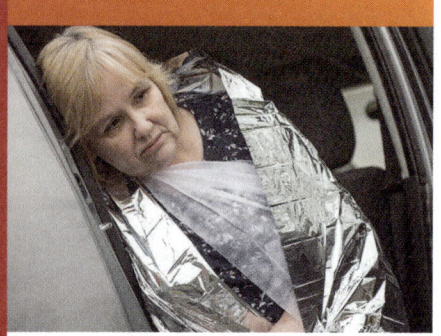

CHOKING

The usual cause of choking is foreign matter lodged in a victim's windpipe. A choking victim will probably panic, which usually makes it difficult to get his cooperation. Try to keep the victim calm so you can decide if your help is needed or if the victim can cough up the obstruction. "Are you choking?" That question is very effective. The victim may be coughing or gasping violently, but if you get an answer, he is probably not choking. As long as he continues to cough, he is helping himself to clear any obstruction. A victim of choking usually cannot speak.

If all you get is a gesture, pointing to the throat, or the universal sign of hands around the throat, the victim probably cannot breathe. Similarly, if the victim's face turns blue or if the victim collapses, the victim probably cannot breathe. In these cases, you need to perform the Heimlich maneuver at once. The Heimlich maneuver operates on the same principle as an air gun. You are using trapped air to pop out the airway obstruction.

- Start by first attempting 5 back blows. Bend the person forward at the waist, and give 5 back blows between the shoulder blades.
- If the back blows do not result in the victim being able to breathe or cough, then find the proper stance—behind the victim with one of your feet planted firmly between the

victim's feet and the other foot further back to brace yourself in case the victim loses consciousness.
- Wrap one of your arms around the victim, and place your hand in a closed fist just slightly above his belly button.
- Place your other hand directly on top of the first.
- Squeeze the victim's abdomen in quick upward thrusts as many times as necessary to dislodge the object.
- If the victim is a young child, you may need to kneel behind him to perform the Heimlich maneuver; otherwise, no change in technique is necessary.

If you are unable to clear the victim's air passage, dial 9-1-1 immediately and continue to perform the Heimlich maneuver until help arrives. If the victim loses consciousness, then begin CPR. Each time, before you give a breath, look to see if you can see the object and pluck it out. Only try to remove an object if you can see it. No blind finger sweeps.

Infant Choking

DO NOT perform these steps if the infant is coughing forcefully or has a strong cry. Strong coughs and cries can push the object out of the airway.

If the child is not coughing forcefully or does not have a strong cry, follow these steps:

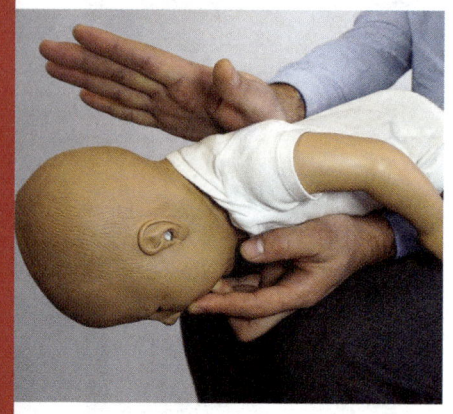

- Lay the infant face down, along your forearm. Use your thigh or lap for support. Hold the infant's chest in your hand and his jaw with your fingers. Point the infant's head downward, lower than the body.
- Give up to 5 quick, forceful blows between the infant's shoulder blades. Use the palm of your free hand.

If the object does not come out of the airway after 5 blows:
- Turn the infant face up. Use your thigh or lap for support. Support the head.
- Place 2 fingers on the middle of his breastbone just below the nipples.
- Give up to 5 quick thrusts down, compressing the chest 1/3 to 1/2 the depth of the chest.
- Continue 5 back blows followed by 5 chest thrusts until the object is dislodged or the infant loses alertness (becomes unconscious).

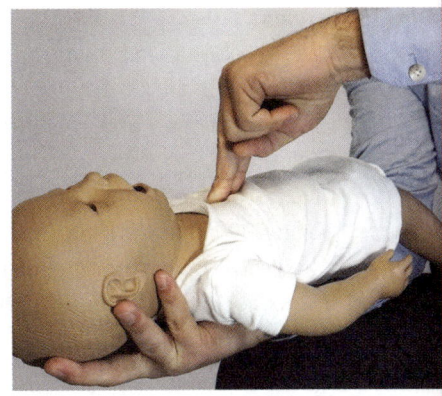

If the child becomes unresponsive, stops breathing, or turns blue:
- Shout for help.
- Give infant CPR. Call 9-1-1 after 2 minutes of CPR.
- If you can see the object blocking the airway, try to remove it with your finger. **Try to remove an object only if you can see it. No blind finger sweeps.**

HEART ATTACK

Symptoms (may experience any or all of the following):
- Uncomfortable pressure, fullness, or squeezing pain in the center of the chest
- Prolonged pain in the upper abdomen
- Discomfort or pain spreading beyond the chest to the shoulders, neck, jaw, teeth, or one or both arms
- Shortness of breath
- Lightheadedness, dizziness, fainting
- Sweating
- Nausea

A heart attack generally causes chest pain for more than 15 minutes, but it can also have no symptoms at all. Many people who experience a heart attack have warning signs hours, days, or weeks in advance.

Treatment:
- Call 9-1-1. Don't wait more than 20 minutes for symptoms to resolve.
- Have victim chew and swallow an aspirin, unless he is allergic to aspirin.
- Give nitroglycerin, if prescribed.
- Begin CPR if the victim is unconscious.
- If you're with a victim who might be having a heart attack and he is unconscious, tell the 9-1-1 dispatcher and begin CPR.

STROKE

A stroke occurs when there's bleeding into the brain or when normal blood flow to the brain is blocked. Within minutes of being deprived of essential nutrients, brain cells start dying—a process that will continue over the next several hours.

Seek immediate medical assistance. A stroke is a true emergency. The sooner treatment is given, the more likely it is that damage can be minimized.

In the event of a possible stroke, use F.A.S.T. to help remember warning signs:
- **Face.** Does the face droop on one side when victim tries to smile?
- **Arms.** Is one arm lower when victim tries to raise both arms?
- **Speech.** Can a simple sentence be repeated? Is victim's speech slurred or strange?
- **Time.** During a stroke, every minute counts. If you observe any of these signs, call 9-1-1 immediately.

SEIZURES

When a victim's body shakes rapidly and uncontrollably, he is having a seizure or convulsion. During convulsions, the victim's muscles contract and relax repeatedly. There are many different types of seizures. Some have mild symptoms and no body shaking.

Some seizures only cause a victim to have staring spells. These may go unnoticed. Specific symptoms depend on what part of the brain is involved. They occur suddenly and may include:

- Brief blackout followed by period of confusion
- Changes in behavior such as picking at one's clothing
- Drooling or frothing at the mouth
- Eye movements
- Loss of bladder or bowel control
- Mood changes such as sudden anger, unexplainable fear, panic, joy, or laughter
- Shaking of the entire body
- Sudden falling
- Teeth clenching
- Temporary halt in breathing
- Uncontrollable muscle spasms with twitching and jerking limbs

Symptoms may stop after a few seconds or minutes, or they may continue for 15 minutes. They rarely continue longer.

Causes

Seizures of all types are caused by disorganized and sudden electrical activity in the brain. Causes of seizures can include:

- Abnormal levels of sodium or glucose in the blood
- Brain infection, including meningitis
- Choking
- Drug abuse
- Electric shock
- Epilepsy
- Fever (particularly in young children)
- Head injury
- Heart disease
- Heat illness
- High fever
- Illegal and prescription drugs
- Low blood sugar
- Poisoning
- Stroke
- Very high blood pressure
- Venomous bites and stings

Care

Most seizures stop by themselves. However, the patient can be hurt or injured during a seizure.

When a seizure occurs, the main goal is to protect the victim from injury.

- Lay the victim on the ground in a safe area. Clear the area of furniture or other sharp objects.
- Cushion the victim's head.
- Loosen tight clothing, especially around the victim's neck.
- Turn the victim on his side. If vomiting occurs, this helps ensure

that the vomit is not inhaled into the lungs.
- Look for a medical ID bracelet with seizure instructions.
- Stay with the victim until he or she recovers or until help arrives.
- If a baby or child has a seizure during a high fever, cool the child slowly with tepid water. Do not place the child in a cold bath.

Call 9-1-1 or your local emergency number if:
- This is the first time the victim has had a seizure.
- A seizure lasts more than 2 to 5 minutes.
- The victim does not awaken or have normal behavior after a seizure.
- Another seizure starts soon after a seizure ends.
- The victim has a seizure in water.
- The victim is pregnant, injured, or has diabetes.
- The victim does not have a medical ID bracelet with seizure instructions.
- There is anything different about this seizure compared to the victim's usual seizures.

FAINTING

Fainting, or syncope, is a temporary loss of consciousness. If you're about to faint, you'll feel dizzy, lightheaded, or nauseated. Your field of vision may "white out" or "black out." Your skin may be cold and clammy. You may lose muscle control at the same time and fall down.

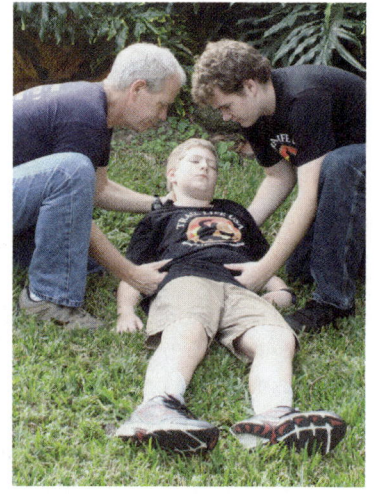

Fainting usually happens when your blood pressure drops suddenly, causing a decrease in blood flow to your brain. It is more common in older people. Some causes of fainting include:
- Heat or dehydration

- Emotional distress
- Standing up too quickly
- Certain medicines
- Drop in blood sugar
- Heart problems

When someone faints, make sure that his airway is clear and check for breathing. The victim should lie down for 10-15 minutes. Most people recover completely. Fainting is usually nothing to worry about, but sometimes it can be a sign of a serious problem. If you faint, it's important to see your health care provider and find out why it happened.

LOW BLOOD SUGAR

Low blood sugar, or hypoglycemia, is a condition that occurs when your blood sugar (glucose) is too low. Blood sugar below 70 mg/dL is considered low.

Causes

Low blood sugar is most common in people with diabetes who are taking insulin or other medicines to control their diabetes. Hypoglycemia in people who do not have diabetes may be caused by drinking alcohol or skipping a meal.

Symptoms

Symptoms you may have when your blood sugar gets too low include:

- Double vision or blurry vision
- Fast or pounding heartbeat
- Feeling cranky or acting aggressively
- Feeling nervous
- Headache
- Hunger
- Shaking or trembling
- Sweating
- Tingling or numbness of the skin
- Tiredness or weakness
- Trouble sleeping
- Unclear thinking

Sometimes your blood sugar may be too low even if you do not have symptoms. If your blood sugar gets too low, you may:

- Faint
- Have a seizure
- Go into a coma (insulin shock)

Treatment

Treatment depends on the cause. Eat something that has about 15 grams of carbohydrates. Examples are:

- 3 glucose tablets
- A 1/2 cup (4 ounces) fruit juice or regular, non-diet soda
- 5 or 6 hard candies
- 1 tablespoon sugar, plain or dissolved in water
- 1 tablespoon honey or syrup

Wait about 15 minutes before eating anything else. Be careful not to eat too much. This can cause high blood sugar.

Follow with a good meal or at least a good source of protein.

ALLERGIC REACTION (ANAPHYLACTIC SHOCK)

Anaphylaxis is a severe—possibly life threatening—whole-body allergic reaction to a chemical that has become an allergen. Anaphylaxis can occur in response to any allergen.

Common causes include:

- Drug allergies
- Insect bites/stings
- Food allergies (Eggs, fish, shellfish, soy, tree nuts, peanuts, and wheat are the most common.)

Symptoms

Symptoms can come on quickly:

- Abnormal (high-pitched) breathing sounds
- Chest discomfort or tightness
- Cough
- Difficulty breathing
- Difficulty swallowing
- Hives or itchiness
- Nausea or vomiting
- Rapid, weak pulse
- Swelling of the face, eyes, or tongue
- Unconsciousness

Treatment
- **Call 9-1-1 immediately.**
- Check the victim's airway, breathing, and circulation.
- Be calm and reassure the victim.
- If the victim has emergency allergy medicine, help the victim take or inject the medication—antihistamine or epinephrine injection.
- Avoid oral medication if the victim has difficulty breathing.
- Take steps to prevent shock.

Possible Complications
- Airway blockage
- Cardiac arrest
- Respiratory arrest
- Shock

Epinephrine injection

CUTS AND SCRAPES

The skin is your primary defense against germs. When it gets broken, bacteria penetrate that outer wall and can cause infection.

Begin treating minor cuts and scrapes by thoroughly cleaning the wound with mild antibacterial soap and water. You can use sterilized tweezers to remove any debris that remains embedded in the wound after rinsing it to reduce the risk of an infection. If you can't remove all the debris, a trip to the emergency room will be necessary.

Cleaning the wound may induce bleeding. If so, use gauze or a clean cloth to apply gentle, continuous pressure for 5–10 minutes until the bleeding stops.

Apply a triple antibiotic ointment such as Neosporin™ to keep the wound from getting infected and to speed healing. Dress the wound with a bandage or sterile gauze to keep out dirt and bacteria. Clean the wound and change the dressing daily. If the wound is very deep or the bleeding is profuse, stitches may be required for the wound to heal properly. This should only be done by a health care professional.

SPLINTERS

1. **Clean wound**
   - Clean the area with mild soap and water.
   - If a small splinter doesn't hurt, let the splinter work its way out over a few days.
   - If it does hurt, touch the area gently with sticky tape and pull away carefully.
2. **Remove larger splinter**
   - Clean a small needle and tweezers with alcohol.
   - If you can see the end of the splinter, grip it with the tweezers and gently pull out the entire splinter.
   - If none of the splinter is sticking out, follow the path of the splinter with the needle. Open the skin and expose enough of the splinter to remove it with tweezers.
   - Clean wound area again. Apply a bandage and antibiotic ointment.

Most splinters do not need the care of a health care provider, but it is important to prevent possible infection *(See Puncture Wounds, below)*.

BITE WOUNDS

A bite from a wild animal, such as a raccoon or squirrel, may require an immediate shot to prevent the possibility of rabies. Seek medical advice. Domestic animals can carry rabies as well. If the animal is unknown to victim, find the owner and get shot records. If you can't find an owner, seek medical advice.

A bite from a domestic pet may be painful but rarely requires a visit to the emergency room. Unless obvious bodily harm was sustained, simple precautionary treatment is enough. Use the same procedures for a human bite.

- Use water and antibacterial soap to thoroughly clean the bite wound.
- Apply antibiotic ointment such as Neosporin™ to prevent infection.
- If the injury resulted in broken skin, dress it with a sterile bandage and replace the dressing frequently.
- If the bite is deep, the victim may need to be treated for a puncture wound.

PUNCTURE WOUNDS

A puncture wound does not usually bleed profusely. While painful, it may appear harmless because the skin around the puncture may close. Yet puncture wounds are very susceptible to infection and if untreated can result in serious complications.

Punctures of the foot caused by stepping on a nail through a shoe are extremely prone to infection. If the puncture was caused by stepping on a nail or glass that has been exposed to the elements, it would be wise to see a doctor, who may recommend a tetanus shot or booster.

Animal bites resulting in a puncture wound are serious. If the bleeding is heavy or the wound or what produced it appears unsanitary, clean the injured area thoroughly with water and a mild antibacterial soap, then seek medical assistance as soon as possible.

If the injury is minor, clean it with soap and water, then apply an antibiotic ointment such as Neosporin™ to prevent infection. Dress the wound with sterile bandage, and replace the dressing frequently. Keep watch for the next few days. If you notice persistent redness or puffiness or if the wound starts to ooze, have the victim consult a doctor right away.

MOUTH AND TOOTH INJURIES

If your tooth is broken, chipped, or fractured, see your dentist as soon as possible. Otherwise, your tooth could be damaged further or become infected, which may result in the loss of that tooth.

In the meantime, try the following self-care measures:

- If the tooth is painful, take acetaminophen or another pain reliever. Rinse your mouth with salt water.
- If the break has caused a sharp or jagged edge, cover it with a piece of wax, paraffin, or chewing gum.
- If you must eat, eat soft foods and avoid biting down on the broken tooth.

Knocked-out Tooth

If a permanent tooth is knocked out, get emergency dental care. It's sometimes possible to successfully reattach permanent teeth that have been knocked out, but only if you follow the steps below immediately—before you see a dentist.
- Handle your tooth by the top or crown only, not the roots.
- Don't rub the tooth or scrape it to remove debris. This damages the root surface.
- Gently rinse your tooth in a bowl of tap water. Don't hold it under running water.
- Try to replace your tooth in the socket. If it doesn't go all the way into place, bite down slowly and gently on gauze or a moistened tea bag to help keep it in place. Hold the tooth in place until you see your dentist.
- If you can't replace your tooth in the socket, immediately place it in some milk, your own saliva, or a warm, mild saltwater solution—¼ teaspoon salt to 1 quart of water.

Bleeding of the Mouth

- Wash your hands well with soap and water, if available.
- Put on medical gloves, if available, before applying pressure to the wound. If gloves are not available, use many layers of fabric, plastic bags, or whatever else you have between your hands and the wound.
- Have the victim hold his own hand over the wound, if possible, and apply pressure to the injured area.
- Use your bare hands to apply pressure only as a last resort.
- Have the victim sit up and tilt his head forward with his chin down.

This will help any blood drain out of the mouth rather than down the back of the throat. Swallowing blood can cause vomiting.
- Remove any visible objects that are easy to remove. Remove chewing gum if it is present.
- Remove any jewelry from the general area of the wound.
- Press firmly on the wound with a clean cloth or the cleanest material available. If there is an object in the wound, apply pressure around the object, not directly over it.
- Apply steady pressure for a full 15 minutes. Use a clock to time the 15 minutes. It can seem like a long time. Resist the urge to peek after a few minutes to see whether bleeding has stopped. If blood soaks through the cloth, apply another one without lifting the first.
- Inner lip bleeding. Press the bleeding site against the teeth or jaw, or place a rolled or folded piece of gauze or clean cloth between the lip and gum.
- Tongue bleeding. Squeeze or press the bleeding site with gauze or a piece of clean cloth.
- Inner cheek bleeding. Place rolled gauze or a piece of clean cloth between the wound and the teeth.
- Avoid spitting, using any form of tobacco, and using straws, which can make bleeding worse.

SEVERE BLEEDING

A severe cut can kill in a matter of minutes. Immediately ask someone to summon help, but if it is just you and the victim, do not leave him before beginning first aid.

With a clean cloth or sterile dressing, use the palm of your hand to apply firm, continuous pressure directly over the wound for 20 minutes. A tourniquet may be used if you're unable to stop the bleeding but only as a last resort. Use an elastic bandage, if you have one, to secure the pad tightly over the source of the bleeding.

If you don't have a clean cloth, use whatever is available. A victim can bleed to death long before he would ever become infected.

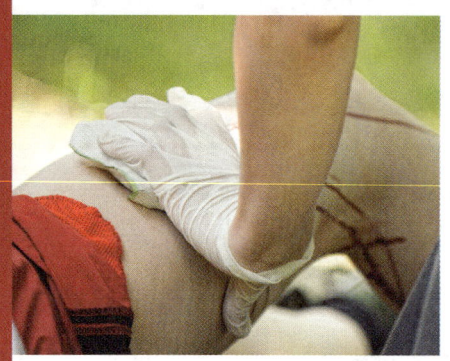

After the bleeding stops, hold the pad in place with a sterile bandage. Bind the pad firmly but not tightly enough to cut off circulation. Immobilize and elevate the extremity above the heart.

When the bandage is on a limb, check farther down the limb every few minutes for a pulse, for warmth, feeling, and color. If you can't feel a pulse or if fingers or toes are numb, pale, or cold, the bandage needs to be loosened.

If a pad becomes soaked with blood, put a fresh pad over it and continue to apply pressure. Do not remove a blood-soaked pad.

As with all other injuries requiring first aid, treat the victim for shock.

INTERNAL BLEEDING OR ABDOMINAL PAIN

Call 9-1-1 if:
- You have pain and tenderness to the touch in the lower right abdomen with fever and/or vomiting. These may be signs of appendicitis. Seek medical attention.
- The person is pregnant and has abdominal pain or vaginal bleeding. This may be a sign of an ectopic pregnancy or miscarriage. Seek medical attention.

Treat symptoms:
- For heartburn from gastro-esophageal reflux disease (GERD), take an over-the-counter antacid.
- For constipation, take a mild stool softener or laxative.
- For pain, take acetaminophen. Avoid aspirin and ibuprofen

because they can cause stomach irritation or bleeding.

Call a doctor if the victim:
- Has severe abdominal pain or pain that lasts several days
- Has nausea, vomiting, fever, or is unable to keep food down for several days
- Has bloody stools or black, tar-like stools
- Vomits blood
- Has difficulty breathing
- Has suffered a blow or injury to the abdomen in the days before the pain started

OBJECTS IN THE EYE

The best way to get objects out of your eye is to avoid getting them into your eye. That's why you wear safety glasses or goggles while using certain types of tools and machines that throw out debris.

If someone does get something in his eye, he should not rub it. If the victim wears contact lenses, they should be removed. Ask the victim to blink his eyes rapidly. This may permit tears to wash the object out. Flushing the eyes with eye wash or clean water from a tap, water bottle, or cup are also useful. If the object will not wash out, cover the affected eye with a dry, sterile gauze pad and get the victim to a doctor.

Certain liquid chemicals in the eye can cause discomfort or damage and should be treated by flushing the eye under a tap. The length of time recommended is often stated on the chemical container.

BLISTERS

The best way to deal with blisters is to prevent them in the first place. While you are hiking, wear shoes or boots that fit you well and have been properly broken in. If your socks get sweaty or wet, change them. Wear work gloves while working outdoors to protect your hands. If you get a blister while hiking, cut a piece of moleskin slightly larger than the blister patch. The moleskin will help protect the spot.

Do not pop blisters unless you have to. Breaking the skin increases the risk of infection. If you must pop them, sterilize a needle with a flame and stick the blister close to its base to drain the fluid. Apply antibiotic ointment and protect with a dressing.

BURNS

Proper care for a burn victim depends on the type and extent of his injury. Burns vary greatly from sunburn to life-threatening third-degree burns caused by open flames, chemicals, or electric shock. Treat the burn according to its type.

First-Degree Burns

Symptoms: First-degree burns are usually caused by overexposure to the sun (sunburn), and they are accompanied by redness and some swelling of the skin. The best way to treat sunburn is to avoid it by applying sunscreen with an SPF of 30 or greater every 2 hours. If you're sweating or swimming, apply the sunscreen more frequently. Wearing a wide-brim hat, sunglasses, long sleeves, and long pants can help as well.

Treatment: Treat a minor burn by first cooling the affected area. If possible, keep the injury under cool running water for at least 10 minutes.

If running water is not available, place the burned area in a container of cold water such as a bucket, tub, or even a deep dish. Using a cool, wet compress made of clean cloth will also work, if nothing else is available.

Keeping the burn cool will reduce pain and minimize the swelling. If the injury is on a part of a body where jewelry or snug clothing is present, carefully remove them before swelling begins. Apply a moisturizing lotion or aloe vera extract, and dress the burnt area with loosely wrapped sterile gauze.

Second-Degree Burns

Symptoms: Second-degree burns will result in deeper, more intense redness of the skin as well as swelling and blistering.

Treatment: This type of burn should be treated as a first-degree burn, but, because the damage to the skin is more extensive, extra care should be taken to avoid infection and excessive scarring. Replace the dressing daily and keep the wound clean. If a blister breaks, use mild soap and warm water to rinse the area. Apply antibiotic cream such as Neosporin™ to prevent infection before redressing in sterile gauze.

Third-Degree Burns

Symptoms: Third-degree burns may appear and feel deceptively harmless, as the victim may not feel much pain due to complete destruction of all layers of skin and tissue as well as nerve endings. The damaged area may appear charred or ash-color and will instantly start to blister or "peel."

Treatment: If the victim's clothing is on fire, shout, "Stop, drop, and roll." If the victim panics and runs, douse him with a nonflammable liquid. Dial 9-1-1. Do not remove burnt clothing from the victim, as this will expose open wounds to the elements and potential infection. If possible, cover the victim's injuries with wet, sterile cloth to reduce the pain and swelling. Do not apply any antibiotic cream or other lotions. If you notice that the victim is going into shock and he loses consciousness, you will need to perform CPR and treat for shock.

FRACTURES

A broken bone is not always obvious. It is important not to mistake a broken bone for a bruise or sprain. Typical symptoms of a fracture are:
- Immediate and excessive swelling
- Injured area appears deformed
- The bone has pierced the skin or bleeding is present (known as a "compound fracture")
- The farthest point of the injured limb turns blue or is numb to

the touch
- Even slight movement or contact with the injured area causes excessive pain

Immobilize the broken bone with a splint. A functional splint can be made of almost any material (sticks, plastic, etc.), as long as it is rigid and is longer than the broken bone. To apply the splint, simply lay it along the broken bone, and wrap it against the limb with gauze or a length of cloth, starting at a point farthest from the body. Do not wrap it too tight, as this may cut off blood flow.

If the break is in the upper or lower arm, loosely wrap a magazine or a thick newspaper around the break, and use a sling fashioned from gauze or a strip of cloth to keep the elbow immobilized.

A break in the lower or upper part of the leg requires two splints, one on each side of the leg (or at least the shin). If suitable material is unavailable, use the victim's healthy leg as a makeshift splint.

In the case of a compound fracture, do not attempt to push the exposed bone back into place. Splint around it to avoid aggravating any internal bleeding.

As much as possible, keep the victim from moving. **Until an ambulance arrives, remember I.C.E.:**

"I" is for ice. If possible, apply an ice pack or ice cubes to the injured area. This will reduce the swelling and pain; it can also help to slow bleeding. Apply ice for 20 minutes at a time and repeat every 3–6 hours.

"C" is for compression. If the wound is bleeding, apply direct pressure with a clean cloth to reduce blood flow (except in situations where direct pressure would be placed on a compound fracture that could increase internal damage).

"E" is for elevation. Keep the injured area as high above heart level as possible. This will reduce blood flow to the injury and minimize swelling.

Broken collarbone or clavicle

The clavicle connects the upper part of your breastbone (sternum) to your shoulder blade (scapula). Common causes of a broken collarbone include falls onto a shoulder, sports injuries, and trauma from traffic accidents.

- **Ice.** Applying ice to the affected area during the first two to three days following a collarbone break can help control pain and swelling.
- **Immobilization.** Restricting the movement of any broken bone is critical to healing. To immobilize a broken collarbone, the victim will most likely need to wear an arm sling. In some cases, a figure-eight strap that fits around both the victim's shoulders helps keep the bone in place.
- **Medications.** To reduce pain and inflammation, use over-the-counter pain relievers.
- **Get to a doctor** for treatment.

Broken Ankle

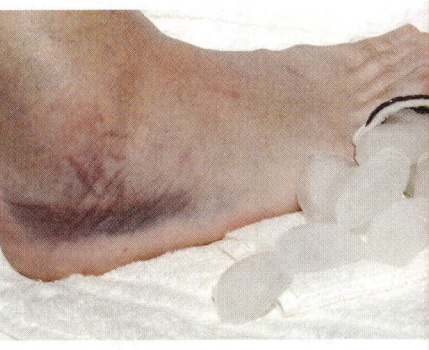

- **Ice.** Applying ice to the affected area during the first two to three days following a break can help control pain and swelling.
- **Immobilization.** Restricting the movement of any broken bone is critical to healing. To immobilize a broken ankle, wrap it in a figure-eight strap to help keep the bone in place.
- **Medications.** To reduce pain and inflammation, use over-the-counter pain relievers.
- **Get to a doctor** for treatment.

SPLINTING AND WRAPPING

When splinting a sprain or fracture in the field, you may need to create a splint using natural materials. It is recommended that your First Aid Kit also include a SAM Splint for quicker and easier splinting.

SAM Splints are foam-covered, foldable aluminum splints that are great First Aid resources.

Tying a Sling

- Bring the wounded arm across the victim's chest.
- Fold or lay a large cravat, shirt, towel, or other cloth into an obtuse triangular shape.
- Take one of the longer sides and lay it between the victim's chest and forearm and over the shoulder of the wounded side. Fold the opposite side of the sling up and over the victim's forearm and over the other shoulder.

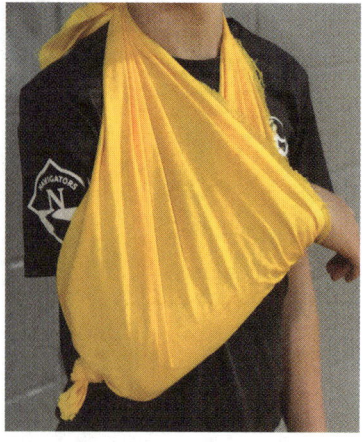

- Take the two long ends and tie them together behind the victim's neck. Ensure that you allow the sling to carry the weight of the wounded arm.
- Tie a knot in the corner of the sling near the victim's elbow bringing that corner of the sling up and around the elbow, trapping it from sliding out the back.

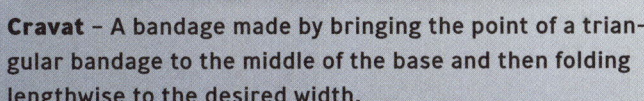

Cravat – A bandage made by bringing the point of a triangular bandage to the middle of the base and then folding lengthwise to the desired width.

Swathe – A bandage or wrapping or the act of wrapping or binding.

To splint a fractured wrist or forearm:

Prepping with Natural Materials

- Keep the wounded wrist or forearm in the most natural position without pain.
- Find several rigid objects slightly longer than the victim's forearm. Tent poles, sticks, branches, hiking poles, and tool handles will work well.
- Place at least two of the rigid objects on either side of the wounded area of the forearm.
- Place a rolled up cloth in the palm of the wounded hand for support.

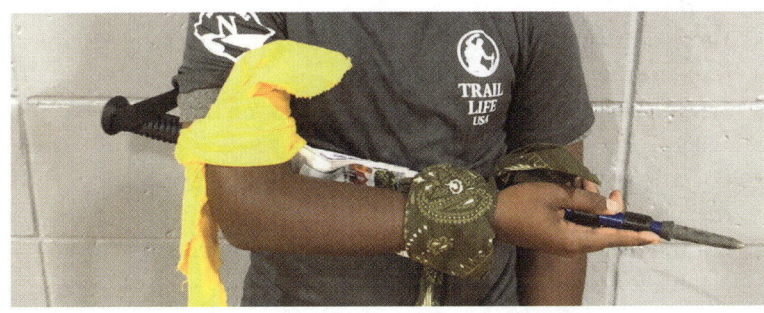

Prepping with a SAM Splint
- If your First Aid Kit has a SAM splint, fold it in half, upon itself, creating a double-layered splint. Leave one side approximately I inch longer than the other.
- Take the folded end of the SAM splint and roll it at least two times toward the side with the shortest end. This will provide a natural curvature for the hand when the splint is applied.
- Shape the SAM splint into a C curve along the long axis from the rolled end to the opposite end.
- Shape the splint until the splint generally conforms to the curve and shape of the limb being splinted.
- Pad the splint and fill in the voids as needed.
- Place the fractured forearm in the splint with the hand in a natural curve on top of the rolled end of the splint.

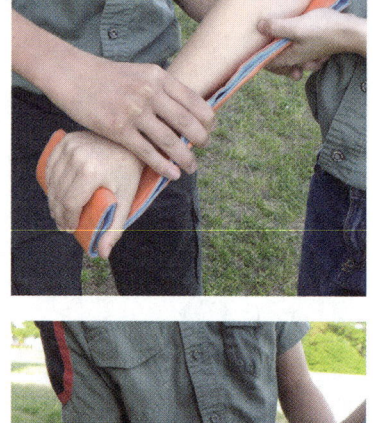

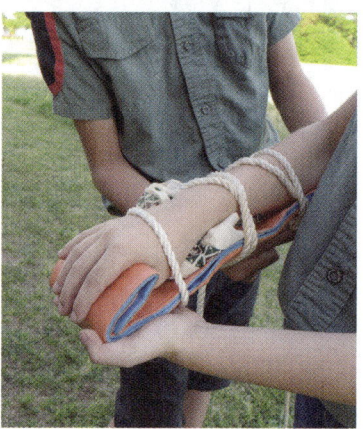

Tying the Splint
- Tie one cravat above (proximal) and one cravat below (distal) the fracture site.
- Tie the tails of the cravats in a nonslip knot on the outside of the splint.
- Check the victim's pulse (at the wrist). Loosen the cravats and reapply the splint if needed.
- Cut the tails of the each cravat to prevent accidental entanglement when the victim is moved.

- Apply a sling and swathe to further immobilize the fractured arm.

To splint a fractured elbow:

Prepping with Natural Materials
- The injured extremity should be placed in a V (bent) position with the forearm across the front of the chest between the neck and the abdomen or placed in a straightened position depending on the type of injury.
- Find several rigid objects longer than the victim's wounded area. Tent poles, sticks, branches, hiking poles, and tool handles will work well.

Prepping with a SAM Splint
- Take one splint and fold in half end-to-end.
- Fold the splint in half again lengthwise.
- Pad around the splint if needed.

Tying the Splint
- Place at least two of the rigid objects or SAM Splints on either side of the wounded area of the elbow, upper arm, and lower arm.
- Place a rolled up cloth in the palm of the wounded hand for support.
- Tie one cravat above (proximal) and one cravat below (distal) the fracture site.

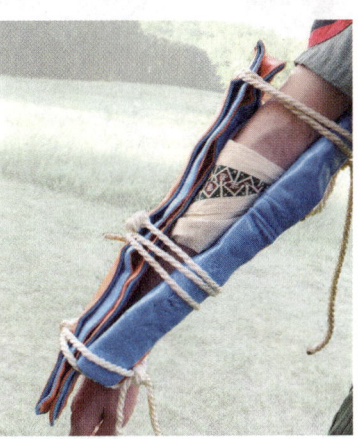

FIRST AID FOR THE TRAILMAN

- Tie the tails of the cravats in a nonslip knot on the outside of the splint.
- Check the victim's pulse (at the wrist). Loosen the cravats and reapply the splint if needed.
- Cut the tails of the each cravat to prevent accidental entanglement when the victim is moved.
- Apply a sling and swathe to further immobilize the fractured arm.

To splint a fractured long-bone (humerus) of the arm:

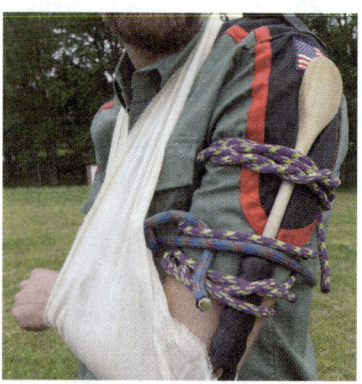

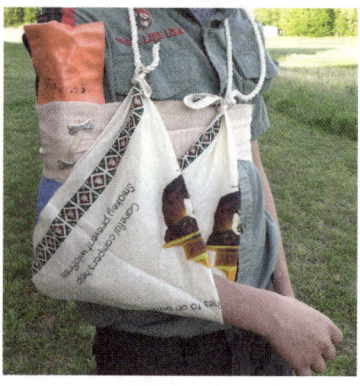

Prepping with Natural Materials
- The injured extremity should be placed in an L (bent) position with the forearm across the front of the mid chest.
- Find several rigid objects longer than the victim's upper arm. Tent poles, sticks, branches, hiking poles, and tool handles will work well.
- Place at least two of these rigid objects along the outside of the upper arm, running from slightly above the shoulder to slightly below the elbow.

Prepping with a SAM Splint
- The injured extremity should be placed in an L (bent) position with the forearm across the front of the mid chest.
- Fold one third of a 36-inch SAM splint upon itself to create a 12-inch section of double-layered splint.

- Bend the double-layered portion of the splint into a J and tape both layers together.
- Hook the elbow with the J portion of the splint, running the rest of the splint along the upper arm toward the shoulder (on the outside of the arm).
- Fold any excess splint—a portion extending above the top of the shoulder—back upon itself (double layer).

Tying the Splint
- Tie one cravat above (proximal) and one cravat below (distal) the fracture site.
- Tie the tails of the cravats in a nonslip knot on the opposite side of the victim's body from the splint.
- Check the victim's pulse (at the wrist). Loosen the cravats and reapply the splint if needed.
- Cut the tails of the each cravat to prevent accidental entanglement when the victim is moved.
- Apply a sling and swathe to further immobilize the fractured arm.

To splint a fractured collarbone (clavicle)

Tying the Splint
- Splints are not practical for a collarbone fracture.
- Apply a sling and swathe to immobilize the fractured collarbone.
- Get medical help.

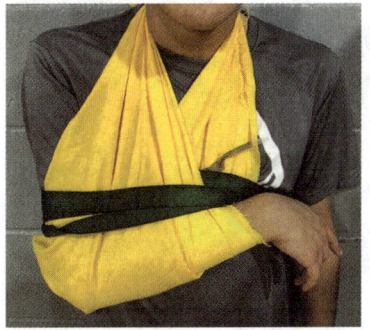

To splint a fractured ankle:

Prepping with Natural Materials
- Have the victim sit or lie down.
- Have another person manually immobilize the fractured extremity.
- Remove the foot gear and expose the fracture site.
- The injured ankle should be placed in the most natural position possible without pain.

- Apply padding to the bony prominence of the middle to outside portion of the ankle.
- Find several rigid objects the length of the victim's lower leg, preferably with a hooked shape on one end to act as a stirrup. Tent poles, sticks, branches, hiking poles, and tool handles could work well.

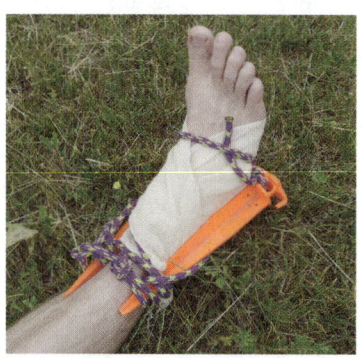

- Place the rigid objects on both sides of the victim's ankle and preferably hooked under the victim's foot.
- If no suitable objects are found, the victim's other leg could be used as splint by tying the legs and feet together. However, this method would require additional assistance in transporting the victim.

Prepping with a SAM Splint

- Fold a 36-inch formable splint to create two equal halves.
- Make sure the middle fold is large enough to accommodate the foot.
- Fold both sides of the splint in a slight C to create rigidity along the length of the splint.
- Apply padding to the bony prominence of the middle to outside portion of the ankle.
- Apply the splint to the ankle by placing the foot in the stirrup position of the splint.
- Form the splint to the length of the lower leg.

Tying the Splint

- Secure the splint by tying

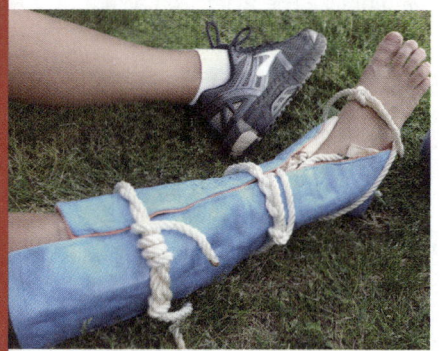

cravats or other cloths around the top and bottom of the foot as well as up the length of the splint.
- Tie at least one cravat above (proximal) and one cravat below (distal) the fracture site.
- Tie the tails of the cravats in a nonslip knot on the outside of the splint.
- Check the victim's pulse (at the ankle). Loosen the cravats and reapply the splint if needed.
- Cut the tails of the each cravat to prevent accidental entanglement when the victim is moved.

To splint a fractured tibia or fibula:

Prepping with Natural Materials

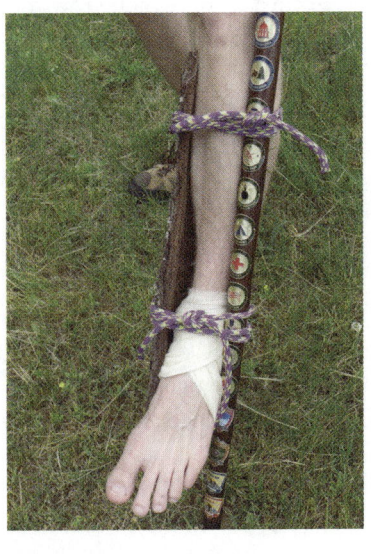

- Have the victim sit or lie down.
- Have another person manually immobilize the fractured extremity.
- Remove the foot gear and expose the fracture site.
- The injured leg should be placed in the straightest position possible without pain.
- Apply padding to the bony prominence of the middle to outside portion of the ankle.
- Find several rigid objects the length of the victim's lower leg, preferably with a hooked shape on one end to act as a stirrup. Tent poles, sticks, branches, hiking poles, and tool handles could work well.
- Place the rigid objects on both sides of the victim's ankle and preferably hooked under the victim's foot.
- If no suitable objects are found, the victim's other leg could be

used as splint by tying the legs and feet together. However, this method would require additional assistance in transporting the victim.

Prepping with a SAM Splint

- Apply padding to the bony prominence of the middle to outside portion of the ankle.
- Completely extend the entire 36-inch formable splint.
- Curve approximately 6 inches of the splint into a J shape.
- Form a C curve along the long axis of the remaining 30 inches of the splint.
- Perform the same steps to another 36-inch formable splint.
- Apply the splint to the outside area of the fractured tibia/fibula.
- Place the foot in the J portion of the splint and run the long axis of the splint up the leg toward the knee.
- Apply the second splint to the inside area of the fractured tibia/fibula.
- Place the foot (with the previous splint) into the J and run the long axis of the splint up the leg toward the knee.

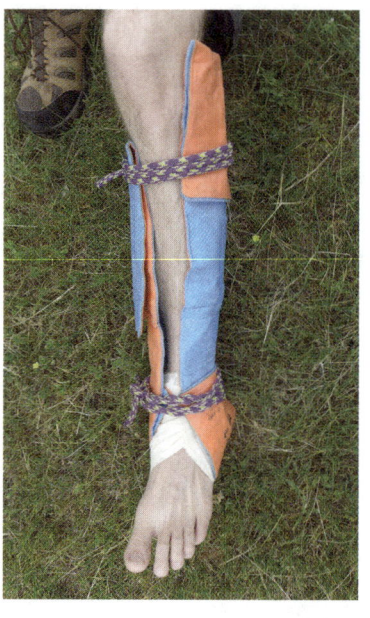

Tying the Splint

- Secure the splint by tying cravats or other cloths around the top and bottom of the foot as well as up the length of the splint.
- Tie at least one cravat above (proximal) and one cravat below (distal) the fracture site.
- Tie the tails of the cravats in a nonslip knot on the outside of the splint.
- Check the victim's pulse (at the ankle). Loosen the cravats and reapply the splint if needed.

- Cut the tails of the each cravat to prevent accidental entanglement when the victim is moved.

To splint a fractured knee:

Prepping with Natural Materials
- Have the victim sit or lie down.
- Have another person manually immobilize the fractured knee.
- Remove the foot gear.
- The injured knee should be placed in a slightly bent position if possible.
- Apply padding to the bony prominence of the middle to outside portion of the knee and ankle.
- Find several rigid objects the length of the victim's lower leg, preferably with a hooked shape on one end to act as a stirrup. Tent poles, sticks, branches, hiking poles, and tool handles could work well.
- Place the rigid objects on both sides of the victim's ankle and preferably hooked under the victim's foot.

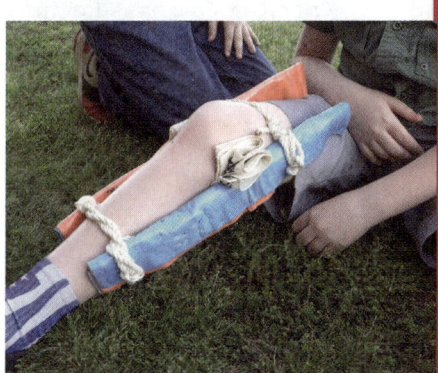

Prepping with a SAM Splint
- Take one splint and fold in half end-to-end.
- Fold the splint in half again lengthwise.
- Apply padding to the bony prominence of the middle to outside portion of the knee and ankle.

Tying the Splint
- Secure the splint by tying cravats or other cloths around the top and bottom of the foot as well as up the length of the splint.

> **Never attempt to straighten or apply traction on the fractured limb. A fractured femur is a medical emergency. Medical assistance must be sought as soon as possible. Moving the victim with a fractured femur may cause further life-threatening injury.**

- Tie at least one cravat above (proximal) and one cravat below (distal) the knee.
- Tie the tails of the cravats in a nonslip knot on the outside of the splint.
- Check the victim's pulse (at the ankle). Loosen the cravats and reapply the splint if needed.
- Cut the tails of the each cravat to prevent accidental entanglement when the victim is moved.

Fractures of the Femur (upper leg):

When a victim has a fractured femur, he should not be moved unless leaving him in place would result in greater injury being inflicted.

- Call 9-1-1 or send a group of Trailmen to go get help.

SPRAINS

A sprain is an injury to a ligament caused by the tearing of the fibers of the ligament. It can have a partial tear, or it can be completely torn apart. Sprained ligaments swell rapidly and are painful.

Treatment

Follow the instructions for R.I.C.E.:
- REST the injured limb.
- ICE the area with a cold pack, a slush bath of ice water, or a compression sleeve filled with cold water. Continue to ice for 15 to 20 minutes, 4 to 8 times a day, for the first 48 hours or until

swelling improves.
- COMPRESS the area with an elastic wrap or bandage.
- ELEVATE the injured limb above your heart whenever possible.

Splinting the injured limb can also help to reduce further injury.

After two days, gently begin using the injured area. See a doctor if the sprain isn't improving after two or three days.

Get emergency medical assistance if:
- You're unable to bear weight on the injured leg, the joint feels unstable or numb, or you can't use the joint. This may mean the ligament was completely torn. On the way to the doctor, apply a cold pack.
- You develop redness or red streaks that spread out from the injured area. This means you may have an infection.
- You have re-injured an area that has been injured a number of times in the past.
- You have a severe sprain. Inadequate or delayed treatment may contribute to long-term joint instability or chronic pain.

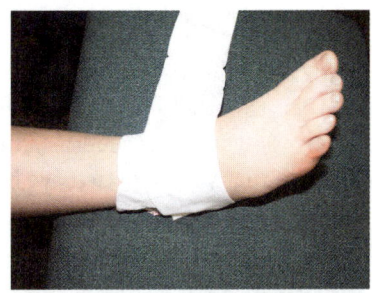
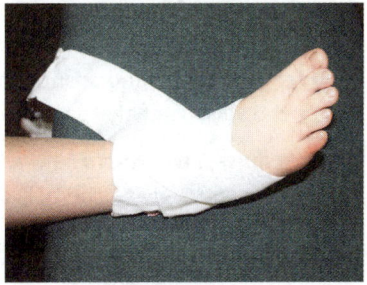
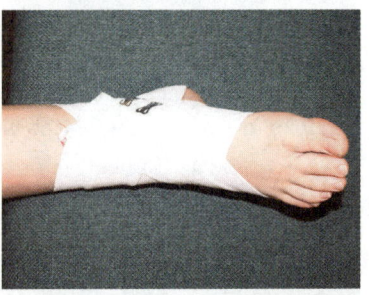
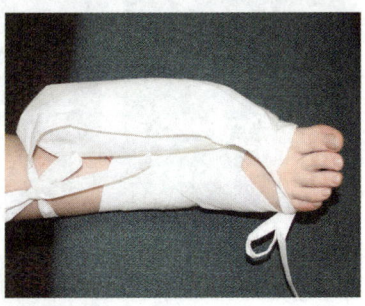

FIRST AID FOR THE TRAILMAN

TRANSPORTING METHODS

There are many ways to carry an injured victim. Choose one that is considerate of the severity and type of injury. Determine your resources: number and size of rescuers, materials available, also size of victim, distance that you have to move him, and the geography and topography. Make sure you don't get hurt or drop the victim. Be careful.

Walking assists:

Conscious—One Rescuer
- Place the victim's arm around your shoulders and hold that hand.
- Place your free hand around the victim's waist.
- Let the victim set the pace and be prepared to stop frequently.

Unconscious—Two Rescuer
- Both rescuers grasp the belt or waistband of the unconscious victim.
- Pull to lift the victim's upper body.
- With both rescuers facing each other, squat next to the victim and place his arm around your shoulders and hold that hand.
- Slowly stand to lift the victim. Keep your back straight and use your legs to help avoid injury.
- Move forward, dragging the victim's legs.

Pack strap carry

One rescuer

Two rescuers

Dragging assists: one rescuer

Blanket—Conscious or Unconscious
- Lay a blanket, coat, or tarp on the ground close to the victim.
- Roll or lift the victim carefully onto the blanket.
- Keep the victim's head and neck aligned while moving him.
- Keep enough material to pull the victim safely. Your grasp of the material should be about 2 feet from the victim's head.
- Keep your back as straight as possible while moving the victim.

Shoulder—Conscious or Unconscious
- Grasp the victim's clothing underneath his shoulders.
- Support the victim's head by keeping an arm along the side of it.
- Pull the victim, keeping his body aligned.

Ankle—Conscious or Unconscious
- Grasp the victim by the ankles or pant cuffs.
- Keep your back as straight as possible.
- Drag the victim in a straight line.
- This carry is not preferred, as it does not support the victim's head or neck. It should only be performed slowly and on smooth ground or grass.

Blanket rescue

Shoulder rescue

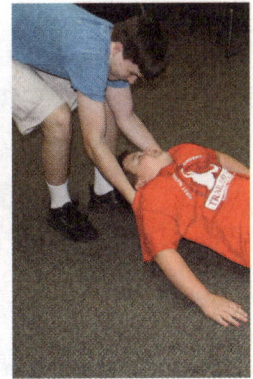

Ankle rescue

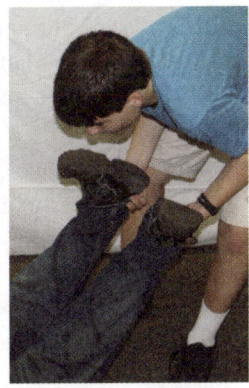

Two-Rescuer Carries:

Two-hand Seat—Conscious or Unconscious

- While facing each other, squat on each side of the victim. Keep your backs as straight as possible.
- Reach under the victim's shoulders with one arm and under his knees with the other.
- Grab your partner's wrists, arm, or shoulder and hold tightly.
- If the victim is conscious, he can place his arms around the rescuers' necks.
- Lift the victim slowly, using your legs and keeping your back straight.

Four-hand Seat—Conscious

- Face your partner and hold your right wrist with your left hand. Grab your partner's left wrist with your right hand. You should have a seat for the victim.
- Lower yourselves by bending your knees, keeping your wrists interlocked so the victim can sit.
- If the victim is conscious, he can place his arms around

Two-hand seat

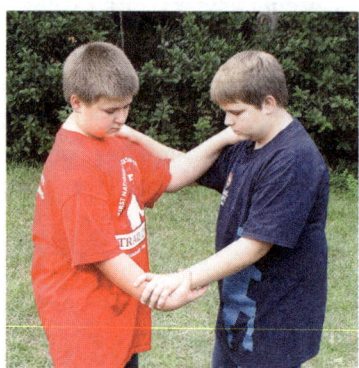

Four-hand seat

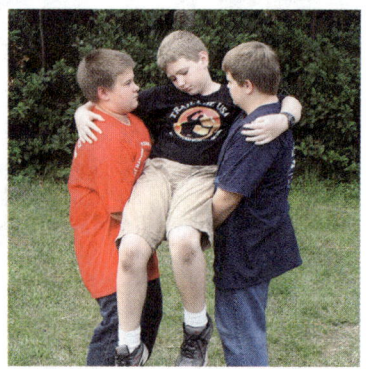

the rescuers' necks.
- Lift the victim slowly, using your legs and keeping your back straight.

Chair carry

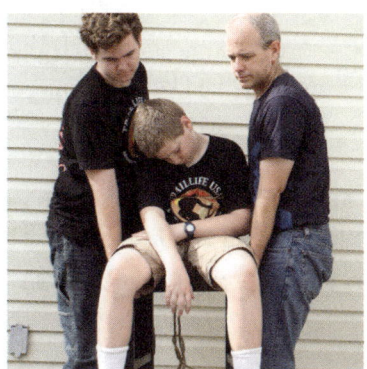

Chair Carry—Conscious or Unconscious
- Help or place the victim onto a sturdy chair.
- The conscious victim should fold his arms across his chest to prevent injury.
- Tie an unconscious victim to the back of the chair using a rope, blanket, or piece of clothing.
- Stand at the sides of the chair. Grab the back of the chair's sides with your palms facing the victim's back.
- Tilt the chair onto its rear legs.
- Each rescuer should grab the front leg with remaining hand.
- Lift the chair off the ground and start walking. Do not walk backward.

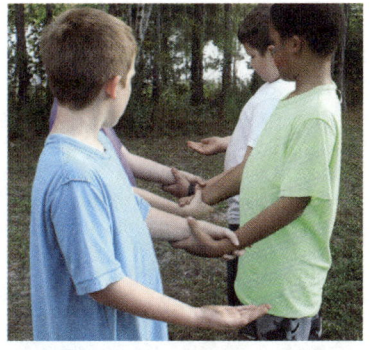

Human Stretcher Carry for 3–6 Rescuers
- 3–6 Trailmen stand on both sides of the victim.
- Squat or kneel on one knee facing each other.

FIRST AID FOR THE TRAILMAN

- Link hands/wrists under the victim.
- Lift the victim slowly, using your legs and keeping your back straight.

Improvised Stretcher: Blanket and Shirt/Coat

- Locate 2 poles that can hold the victim's weight: tent poles, car-rack poles, or two sturdy pieces of wood.
- Then locate a blanket, unzipped sleeping bag, tarp, shirts, pants, or coats that are able to hold the victim's weight.
- Using clothing, zip or button it, then stick the poles through the bottom and

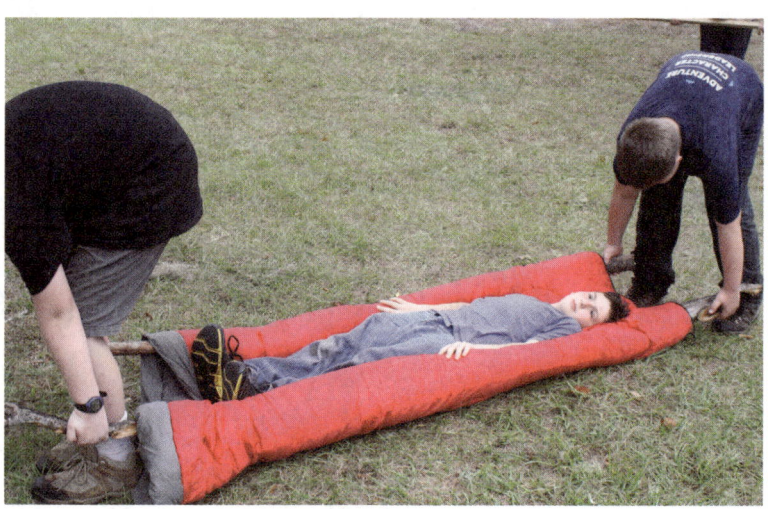

through the sleeves or pant legs. You need enough garments to cover the height of victim.
- Spread the blanket out on the ground. Place one "pole" about 1 foot from the center of the blanket.
- Fold the shorter end of the blanket over the first pole.
- Put the second pole about 2 feet from the first pole. Or adjust size to accommodate victim and blanket.
- Fold both halves of the blanket over the second pole.
- Trailmen should stand at each end of stretcher.
- Squat down and grasp the poles. The Trailman at the head should face away from victim.
- Lift the victim slowly, using your legs and keeping your back straight.

HEAD INJURY

The majority of minor head injuries—caused by a small fall or a bumping of the head, which may cause a bump or a bruise or a short-term headache—are not dangerous. It is very important, however, to pay close attention to head injuries, especially those with the following symptoms:
- Excessive bleeding from an open wound, ears, or nose
- Clear fluid coming from ears or nose
- Loss of consciousness
- Prolonged disorientation, apparent memory loss, irritability, slurred speech, dizziness, or drowsiness
- Unequal pupil size, blurred or double vision
- Nausea or vomiting
- Weakness in hands or feet
- Interruption of breathing or change in rhythm

If you detect any of these symptoms, you should assume the victim has sustained serious head trauma and needs medical attention. Dial 9-1-1 immediately. Until the ambulance arrives:
- If possible, place the victim in a dim, quiet area.
- Lay the victim down, head and shoulders slightly elevated.
- If the wound is bleeding, dress it with gauze or a clean cloth.

- Apply ice for 20 minutes every 2–4 hours.
- Do not leave the victim unattended during the first 24 hours.
- Awaken the victim and check for alertness every 2 hours.
- If the victim loses consciousness, you may need to perform CPR.

NECK AND SPINAL INJURIES

If you suspect a back or neck (spinal) injury, **do not move the victim.** Permanent paralysis and other serious complications can result. Assume the victim has a spinal injury if:
- There's evidence of a head injury and any change in the level of consciousness.
- The victim complains of severe pain in his neck or back.
- The victim won't move his neck.
- An injury has exerted substantial force on the back or head, especially a fall from elevation.
- The victim either exhibits or complains of weakness, numbness, or paralysis, or he lacks control of limbs, bladder, or bowels.
- The neck or back is twisted or positioned oddly.
  If you suspect someone has a spinal injury:
- **Call 9-1-1 or emergency medical help.**
- Keep the victim still. Place heavy towels on both sides of his neck or hold his head and neck.
- Provide as much first aid as possible without moving the victim's head, neck, or back.

If the victim is unconscious and shows no signs of circulation (breathing, coughing, or movement), begin chest compressions, but do not tilt the head back to open the airway. Use your fingers to gently grasp the jaw and lift it forward.
- If the victim is wearing a helmet, don't remove it.
- If you absolutely must roll the victim because he is vomiting, choking on blood, or in danger of further injury, you need at least one other Trailman. Work together to keep the victim's head, neck, and back aligned while rolling the victim onto one side. Roll him like a log.

NOSEBLEED

A human nose is rich with small, fragile blood vessels that are susceptible to damage. A nosebleed may be caused by a fall, a strike to the nose, or even from breathing excessively dry air.

If the nosebleed is not a symptom of a more serious injury, it is rarely dangerous and can usually be stopped by continuous pressure.
- Do not tilt the victim's head backward.
- Have the victim sit or stand upright to slow the flow of blood.
- Loosen any tight clothing around the victim's neck.
- If possible, have the victim spit out excess saliva—swallowing may disturb the clot and cause nausea.
- Pinch the nostrils shut and press the tip of the nose against the bones of the face.
- Maintain pressure for 5 to 10 minutes.
- Once the bleeding has stopped, the victim should avoid blowing his nose or otherwise straining himself for at least an hour.

If the victim's nose continues to bleed, if the blood flow appears to be excessive, or if the victim feels weak or faint, the damage may be more serious than it appears. You should call 9-1-1 or take him to the nearest emergency room as soon as possible.

POISONOUS PLANTS

Poison ivy, poison oak, poison sumac, and stinging nettle are the most common skin-irritant plants found in North America.

Poison ivy, poison oak, and poison sumac have oily sap in their leaves, stems, and roots, which may irritate your skin. If you can wash the sap off with soap and water within ten minutes, you can spare yourself a lot of misery. Remember that the oil clings to clothing too, so make sure any clothing that comes into contact with these plants gets a thorough washing.

Stinging nettles inject a combination of chemicals (mostly histamine) that cause a stinging sensation and a rash. Due to the complex mixture of irritants, treating the discomfort is more complicated. Common anti-itch drugs may or may not help. As a backup, calamine lotion often brings relief.

If you've had contact with any of these plants, avoid scratching your skin. If the reaction is severe, if the eyes or genital region is affected, or if parts of the plant were chewed or swallowed, seek immediate medical attention.

Prevention: Wearing long sleeves and long pants can help protect from the plant oils.

Some people are especially allergic to poison ivy, poison oak, or poison sumac. For them, smoke from burning these plants or even a strong wind passing by may cause a reaction. Dead plants and dried roots can still cause irritation.

Poison ivy can vary somewhat in its appearance. It may or may not be shiny. The plant may have white berries. It is best to have a Trail Guide point out several examples of poison ivy on hikes or campouts so that you are better able to recognize the plant.

Generally, poison oak is more toxic than poison ivy, and poison sumac is so toxic as to be extremely dangerous.

Poison Ivy

Poison Oak

SPIDER BITES

Most spider bites cause relatively minor pain and itching that soon go away. Some spider bites are more serious.

A bite from a brown recluse spider may not hurt at once, but it may cause pain, redness, and swelling at the wound within 2 to 8 hours. An open sore is likely to form, and the victim may suffer fever, chills, nausea, joint pain, vomiting, and a faint rash.

The bite of a female black widow spider might cause sharp pain and redness at the wound. Symptoms may include sweating, nausea, vomiting, stomach pain, cramps, severe muscle pain, spasms, and shock. It may cause difficulty breathing.

Treat all spider-bite victims for shock, recheck the bite area periodically, and have the victim seen by a doctor as soon as possible.

SCORPION STINGS

Scorpion stings, although painful, are mostly harmless. As many as 1,500 species of scorpions have been described worldwide, but only about 30 of these are considered dangerous. In the United States, only the bark scorpion—native to Arizona, New Mexico, and the California side of the Colorado River—has venom potent enough to cause severe symptoms. Elsewhere, lethal scorpion stings occur predominantly in Mexico, South America, parts of Africa, the Middle East, and India.

Scorpion stings are most serious in young children, older adults, and pets. In the United States, healthy adults usually don't need treatment for scorpion stings, but if a child is stung, always get immediate medical care.

Symptoms

Children who have been stung by a bark scorpion might experience:
- Pain, which can be intense, and numbness and tingling in the area around the sting, but little or no swelling
- Muscle twitching or thrashing
- Unusual head, neck, and eye movements
- Drooling
- Sweating
- Restlessness or excitability and sometimes inconsolable crying

Adults are more likely to experience:
- Rapid breathing
- High blood pressure

- Increased heart rate
- Muscle twitching
- Weakness

When to see a doctor

It's always best to be safe. Anyone stung should follow these guidelines:
- Make a note of the time stung and, if known, a description of the scorpion.
- Get immediate medical care for any child stung by a scorpion.
- Get prompt care if you or an adult has been stung and begins to experience widespread symptoms.
- If you're concerned about a scorpion sting—even if the reaction is minor—call your local poison control center for advice.
- Seek medical attention right away if stung while traveling in another country.

SNAKE BITE

If someone is bitten by a snake or lizard that is known or thought to be possibly venomous, call 9-1-1 or another emergency service immediately. Do not wait for symptoms to develop. Symptoms may progress from mild to severe rapidly.

If you are not sure what type of snake or lizard it is, take a picture of it. But do not do this if it will delay treatment or put someone at risk for additional bites.

- Keep the victim calm and resting quietly.
- If you are not sure what type of snake or lizard it was, call the Poison Control Center (800-222-1222) to help identify the snake or lizard and find out what to do next.
- Remove any jewelry. The limbs might swell, making it more difficult to remove the jewelry after swelling begins.
- Use a pen to mark the edge of the swelling around the bite every 15 minutes. This will help the doctor estimate how the venom is moving in the body.

TICKS

Ticks are small, hard-shelled creatures (related to spiders) that bury their heads in the skin. Some are larger and easier to spot; others are tiny "seed ticks" that are hard to spot during a casual inspection.

The best way to treat ticks is to properly apply repellant in the first place. Wearing long sleeves and long pants can help too. Sometimes we forget and or miss a spot, and ticks are always ready to remind us.

Remove ticks with tweezers, grasping the tick close to the skin and gently pulling until the tick comes out. If you squeeze, twist, or jerk the tick, its mouthparts may break off in the wound and result in an infection or blood poisoning.

Wash the wound with soap and water, then apply a triple antibiotic ointment.

Ticks may spread Lyme disease, Rocky Mountain spotted fever, or other illnesses. If flu-like symptoms or a rash develops or the victim otherwise feels unwell in the following days or weeks, they need to see a doctor.

CHIGGERS

Chiggers, if you even see them, look like tiny red dots. Feeling them is much easier. Using repellant sprays correctly is far less trouble than resisting the urge to scratch the small bumps that form on the skin. Wearing long sleeves and long pants can help too. Cover the bites with calamine lotion or dab them with clear fingernail polish.

INSECT STINGS

If someone is stung by a bee or hornet, the stinger and poison sack are often left in the wound. Remove the stinger by scraping it out with a driver's license, credit card, or the side of a knife blade. If you try to pinch it out or scrape it with a finger, you may push more venom into the wound. An ice pack may help reduce pain and swelling.

Anyone that has trouble breathing after an insect sting must be treated immediately for anaphylactic shock. Call 9-1-1 or your local emergency number. If the victim has a kit for treating anaphylactic shock such as an EpiPen, follow the instructions in assisting them to use it.

FIRE ANTS

Fire ants are not native to North America, but unfortunately they are spreading in the southeastern and southwestern US.

The best way to treat fire-ant stings is to stay away from the ants. Keep your shoes on when playing near fire-ant mounds. If you come across a fire-ant mound, don't poke at it or play with it. You will easily recognize the mounds because they can be up to 18 inches high and over 2 feet wide.

Fire-ant stings cause sharp pain and burning. If the victim steps on a fire-ant mound, he may be stung several times at once. Each sting will turn into an itchy white blister over the next day.

Tell an adult immediately. The venom in the fire-ant stings may cause quite a bit of swelling, and a doctor may need to look at the infected area to make sure the victim is not having an allergic reaction.

If the victim develops hives (red patches on the skin that itch and sting), nausea, dizziness, or a tight feeling in the throat or if he has difficulty breathing, the victim needs medical attention right away.

People with known allergies to fire ants may carry a kit for anaphylactic shock, which they can administer to prevent a severe reaction.

For most people under most circumstances, the stings can be treated by washing the area with soap and water, then applying ice. Only check with a doctor if there is severe redness, swelling, or itching.

INGESTED POISONS

Symptoms: A victim who has been poisoned may feel nauseated and suffer stomach pains. The victim may vomit, and there may be burns around the mouth. Breathing may be abnormal.

If you suspect someone has been poisoned, look for spilled liquids, pill bottles, or other evidence that may be useful to medical professionals in identifying the poison and choosing the right treatment.

Swallowed Poisons

Treatment must be immediate. Take any poison containers to a telephone and call the poison control center at 1-800-222-1222. Otherwise, call 9-1-1 or your local emergency response number and carefully follow any instructions you are given.

Treat the victim for shock and monitor his breathing. Save any vomit in a bowl, cook pot, or plastic bag to turn over to a health care professional.

Inhaled Poisons

Smoke and certain gasses or fumes are poisonous. A victim of inhaled poisoning may have trouble breathing and may lose consciousness.

Symptoms may include headache, dizziness, and nausea. The victim may lose consciousness without realizing he is in danger.

Treatment must be immediate, as long as safely possible. Approach the scene carefully to ensure that the poisonous gases or fumes are not still present. You do not want to become the next victim. If you are unsure if the inhaled poison is still an active hazard in the area, do not enter the area, call 9-1-1, and wait for help to arrive. If safely possible, move the victim to fresh air or vent the enclosed space. Get medical help or call the poison control center, 1-800-222-1222.

While waiting for help to arrive, regularly check that the victim is still breathing and has a heartbeat. If necessary, perform rescue breathing or CPR.

ELECTRICAL SHOCK

Minor electrical shock is a common household hazard. Fortunately, it is usually more surprising than dangerous and does not require medical attention. However, some basic precautions should be taken to ensure that the shock does not interfere with the body's normal electrical impulses, including the functions of the brain and the heart. Prolonged exposure to a direct source of electricity can also cause severe burns to the skin and the tissue.

In the event of electric shock, do not rush to assist the victim until you are certain that he is no longer in contact with electricity. Otherwise, the current will pass through the victim directly to you.

- If possible, turn off the electricity. If this is not an option, use non-conductive material, such as plastic or dry wood, to separate the source of electricity from the victim.
- If the injuries appear serious or extensive, dial 9-1-1.
- Check the victim's vital signs, such as the depth of his breathing and regularity of his heartbeat. If either one is affected by exposure to electricity or if the victim is unconscious, begin to perform CPR.
- Treat any areas of the victim's body that may have sustained burns.
- If the victim is responsive and does not appear seriously injured but looks pale or faint, he may be at risk of going into shock. Gently lay him down with his head slightly lower than his chest and his feet elevated.

BRUISES

A typical bruise is caused by traces of blood escaping from small vessels that lie close to the skin's surface. Since our blood vessels become more fragile with age, the elderly tend to bruise easier than healthy adults and children. If a child sustains excessive bruising, it may be an indication of a more serious injury and should be treated accordingly.

If the bruise is on the victim's head, he may have sustained a concussion and should be checked for head trauma.

To reduce the bump and minimize the pain, have the victim elevate the injured area and apply a commercial ice pack or ice cubes wrapped in a towel for 15 to 20 minutes. You may repeat this step every 2–4 hours as needed. Depending on the extent of the injury, this process should be repeated for a few days or until the swelling and the pain begins to dissipate.

DEHYDRATION

There are several ways our body loses water such as sweating, urination, and evaporation as we breathe. Under certain conditions, we can give off more water than we take in, and that causes dehydration.

Dehydration is serious and should be treated right away. Symptoms of dehydration include:
- Dark urine or decreased urine production
- Severe thirst
- Tiredness or weakness
- Dry skin and lips
- Decreased sweating
- Loss of appetite, nausea, or fainting
- Confusion or dizziness
- Headache, body aches, and muscle cramps

You should protect yourself from dehydration by drinking plenty of fluids before you feel thirsty. Make sure your urine stays clear.

Encourage a victim of dehydration to drink fluids and rest. In hot weather, get the victim to a shady place or into an air-conditioned building or vehicle. Watch the victim until symptoms clear up.

When hiking and camping in remote areas, you must be able to filter your water or chemically decontaminate it.

HEAT INJURIES

Heat Cramps

These cramps are probably related to electrolyte imbalances including sodium, potassium, calcium, and magnesium.

Symptoms of Heat Cramps

Muscle spasms are typically painful, involuntary, brief, intermittent, and usually self-limited (go away on their own).

Heat Cramp Treatment
- Heat cramps usually go away whether you do anything or not.
- Have the victim rest in a cool place.

- Commercially available electrolyte beverages will provide adequate electrolyte intake.

Heat Exhaustion

Heat exhaustion is caused as the body struggles to keep its internal temperature down. It can be made worse by dehydration.

Symptoms include skin that is pale and clammy from heavy sweating, nausea, and tiredness, dizziness and fainting, headache, muscle cramps, and weakness. It may resemble symptoms of shock.

Treatment includes having the victim lie down in a cool, shady place with his feet raised. Remove excess clothing, then cool the victim by applying wet cloths to his body and fanning him. If the victim is alert, let him sip some water.

Recovery should be quick, but if symptoms remain or progress to fainting, confusion, or seizures, call 9-1-1.

Heatstroke

Heat exhaustion, if not treated, can go into heatstroke. The body's cooling system starts to fail and its internal temperature rises to dangerous levels.

Symptoms include skin that is very hot to the touch, is red, and is either very dry or damp with sweat. The victim may have a rapid pulse and rapid, noisy breathing. The victim may be confused and unwilling to cooperate. Ultimately, the victim may become unconscious.

Treatment begins with immediately calling for medical assistance. Meanwhile, move the victim to an air-conditioned or shady area, loosen tight clothing, and cool the skin by fanning and applying wet cloths. If you have ice packs, wrap them in a towel, shirt, or other thin barrier, and then place them under the victim's armpits and against the neck and groin to have the greatest effect. If the victim can drink, give him small amounts of cool water. Keep an eye on the victim's condition and be ready to provide further first aid if necessary.

COLD INJURIES

Frostbite

Frostbite occurs when skin and tissue get cold enough to freeze. The injury may hurt or it may be numb.

You can tell when frostbite is beginning as grayish-white patches form on the skin. This is a sign that ice crystals are forming.

Move the victim into a shelter. If the injury is on an ear or cheek, warm the injury with the exposed palm of your hand. Put a frostbitten hand under clothing against warm skin.

If you suspect that the frostbite is severe, get the victim into dry clothing, wrap the injured area in a blanket, and get the victim to a doctor as soon as possible.

If you are certain the injury will not have a chance to refreeze, place it under water that is warm to the touch (not hot) and watch for normal color to return.

If the injury is on a hand or foot, place dry, sterile gauze between the fingers or toes and cover with a loose bandage.

Hypothermia

When the body's ability to produce heat is overtaken by heat loss, the core temperature will drop. This condition is called hypothermia.

It may happen from not wearing warm enough clothing or wet clothing. The danger is increased by wind, rain, hunger, dehydration, and exhaustion.

Hypothermia can happen when you don't expect it. If you don't have rain gear, a cold rain may chill you. Swimming in cold water or capsizing in cold water may start uncontrollable shivering.

Symptoms include feeling cold or numb, tiredness, inability to think straight, uncontrollable shivering, poor decisions, irritability, stumbling, and loss of consciousness.

Treatment starts with preventing a further drop in temperature. It continues with help in slowly bringing the body temperature back up to normal. You can try any or all of these techniques:

- Move the victim into a shelter. Replace wet clothing with warm, dry clothes. Wrap the victim in a sleeping bag, blankets, jackets, or anything handy.
- If the victim is conscious and able to swallow, give him warm liquids to drink.
- Put towels or t-shirts around bottles filled with warm water, then put the bottles in the armpit and groin areas. Do not attempt to warm arms and legs because that will drive cold blood toward the core.
  - Watch the victim closely for changes in his condition. Call for help.
  - Begin CPR if breathing stops or is inadequate.

Prevention: Wearing synthetic insulating layers and nylon/GORE-TEX™ outerwear and gloves can protect you from the elements and keep you warm.

THE BEST FIRST AID

The best way to treat injuries is to avoid them. Know and use the safety rules for the activities you do. Look for hazards around your home, school, and campsite. Make sure they are corrected or at least pointed out to others. Safety first—always!

The Patrol Leaders' Guidebook

WALK WORTHY!

PATROL LEADERS' GUIDEBOOK

WELCOME TO A LIFE-CHANGING OPPORTUNITY!

Congratulations, Trailman. You've been selected to a leadership position within your Troop. Over time, you'll learn to lead with a skillful blend of wisdom, patience, and kindness.

You'll see a lot of language here that addresses the Patrol Leader, as this is the largest group of youth Trailmen in leadership. There are also sections devoted specifically to other youth leadership positions.

You should read every page of this guidebook. It will help you become the best youth leader you can be and, in the process, you'll be developing leadership skills that will serve you and others your whole life.

Take a deep breath. Let it out. Now consider these five things:

- Nobody's perfect.
- The best leaders commit to continual growth as a leader.
- You're not in over your head.
- You're not going to make a fool of yourself in front of your friends.
- You're not in this alone.

Your leadership role will challenge you—it was designed to do that. It was also designed to work under the supervision of adult leaders who believe in the Trail Life process that grows better leaders. These adults are familiar with patrol leadership and the Patrol Method, and they will mentor you.

But it's up to you to make the most of this opportunity. Reading through this guidebook can help prepare you to do the best job you can. You'll learn from those who have gone before you, and you'll set an example for Trailmen who will follow in your footsteps.

Give it your best shot. Strive to avoid making the same mistakes twice. Learn from both your successes and your failures, and be honest with yourself and others.

You'll find that part of your time will be spent teaching campcraft—the nuts and bolts of being safe, comfortable, and fully engaged in God's great outdoors.

The skills you learned from your own Patrol Leader not long ago will be passed on to Patrol Leaders of the future. You'll want to have a solid understanding of the basics so you can do a good job. Your leadership role implies that you have some expertise in those areas. Pay attention to the skills you've learned and review them. Make sure you know where to find the answer, which includes familiarizing yourself with this entire guidebook and the advancement process.

Part of your time will be setting the course, whether you're drawing lines on a map or modeling good behavior in the way you speak and act.

You'll listen, observe, and evaluate. As Patrol Leader, you'll be acutely interested in what's going right, what's going wrong, what works, and what doesn't. After every event, ask your Patrol Members what they liked most and what they liked least. The Patrol Members are your eyes and ears—miss their feedback and you're flying blind.

You'll also settle disputes. This is never fun, but when you restore order to a chaotic situation and everyone is at peace with your decision (don't expect them all to like it), you'll experience a deep sense of satisfaction.

Wielding authority will be awkward at first, like the first time you shot a basketball. But you'll get better with study and practice.

So, what exactly is leadership? **Leadership is exercising the gift of guidance.** While a boss is busy directing his power, a leader directs the power of others. The best leader becomes a treasure map that directs others to hidden riches.

As your leadership skills grow, you'll become better able to sense the potential God has hidden inside you and every other Trailman; you'll then use your skills to reveal it. This Patrol Leaders' Guidebook will equip you with what's necessary to head out on this trail.

So, let's get started!

WHAT IS THE PATROL METHOD?

Even though you may have served in a patrol as a member, its purpose may not be clear to you.

Patrols are divisions of a Troop, ideally made up of six to eight Trailmen who work together the way systems in your body work together. Just as your body needs its systems to work in balance,

your Patrol Members need to work in harmony. Just as your body has blood to send energy and life to all its parts, your group needs patrol spirit as its energy.

The best way to get your patrol in balance and give it spirit is to believe in and rely on the **Patrol Method**. It can be stated like this:

> **The Patrol Method splits a Troop into small groups that explore _the theory and practice_ of _leadership_, while using the _gifts of individuals_ to build _group wellbeing_.**

Wow, that's a mouthful. Let's break this statement into its parts and look at each one.

Under the Patrol Method, the leader is guided by the wishes of the Patrol Members, but ultimately the decision—and responsibility—is his. As a Patrol Leader, you must process discussion through the filters of your training, experience, and conscience, then exercise your best judgment.

The difference between _theory and practice_ is like the difference between knowing the rules of a sport and playing it well. As Patrol Leader, you should make a special effort to attend as many outings as possible to get that practice, doing your best work and striving to make your best even better. True skill comes from testing your ideas in the real world, and then committing to improve them.

> **Leadership is exercising the gift of guidance.**

Leadership is exercising the gift of guidance. It is undertaken in an attitude of generosity and servanthood. From time to time, it involves handing out unpopular assignments and saying no. That won't be a problem if you remember your other important title, Patrol Member. Accept your share of the work and obey your own guidelines with the same attitude you expect from others.

Gifts of individuals are the unique set of talents and abilities God gave each of us to be successful in the adventure of life. Great things happen when people with different skills work together. An engineer, a mechanic, an electrician, a welder, and a pilot can build a plane and fly it wherever they want to go. None of them working alone could

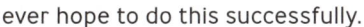

ever hope to do this successfully.

Group wellbeing is a kind of joy, belonging, and self-worth you can only experience through a community such as a family, a church, or a well-run patrol.

Read the definition of the Patrol Method again. Does it make a lot more sense the second time?

> **The Patrol Method splits a Troop into small groups that explore <u>the theory and practice</u> of <u>leadership</u>, while using the <u>gifts of individuals</u> to build <u>group wellbeing</u>.**

Maybe you thought a patrol was just a group of Trailmen. Remember, in God's eyes, there is no such thing as "just a group of Trailmen."

Now that you are in the right mindset, let's dive into the nuts and bolts of how patrols work.

WHY DOES TRAIL LIFE USE BOY-LED PATROLS IN THE OUTDOORS?

If Trail Life USA were a camping club, adults could and would cut out middle management—youth Patrol Leaders—and do everything their way.

But the developers, founders, board of directors, home office staff, and area and regional volunteers in Trail Life USA trust you and the other young men who are growing through the Trail Life experience to take on the difficult challenge of leadership.

Boy-led patrols are an important element in helping Trailmen grow. Adult leaders don't pass off work to your patrol for speed or convenience. They insist on your opportunity to lead because it is a skill that goes beyond knot-tying or mastery of another outdoor skill. It's bigger than that. It's designed to give you experience that will aid you as you mature and, if you choose, will help you lead a business, a church, your family, or maybe even the entire country.

You're being prepared to lead well because Trail Life USA is a youth development organization. Conveying the skills of leadership is so important that many other considerations take a back seat. Every decision you make involves leadership, and every righteous or sinful act is commentary on how well you lead yourself and others.

The Trail Life Mission puts going through the motions of patrol life into perspective:

> "Our mission is to guide generations of courageous young men to **honor God,** **lead** with integrity, **serve** others, and **experience outdoor adventure**."

Experiencing outdoor adventure, while important, is only one goal. Notice the biblical virtues mentioned in the mission statement that will continue to resonate long after your success in tying that knot or climbing that crag gets filed under *"M"* for *Memories*.

The Trailman's Oath states it in a compelling way:

> **On my honor,**
> **I will do my best**
> **to serve God and my country;**
> **To respect authority;**
> **To be a good steward of creation;**
> **And to treat others as I want to be treated.**

Where does the oath mention anything about selecting the perfect campsite, staying under budget on food, or advancing in rank?

Does this mean that outdoor adventure is merely an afterthought? No. Outdoor adventure is one of the best environments in which to learn how to lead with integrity, serve others, respect authority, and treat others as you want to be treated.

Outdoor adventure is a place where character is built through apprenticeship. The outdoors is an environment directly designed and constructed by God. Outdoors there is no social promotion, no participation award. *Almost* erecting a tent, picking a *sort-of good* spot to lay your bedroll, and getting your bacon and eggs *nearly* edible has consequences.

The elements of a good outdoor adventure all have a point: tying a taut line hitch correctly makes a tent stay firm. A more important point is that you should not give up on learning a skill after a couple of failures. You can apply that lesson to doing well in school, getting a good job, or having a good marriage someday. That makes the experience of outdoor adventure more, not less, important.

When Christ taught the parable of the sower[1] who threw seeds on the rock, the path, and the fertile ground, he gave sound agricultural advice. But it means much more when you recognize the spiritual truths contained in that parable. The same thing can be said about the assignments on your duty roster or the other tasks and activities your patrol will carry out. There is much to be learned from every experience in your patrol.

Leading well is something you should be proud of. And one day, when you need to deal with the behavior of your son or daughter,

---

[1]   *Mark 4:1-20*

you'll use skills you developed in a boy-led patrol.

In summary, some of your personal growth involves relationships with other people. As you lead, your Troop helps you relate to others, so everyone can grow in wisdom and stature. The boy-led Patrol Method is not *one* way of running a Troop; it is *the* way to lead a Trail Life Troop. It ensures that the adult leaders don't end up running the show when you and other Trailmen should be participating and growing in a vibrant boy-led patrol and Troop.

Your leadership role prepares you for life as a free man in a free nation, where success and failure are less about your circumstances and more about your decisions and the way you interact with others.

Participating in a boy-led patrol could be one of the greatest learning opportunities of your life.

WHAT DOES PATROL LIFE LOOK LIKE?

Your patrol is like a family within your Troop. And families are meant to have fun and enjoy one another's company. This fun may lead to friendly competition with other patrols in your Troop or with other Troops at area and regional gatherings.

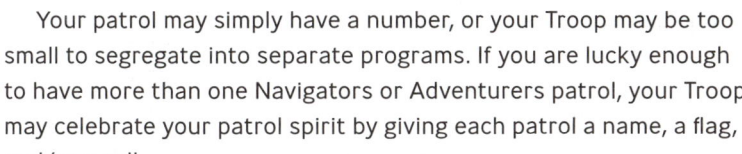

Your patrol may simply have a number, or your Troop may be too small to segregate into separate programs. If you are lucky enough to have more than one Navigators or Adventurers patrol, your Troop may celebrate your patrol spirit by giving each patrol a name, a flag, and/or a call.

A symbol is something you can see or hear that represents an important idea that can't be seen or heard. The flag of your country is an important symbol. So is the cross. If you believe in your patrol and what it stands for, you'll want fitting symbols to represent it.

Patrol Name

Work together to determine a patrol name that is fun and exciting. It should never demean or disrespect anyone; neither should the name be beneath the dignity of the Trail Life USA program. Patrol names convey the identity of the patrol. For example, your patrol might decide to use an animal name. Consider an animal's dominant personality trait (a clever raccoon, a sneaky viper, or a powerful buffalo). Remember, your patrol's name can be changed at a later time, so have fun as you create this identity.

Patrol Flags

More than a simple way to identify patrols at large events, patrol flags may be a visual representation of something important to the Patrol Members that fosters unity among them. Working to design and make a patrol flag is a great exercise in listening, brainstorming, and recognizing talents. Get creative with the materials and type of flag your patrol chooses.

Patrol Call

The patrol call originated in ancient times when groups hiding in the brush or woodlands needed to signal one another without giving themselves away. Come up with a call to gather your patrol or celebrate a job well done.

Patrol Bonding

Patrols may perform skits at campfires, form teams in games at area and regional events, or perform service projects. Patrols build stronger ties when the Patrol Leader recognizes members by presenting insignia and awards. Patrols also forge closer bonds when they camp and eat as a group. This is living proof they are more than just an administrative unit. They do it to learn and display successful mastery of finances. They do it to learn and display skill at woodcraft. They do it to show esprit de corps, or patrol spirit.

Patrol Camps/Hikes

Your patrol may have activities that it especially enjoys. Maybe that means you will want to plan a hike or camping trip that involves only your patrol. Work with your Troop adult leaders to make something this special happen. Remember, you'll also need adults to accompany you.

Spreading Cheer

As **Patrol Leader,** you must be especially watchful for the potential to make some lemonade when life deals you lemons. And you don't just spread cheer because happiness is more joyful than sadness. There are unpleasant or even tragic moments in life, and these do not dissipate when you whistle a happy tune. At such moments, you need happy memories to lean upon. Setting aside as many happy memories as you can on sunny days will help carry you through dark, rainy times.

Triage for Morale

Triage can be defined as a fancy word for dividing things into three groups. Where morale is concerned, you could be a pessimist and

always find the worst in every situation. Your motto would be, "The glass is half empty." On the other hand, you could be an optimist and always look for the best in every situation. Your motto would be, "The glass is half full." Fact is, as a Patrol Leader you want to take the third approach: evaluate the situation objectively, and look for ways to improve it. Then your motto can be, "Let's see if we can fill this glass to the rim!"

Empowerment

This is all about giving your Patrol Members the can-do attitude and direction they need to make some decisions rather than being completely reliant on you. You can begin by constructing the Leadership Triangle: **Morale, Confidence, and Experience**. Build morale because proper leadership yields satisfaction. Build confidence because a leader's attitude is usually a self-fulfilling prophecy. Build experience because it is the toolkit that meets challenges.

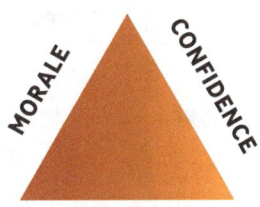

WHAT ARE THE PATROL ROLES AND RESPONSIBILITIES?

Woodlands Trail has patrols led entirely by adults who model fair, wise, and patient leadership. While this age level does not use the full Patrol Method, members learn the first great leadership skill: *the most important person you lead is yourself.* Each Fox, Hawk, and Mountain Lion Trailman is expected to grow toward leading himself well, whether anyone else is watching or not.

Navigator patrols give the first taste of authority. A **Navigator Junior Patrol Leader** makes decisions that affect the health, safety, comfort, and morale of his patrol. He knows what it feels like to turn a duty roster on paper into real people performing real functions. He is a member of the Officers' Conference, and once a month he will meet with other Troop Leaders to discuss the direction of the Troop and see how well the Annual Program Plan is being carried out.

Adventurer Patrol Leaders do everything Navigator Junior Patrol Leaders do and also work closely with the First and Second Officers to set the Annual Program Plan and draw up the Troop calendar. Basically, the leadership emphasis of the Adventurers is on leadership of the entire Troop through heavily influencing the Annual Program Plan and keeping it on track.

Finally comes the position of **Patrol Member**, which isn't an office and doesn't sound like a big deal, but it is. The job of the **Patrol Member** is to experience adventure, growth, joy, responsibility, and personal accountability. **Patrol Members** give the best picture of the success of a patrol by how active, engaged, and excited they are as a part of a healthy patrol. Their collective attitude has a great influence on whether or not new boys wish to continue to be a part of Trail Life.

> A good Patrol Leader will hear suggestions and debate through the filters of his training, experience, and conscience, then use his best judgment.

In a patrol, each Trailman should have the opportunity to express his viewpoint before a major decision is made. The decision should take everyone's view into account; however, the final decision—and the ultimate responsibility—belongs to the **Patrol Leader**. A good **Patrol Leader** will hear suggestions and engage in debate through the filters of his training, experience, and conscience, then use his best judgment.

Each member of the patrol has a job to do. These jobs not only help the patrol function, but they also help its members grow by teaching and learning important life lessons. While few Trailmen will ever make a living as a camper, the skills they learn, the confidence they build, and the responsibility they handle will point them toward future success.

PATROL LEADERS' GUIDEBOOK   275

First Officer

The **First Officer** holds the highest office a youth Trailman can hold. As such, he chairs the Officers' Conference, speaks at Troop meeting openers, and plays an important role at advancement and award ceremonies. He is the last Trailman to counsel a truant youth before an adult leader gets involved. In short, he is the voice of the Troop.

> The First Officer is the voice of the Troop.

As chairman of the Officers' Conference, his job is not to rule the meeting but to give it structure. While different Troops handle the rules of order in their unique way, from very formal to very informal, it is the **First Officer's** job to put items on the agenda, call for them to be discussed, act on motions to bring an end to discussion, and call for a vote.

Last, but certainly not least, the **First Officer** represents everything that is best about Trail Life and his Troop. A **First Officer** who shines in his role makes the whole Troop look good. And a **First Officer** who gets into trouble or acts irresponsibly can bring the whole Troop down. Remember, for those who achieve more, more is expected.

Second Officer

The **Second Officer** basically does three things. He learns by watching the First Officer so that he can lead the Troop someday. He ably assists the **First Officer**, who sometimes wishes he could be in two places at the same time. He also stands in as the highest-ranking Trailman when illness or scheduling conflicts keep the **First Officer** from attending.

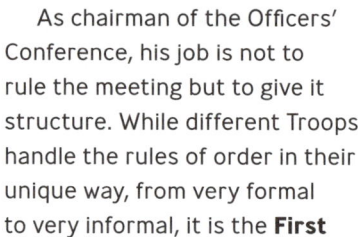

> The Second Officer assists or stands in for the First Officer.

276 THE TRAILMAN'S HANDBOOK

Quartermaster

The **Quartermaster** has the important job of keeping every patrol's gear in working condition, reporting breakage and loss, and checking assets in and out. He is a good steward who reports on the status of the patrol's gear when required by his **First Officer**.

The Quartermaster is responisble for every Patrol's gear.

WHAT IS THE OFFICERS' CONFERENCE?

Patrol agendas are set by the Officers' Conference, a gathering of Troop youth leadership together with the **Troopmaster, Advisor, Trailmaster, and Trail Guides.**

PATROL LEADERS' GUIDEBOOK   277

The Officers' Conference leads the development of an exciting **Annual Program Plan** that encourages fun, fellowship, and personal growth within the framework of the Trail Life USA program.

The **Patrol Planning Guidebook** is a helpful tool for making an Annual Program Plan. Ask your Advisor or Trailmaster to provide copies for your Officers' Conference. See a sample on page 306 in the Appendix.

Suggested Order of Officers' Conference Meeting

1. Opening Prayer
2. Pledge of Allegiance
3. Trailman Oath
4. Any Old Business?
5. Any Discussion of the Last Activity?
6. Cover the Agenda
7. Motion to Close
8. Closing Prayer

Monthly meetings of the Officers' Conference include evaluating each activity as well as the direction of the Troop in general. It is an excellent opportunity to gauge the health and effectiveness of your local Trail Life family. It is also the appropriate time to address unforeseen circumstances and to apply course corrections. The individual patrol meetings are planned out as well. The Navigator/Adventurer Patrol Meeting Plan Pads are a great tool to assist in planning patrol meetings. See a sample on page 307 in the Appendix.

Within the Officers' Conference, only the youth leaders have a vote. The Troopmaster has veto power. It is his job to make sure the plans are consistent with the aims and methods of Trail Life USA, meet the guidelines specified in the *Health and Safety Guide,* and agree with the mission of your Chartering Organization. He will not use this veto to impose his own decisions but to ensure that the decisions of the youth are well-thought-out.

Everyone has a say. Everyone has a vote. But not everyone gets what he wants. Life is like that.

One Voice

The Officers' Conference has one hard and fast rule: once a vote is held, everyone abides by the decisions of the group. It is essential that individual attendees avoid discontent by saying something like "my idea got voted down" or "don't blame me—it's not my fault." This kind of murmuring does not reflect well on your Troop or on you.

Modeling unity in your Troop is one of the most valuable things you can do as a leader. It takes patience and humility—character traits that will serve you well your entire life.

HOW CAN I BEST LEAD IN MY TROOP OR PATROL?

LEAD BY EXAMPLE

Your behavior is both a model for other people to follow and permission for them to do likewise. What they see you do is what they will want to do. Always make sure you behave the way you want others to behave.

Of course, you'll want to be liked by your Patrol Members. That's fine. They want to like you too, and they'll seek your approval. Problem is, there will be times when you must say "no." Consequently, you may often sense a momentary drop in your prestige. Those clouds will pass, and each time your "no" proves to be a wise answer for the Troop, the dip will be shallower and pass more quickly. Eventually, your wise decisions will earn the total respect of your Patrol Members, and when you say no, they'll assume you have a good reason.

Lead with humility. The praise of others is always far superior than your own bragging. Wait for them to tell you how well you're doing.

The way you wear your uniform, the way you arrive on time, the way you wake up at your campsite with a smile, the tone you set with your morale—those are all important. So is the way you hold yourself to the same, or higher, standards than you set for others. People notice that kind of behavior.

Remember, part of your job is to be the treasure map that helps Trailmen find their hidden talents. Sometimes the best way to help them get the gold is to take them there yourself. Use your skills and character strengths to recognize landmarks, overcome obstacles, and meet challenges. People react strongest to what they see. You can tell them the right thing to do morning, noon, and night, but if you stand around with your hands in your pockets, don't be surprised if others do too. If you do the right thing and prosper for it, others will want to follow your example.

> **Remember, part of your job is to be the treasure map that helps Trailmen find their hidden talents.**

Never forget for a moment that your other title is **Patrol Member**. Always take your turn at every duty, from cooking to dishwashing to carrying gear. But while you are functioning as "just another **Patrol Member**," you should always keep a discreet but watchful eye on things. If you see someone struggling, shift your attention to helping him. If you see something unacceptable happening, intervene. When someone stops you with a question, don't act like he's interrupting your duties. Giving guidance is always your duty.

You can make the most irksome jobs easier with a kind word. It takes so little to spice up a bland job with a little encouragement. "Wow, that bacon smells good!" can give a new chef more confidence and boost his feelings of self-worth. Even though it's Bill's job to fill the water containers, thank him when he returns. If you're happy with the nuts and bolts of running a campsite, camping becomes an integral part of the adventure, whether you're kayaking, rock climbing, or hiking.

If you want a friend, be a friend. If you want an effective patrol, be an effective **Patrol Member**. As the Scriptures say, "for whatever one sows, that will he also reap."[2]

You should avoid double standards. If you don't feel comfortable telling that joke or relating that story to a Woodlands Trailman, don't tell it to your Navigators, Adventurers, or an adult leader.

Avoid irresponsible traditions. Whether it is pranking the waterfront staff at camp or hazing anyone, practical jokes are never practical, and no irresponsibility deserves to become a tradition. Trail Life has many rich traditions that deserve to be carried on in the campsites you visit, but misbehavior is not one of them.

You should always strive to pass your uniform inspection with 100% accuracy and to keep your personal appearance top-notch. Your tent should be ready for inspection, and your trash should never be strewn across God's great outdoors.

The Bible tells us to pray always. That doesn't mean to keep your head bowed and your hands clasped. It means that if something should happen to you, the last thing you were doing should reflect well on you as a person and as a setter of priorities.

Remember the importance of slaying the dragon in your own castle before questing abroad. Taking the moral high ground will make all the difference when you impose discipline or ask sacrifices of others for the common good. If you lose that high ground by a shameful act you think nobody else saw—even though you know (and God knows)—you'll have that sinking feeling of being a hypocrite. And if that shameful act, in turn, becomes such a common occurrence that it ceases to bother you, the lack of shame becomes a tragedy in and of itself. Pray that God will give you strength, but also pray that God will give your conscience the strength and courage it needs to confront you when you are about to do something wrong.

A good leader is willing to work hard and to lead by example, yet he should also know when to delegate. In Exodus 18, we learn that Moses judged disputes between the people from morning to evening, not only wearing himself out but also wasting other people's time. Moses' father-in-law advised him to concentrate on being the

---

[2] *Galatians 6:7*

people's representative before God and to select other capable, faithful, and honest men to judge routine cases. It was a win-win situation that accelerated the wheels of justice and shared the load of responsibility. What worked for Moses will work for you.

In the short term, it may be easier to do things yourself, but it's not always the best course of action. When you delegate a task, you give others the opportunity to develop their skills and to serve God. Delegation is perhaps the hardest challenge you'll face. Identify good prospects who can get the job done with a little help. You'll lead them toward becoming **Patrol Leaders** themselves while you experience managing a multi-level leadership structure the way you might as **Second and First Officer** someday.

The members of your patrol look up to you, with good reason. Not because of what you know or what you're willing to learn but because you took your obligation to help other people seriously. You'll want to do everything in your power to be worthy of that respect.

You may be new to patrol leadership, but there are boys new to patrol membership who count on you to bring them up to speed. You'll want to be their hero.

You'll come to realize how important the assignments on your duty roster are to the personal growth of each **Patrol Member**. As much as you respect your patrol's wants, you'll also want to consider their needs in making decisions, even when they don't.

You'll be the doctor who keeps a finger on the pulse of your patrol. When it's time to point out something wrong, you'll want to point out something right to put those problems into perspective. That includes recognizing any improvement as an accomplishment.

You'll also want to take an active role in your Officers' Conference, faithfully representing the needs and desires of your patrol.

PRACTICE YOUR LEADERSHIP STYLE

You can pursue many styles of leadership. You can try to be **popular** by letting members vote on everything. Doing what everyone else wants to do is a sure way to become popular—until you run into trouble. You can try to be **masterful** by choosing what seems right to you and barking out orders, but soon you'll be leading a group of one. The best leaders are **unifiers**. They harness the experience and enthusiasm of the team while giving it clarity and direction. Leadership should be a service you perform for others.

RECOGNIZE THE SUBTLE DIFFERENCE

No matter how fair you try to be and no matter how mature and enlightened your **Patrol Members** try to be, there will be a subtle change in your relationship with your peers.

For one thing, you now have **authority**. Every leadership position in your patrol or Troop carries a certain weight, and Trailmen will come to you to settle disputes or seek your approval. Always use this authority fairly and impartially, and never act like it is interrupting your work. This *is* your work, and you should strive to do it well. That means cultivating **servant leadership**.

Also, you have **responsibility**. If you allow your patrol to run amok and get into trouble, people will want to know what you're going to do about it and why you didn't do it before. That's why it's important for you to work well with your adult leaders and seek their guidance on how you can best guide others. Admitting you don't know the answer or that you made a mistake is not a mark against your leadership. It's a sign of leadership in action. Every problem you encounter is one that someone else already has faced and resolved with justice and kindness.

Lastly, as a leader you experience, perhaps for the first time, the **dignity** of office. If you were the one who joked around too much or tended to slack off or complain or bend the rules, you'll want to shed that image and be taken seriously as a leader. Your **Patrol Members** may have elected you because of your popularity rather than your skill. And they may be unpleasantly surprised that popularity is no longer your top priority. There is one remedy for that. Give them other, more important reasons to be glad you are their **Patrol Leader**. When you use your personality as a tool to make friends, you're forced to adapt to the needs and expectations of others. When you start making friends by *being* a friend, your personality is set free, and you can become truly you. Christ died to save the person you truly are, not the person you become to win friends. If Jesus likes the *real* you, other people—including yourself—can learn to like the real you too.

USE THE DISCIPLESHIP SQUARE

Every skill learned goes through three stages: when you *can't get it right*, when you *can get it right*, and when you *can't get it wrong*. You were born at stage one. To get yourself and your patrol to stage two

where you can get it right, use the **Discipleship Square,** illustrated here.

Don't deny others the use of their God-given gifts.

I Do, You Watch.

When you teach a skill, avoid jargon, although you may need to teach Trailmen new terms so they can communicate clearly. One thing you want to tell the Trailmen is why the skill is important. Before you teach someone to tie a bowline, mention that it forms a non-slip loop for rescue. If he understands that a knot that slips may cause someone to fall to his death, he'll pay closer attention.

I Do, You Help.

When you exhibit a skill, don't do it quickly. Make sure the individual parts that make up the entire skill are clearly shown. As you tie the bowline, you might recite a mnemonic (memory aid) such as "the rabbit comes out of the hole, goes around the tree, and back into the hole." Ensure that your movements are clearly visible. Identify what you are working with. For example, point to the end of the rope and say, "take the free end," then give the middle of the rope a slight twitch as you say, "pass the free end over the standing part." When you make a small loop, refer to it as "wind the key in this direction," and repeat the motion. After your first exhibition, do a second one a little more quickly but still show all the steps clearly.

You Do, I Help.

You may stand behind the Trailman to show him how to tie a bowline on himself rather than tie one around yourself while facing him. If a Trailman doesn't have to reverse the knot, he learns the skill more easily.

- Emphasize certain behaviors that you want Patrol Members to notice.
- Give gentle encouragement and positive affirmations.
- Take their hands or arms to guide them into position.
- Exaggerate or slow your movements.
- Repeat.
- Exercise patience.
- Use hand gestures to illustrate a point.

You Do, I Cheer.

You want your Trailmen to succeed, but success means they can perform the skill when you're not around to prompt them with spoken hints, hand gestures, or any other body language. When they can pass the test cleanly, they truly have reason to be proud.

To get your Trailmen to the stage where they can't get it wrong, use the "Three P's": practice, practice, and more practice.

There's another "P" to consider: Promotion. You're not doing a Trailman a favor to pass him on a test simply because he tried hard. When he moves out into the world, his boss, and his clients will not give him points for trying hard. Were the orders carried out? Don't raise false expectations about what quests Trailmen can win armed only with the sword of good intentions.

Always remember, you don't promote Trailmen; they promote themselves by meeting the standards of advancement and the criteria of personal growth.

MASTER EFFECTIVE COMMUNICATION

If the Troop is a body, communication is the nervous system that carries information from the brain to the arms and legs and returns feedback to the brain: Were the orders were carried out? Were they successful? Without communication, a patrol is only a group of people who happen to be in the same area.

Communication, therefore, is the heart, mind, and soul of the patrol:

> The **heart** because you must relate to one another.
> The **mind** because you must think as a group.
> The **soul** because a patrol needs a shared purpose.

A good plan becomes a great plan when everyone understands it and everyone is updated on last-minute changes. A great plan becomes a great project when there is coordinated effort and effective evaluation.

Parts of Communication

Whether he's asking you something or telling you something, the **sender** needs to know what he wants. If he's not sure, he can't be sure he'll get what he wants. The sender needs to make sure the receiver is paying attention so that he is speaking to him rather than at him.

The **receiver** should listen carefully and make sure he understands. If the receiver says, "got it," the ball is in his court. If he understood the message incorrectly, he has no one to blame but himself.

The **medium** is how the communication is passed on. It needs to be something the sender and receiver both understand, and it needs to be appropriate. Sometimes the medium will be calling across a valley; sometimes the medium will be a phone call or maybe an email. Match the type of communication with the proper medium. Sensitive communications should be face-to-face. Broad announcements can be emails or postings on a board.

The **message** itself is the heart of communication. News reporters talk about the "Five W's and an H," and you should learn to use them when you communicate:

- Who is involved
- What is happening
- Where it is going to occur
- When it will happen
- Why is it being done
- How will it be done

> ### "Tappers and Listeners" Game
>
> **Tapper taps out or drums a common song that anyone knows with no music. Listeners must guess what the song was. Nearly all fail. Once named, the tapper taps it out again humming or singing as he goes. This game exemplifies effective and non-effective communication.**

Communication Tips for Addressing Your Patrol or Troop:

- Organize your thoughts first. Write down the key points.
- Move your audience away from distractions, and wait until you have their attention. Use the Trailman Sign if needed.
- Make eye contact with your audience and speak clearly.
- Ask questions to make sure everyone understood the key points.

- Repeat important points such as dates, times, and places.
- If possible, ask someone to take notes of the discussion.
- Ask the receiver to repeat information to prevent mistakes.
- Important messages should be sent by multiple channels—email by itself or Facebook posts are not enough. Very important messages need to be sent through multiple channels such as a phone tree, a Troop meeting flier, and an email.

Good communication not only helps the patrol and Troop run more smoothly, but it also builds stronger careers, families, communities, and faith.

Know Who's Receiving the Message

It's important to know that, although you say exactly the same thing to a number of people, each person may hear what you're saying differently.

Especially in critical written communications and action proposals, take the time to

craft a message that addresses the different types of receivers and answers their concerns and questions in advance.

At any one time, you can be addressing at least four types of receivers. Here's a helpful diagram on the previous page.

Develop your message so it speaks to each type of receiver:
- The highly involved and low idealistic person. He is very pragmatic. He will say, "Let's get something done."
- The highly involved and highly idealistic person. He is the activist. He says, "We have to do something about this!"
- The low involved and low idealistic person. He is the reservist. He says, "What do you think we should do? I'm fine with that."
- And the low involved, highly idealistic person. He is the theoretician. He says, "Let's study it more."

Read or rehearse your message to make sure you've answered each receiver's questions and concerns. When you craft your message this way, your patrol will move to consensus a lot faster.

When you lead a discussion, make sure each type of receiver is heard.

WHAT ARE THE ACTIVITY AND PROJECT ESSENTIALS?

These habits and skills, when mastered, will serve you your entire life.

PLANNING

When you reach the office of Patrol Leader, you'll need to understand how to plan successful events.

Proper planning begins long before the campout. During the Officers' Conference, the Patrol Leaders and Officers should be planning events at least three months out. See an explanation on page 305 in the Appendix. When the Officers' Conference determines the calendar of activities for the year, the feasibility of each outing should be checked. Certain attractions are not open year-round; others have long waiting lists or may be closed for refurbishment. There may be age limits or restrictions in place. It is better to find out these things well in advance.

After you've made the reservations and paid the fees, life may still throw you a curve. Inclement weather, a wildfire, or other unforeseen circumstances may come into play, and, suddenly, your reservations are worthless. You should always have Plan B to fall back on. You don't need a new Plan B every month. You can just have one trip ready to pull out of your back pocket whenever it's needed. Perhaps there's a local campground or park you could visit that has some trails or other activities to enjoy.

When you arrive at your destination, the weather may not be what you expected. Instead of sunshine, you have rain or an early snow. Instead of warm temperatures, it is unseasonably cold. Monitor the weather forecast right up to the day you leave and be prepared for the unexpected so Patrol Members don't end up miserable or disappointed.

To be prepared means to be able to concentrate for at least several minutes at a time on things other than the weather and your feelings. It also means that your activities don't center on keeping warm and dry. Standing next to the burn barrel for long periods of time to stave off a chill is not ideal camping.

Board games, cards, and other foul weather activities can help you enjoy rainy hours. Be sure games with lots of pieces are properly bagged and carefully stored after use.

Know—don't assume—what the rules are about camping, fires, trailer access, water access, and expected behavior. Be aware of any curfews or quiet times.

To have a successful event, you need the proper equipment. Wouldn't it be disappointing to show up for a backpacking trip with heavy Dutch ovens or arrive for a

canoeing trip without PFDs? It's all about being prepared for the task at hand. So keep the following in mind:
- Is the event season-appropriate?
- What is the cost per individual, and how much of the cost will the Troop cover?
- Who is going?
- Transportation (number of seats, 4x4 vehicles, cargo trailers)
- Who's in charge, and who are the event coordinators? (transportation, reservations, food, equipment)
- Individual gear list
- Patrol and Troop gear lists (Checklist on page 308 in the Appendix)
- Special equipment (canoes, climbing equipment, snow skis, safety equipment)
- Permissions slips
- Special permits or reservations (fishing licenses, backcountry permits, campground reservations)
- Points of contact for each event location
- Other important topics unique to your situation

Some tasks may be accomplished during weekly meetings to help you prepare for the event:
- Is there anything special or a set of skills we need to know before the event? (swim checks, cold weather camping, or orienteering)
- What equipment is required for the weekly skills training?
- Menus
- Food shopping lists
- Assignments, such as tents or canoe partners
- Plan to clean and inventory gear at the end of the event
- Health and safety concerns

Detailed Schedule

If you want your event to be a success, you need a detailed schedule. Make sure you create and share the schedule so each Trailman knows what his role is and what he should expect.

Remember the Basics

Your patrol doesn't have to do everything on a schedule, but certain things should be put on a duty roster and accomplished in a structured manner. See an example on page 311 in the Appendix.

Cooking

Over the course of his career, each boy should gain the skills and confidence to prepare a variety of breakfast, lunch, and dinner menus. Success is measured in safety, appeal, timeliness, and efficiency. An ideal cook prepares food that is properly done and tastes good. The meal should also include foods that require different cooking times yet finish about the same time. This is an enormously important skill for learning self-reliance and project management.

Cleanup

Properly washing implements used for cooking and serving food is a health and safety issue. The feeling of accomplishment after cleanup may be less than the satisfaction of cooking a full meal, but, in the overall scheme, cleanup is equally important.

Fire Tending

Starting, feeding, and putting out a fire are big responsibilities, and they should be taken seriously.

Errands

Whether it is filling the water containers or retrieving equipment from the Troop trailer, there are no bad jobs, just bad attitudes. When a Trailman is doing unpleasant tasks, his fellow **Patrol Members** get an idea of what sort of leader he would be. A Trailman who is prompt and cheerful stands a much better chance of being elected **Patrol Leader** than one who procrastinates or gripes.

Layout.

Every Trailman should have real-world practice in the art of selecting a proper patrol campsite and determining the correct layout of patrol resources such as tents, campfires, and cooking supplies.

See the Field Guides for more detailed information on these duties.

Types of Outings

Your other youth leaders as well as your Troop leaders will be great resources when planning an outing. One way people classify outings is by the way they are carried out:

Field Trips
These involve traveling to an attraction such as a museum, town hall, amusement park, or farm tour.

Service Projects
The goal of these activities is to improve an aspect of the community.

Day Hikes
Generally, these are short trips by foot involving a day pack or rucksack, comfortable shoes, and no cooking.

Backpacking Treks
These trips last longer than day hikes. They involve a full backpack, boots, sleeping in a tent or shelter, and cooking over a campfire or portable stove. Shelters are individual.

Stationary Camping (short-term/long-term camp)
Gear is brought in and out by vehicle. Shelters may be individual or group tents. Frequently, large structures such as dining flies, propane

---

People also classify outings by the degree of difficulty:

Easy. Pre-packaged, simple adventures such as visiting the zoo. Supervision is augmented by staff members, clearly marked walkways, and adequate signage.

Moderate. There may be a few health and training considerations, but it is extremely unlikely that an emergency will arise, and help is nearby, just in case.

High Adventure. There is potential danger on this activity, but it can be minimized through use of proper equipment, training, and safety rules.

Extreme. On this activity, risk can be reduced but not minimized. Make sure you consult the **Health and Safety Guide** (on line) so you take the proper precautions, and don't plan an activity that is not permitted by Trail Life USA.

stoves, lanterns, and chuck boxes are used.

Water Voyages
Participants put in at one place along a waterway and raft, float, motor, canoe, or kayak to another place where they take out.

Tours
These travel plans involve touring across a part of the country. Trailmen can combine visiting interesting places with camping along the way. Participants may only stay for a night or two in each location.

Year-Round Activities

Four seasons mean four different opportunities for fun, adventure, and growth. The secrets to being able to enjoy the Trail Life year-round are weather and opportunity. Coping with weather is easy if you find something unique about each season that you love and capitalize on it or if you select activities for which the weather is irrelevant. Utilize your older youth leaders and your Troop leaders when planning for various year-round activities.

Trailmen will enjoy fair weather campouts more, but they will learn more from challenging conditions. This is an extremely important lesson since some things in life—a career, a marriage, a new baby—will have both sunny and rainy moments. It is not surprising that the expression "fair-weather friend" describes someone who lacks the commitment to stick with you when the chips are down.

Winter

If skiing, survival camping, or snowball fights are things you love to do, winter is an opportunity not a wet blanket. Winter is also a great time for caving trips since the temperature underground is usually steady year-round. Proper diet, proper shelter, and proper clothing will keep you warm and dry.

Spring

Early spring days may be beautiful, but the weather is temperamental. You can expect rain, and, if it comes, you can break out cards, board games, or other forms of recreation ideal for sitting under the dining fly. Dress in layers that you can easily add or remove. Expect chilly temperatures early in the morning or late in the evening.

Summer

The main challenges of summer are heat, insects, and sunburn. You can easily prepare for bugs and burns. Heat can be kept at bay too if you make sure you stay hydrated, seek shade during the hottest parts of the day, and recognize the warning signs of heat exhaustion and heat stroke.

Fall

Some of your best hiking and camping experiences take place in the fall, especially when trees turn the hues of flame and sun. Dressing in layers is important, as is good rain gear. With a little forethought and an extra change of clothes, you'll be fine.

These descriptions of the four seasons may not describe the seasons in your area of the country, but you get the

idea. Experience both the challenges and the rewards of year-round camping where you live.

After the Event

Keep notes and documentation of what worked well and why, what failed badly and why, and what was good but could have been better. Build on your successes and learn from your mistakes. If you rate the good points and bad points of every activity, you'll eventually find what works for you and your Troop.

Get used to the fact that tents will often be wet and need to be dried out. The best way to do this may be to have Trailmen take them home and set them up until they dry in the sun and wind, then repack them and return them at the next Troop meeting.

Periodically, have a shakedown to inspect the condition of Troop camping equipment. Make sure that you have sufficient propane, that tents have the required number of parts (including tent stakes), and that none of the perishables in chuck boxes have expired. An effective way to do this is to check out tents as they are packed up and to check propane cylinders as they are loaded.

The first Troop meeting after a campout is a great time to get your patrol to talk about what went right—and wrong—with a campout and to see if they would consider doing that trip again. It is also worthwhile to use Boards of Review and Conferences to ask Trailmen what their favorite trip of the year was, what their least liked trip was, and why.

Evaluation is not something you do at the end of an activity; it's an ongoing process. Think about the manned missions to the moon where, halfway out, the trajectory of the spacecraft is checked. The key is to check progress when there is enough information to do something with it and early enough to do something about it.

Learning something from one backpacking trip will help you the next time you travel. In fact, even if your patrol is remarkable and gets everything right the first time, you're wearing fabrics and carrying backpacks developed by those who traveled before you. Even if you don't need to learn from your mistakes, you learn from the mistakes of others.

You should fairly assess how well your patrol did on each outing. What went right, what went wrong, and what went better or worse. Start by asking your **Patrol Members** what they liked most and least about the outing. Then you should either concur with the general view or offer your own interpretation. You learn something new with every outing—what to do and what not to do. This should logically lead you to decide what, if anything, should be done differently next time.

> You learn something new with every outing—what to do and what not to do.

Evaluations should also focus on the value of the outing itself. If it always rains when you visit Campbell Forge Military Battlefield Park in November, consider other times of the year to visit. If Sewanee Water Park consistently disappoints, stop going there.

You also must evaluate the success of skills instruction. It's a hindrance, not a help, to pass someone on a skill for the wrong reasons. We'll go into how to measure a skill later. That includes how to objectively measure, to define success, to determine progress, and to check up on retention.

PROJECT MANAGEMENT

"Packing" Your Schedule

When you put gear in your backpack, the shape, the sturdiness, and the size of the items determine how you place each one and how much you can carry. When you assign duties, manpower and time requirements also have a shape and size that determine how you pack them into your schedule and how much can fit.

How do you "pack" your campsite setup or mealtimes so that everything fits? For one thing, you pack with the event in mind. Some things take a long time to cook. If time is at a premium, don't prepare foods that require a long time to simmer and a lot of work to clean up. You may want every second for that long hike or orienteering event. However, if it is appropriate to work on your outdoor cooking, give it the time it needs and look for other jobs that can be done while the meat cooks or the stew simmers.

Delegation

Delegation is a key project-management skill. You are not shifting your responsibility to others; rather, you are trading the responsibility for performing a task for the responsibility of recognizing and developing talent in others and giving their talents an outlet. Leadership has fitness just like your body or mind has fitness. All three of these things need plenty of exercise, adequate rest, and a good diet. You exercise leadership by making crucial decisions, but you also rest it by dividing the work of giving guidance. As for a good diet, you feed your leadership skills by choosing good role models and getting guidance fresh from God. Think about this: Are you fully giving the gift of guidance when you're calling all the shots? Isn't teaching a younger Trailman how to carry out a mission at least as important as teaching them how to tie a bowline?

Types of Assignments

Sequential assignments must be done one at a time. Select your campsite and then lay out your tarp.

Parallel assignments can be done together. One person can erect a tent while another builds camp gadgets.

Triage

The word *triage* means "dividing by three." It can refer to a lot of things you'll encounter in life. When you're setting up camp, it usually means this:
- First, you set up the things that are **essential and time critical.**
- Second, you set up the things that are **essential but not time critical.**
- Third, you set up optional things you may **want but not necessarily need.**

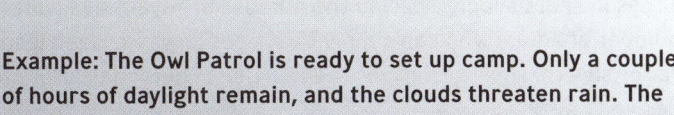

Example: The Owl Patrol is ready to set up camp. Only a couple of hours of daylight remain, and the clouds threaten rain. The Patrol Members are prepared to meet the challenge since they are skilled in triage.

First Steps: They pitch the dining fly and light the lanterns. In fact, they do this whether or not it is stormy. If it starts raining, they have a place to quickly stow their gear and put on their ponchos. Next, they pitch the tents, being careful to put them in the best place with the doors facing away from the wind and rain.

Second Steps: Personal gear, such as sleeping bags, is carried to the tents and set up. Next, tables, chuck boxes, sanitation trays, and the first-aid kit are set up under the dining fly. The duty roster and event schedule are posted. Doing these steps in this order reduces the possibility that it will start raining while Patrol Members are carrying their personal belongings around under the sky. They save tasks that will be done under shelter for later. Then they announce to the First Officer that the Owl Patrol is ready for inspection.

Third Steps: With everything well in hand, you can bring out the board games or chat without fear of a miserable setup in the driving rain.

Scope of a Project

The scope of a project is important. It can involve time, resources, scheduling, preparation, and resolve.

Resources

If you have enough money to buy a hundred jars but no money for lids, you'll never finish that delicious jam for the Troop fundraiser. It would be better to buy fifty jars and fifty lids. There may be other resources in short supply, such as the number of kayaks available, the number of adults who can supply the necessary two-deep leadership for several small groups, or the number of personal flotation devices you have.

Time

You should have an estimate of how long it takes you to travel, hike, set up camp, have your activities, eat, and retire. If all the necessary times add up to more than the time you have, something needs to be scaled back.

Scheduling

If you have a rappelling course available in August and you want to go rappelling in June, you must decide to change either the date of your activity or the type.

Preparation

This can cover a wide range of things. Perhaps you want to do an activity that has a two-year waiting list. You must look far ahead in setting this goal. You may want to engage in an activity that requires a certain level of physical fitness or a certain amount of experience. Clearly, you can't enter a marathon or go rock climbing next week if you aren't in proper physical condition. There is also little you can do about your age except wait until you're 14 if there are age limits on certain activities.

Work with your leaders in fundraising plans so you have plenty of money to pursue your dream adventures. Plan in such a way that every Trailman has the opportunity to attend; a lack of money should never be the reason he can't attend.

Resolve

Here we get into a long, hard look at how badly you want to overcome all the obstacles to do something. Preparing for a complex, expensive project is exciting at first, frustrating as you take on the challenges, and then exciting once more when you near the starting gate. Nothing is sadder than a Troop trailer full of backpacks and portable stoves that would have gone down the Appalachian Trail if boys had not burned out from all the preparation. Choose your challenges carefully, but once you choose them, charge forward with a can-do attitude that overcomes every obstacle and gets you to the summit. There should be no hands in pockets when there is work to be done. There should be no skimping on tests to verify skills. You can build great things if you lay a solid foundation.

Working Together

An important part of project management is to know your resources. That includes knowing the strengths and weaknesses of your Patrol Members. Use their strengths and work on bolstering their weaknesses. But also realize that it is normal and natural for different people to have different gifts. Manage those gifts to achieve synergy, which is the ability to get more out of the group than the sum of its parts.

This does not mean that everyone only does what they do best, especially if that involves less pleasant chores such as washing dishes. Even people with a natural talent need to develop it. They develop talents the way you develop biceps—by exercising them.

WHAT ELSE SHOULD I KNOW?

TRAILMAN ANTI-BULLYING POLICY

Boys may be subjected to inappropriate situations every day that may include:

- Physical striking or ruffling the hair
- Aggressive, sexual, or otherwise inappropriate gestures
- Sarcasm, insults, put-downs, or name calling
- Exclusion from the group
- Laughing at a person or joking about a person
- Commenting on a person's physical attributes, imitating or mocking a person
- Inappropriate internet comments

The Troop is supposed to be a refuge from these types of abuse. Trailmen, Patrol Leaders, and Troop Leaders must work together to identify and eliminate such behavior. There are four defenses:

- **First Defense.** Trailmen must avoid hurtful behavior. "A Trailman treats others as he would want to be treated." If a Trailman is sarcastic or inconsiderate, the Troop expects him to catch himself and make amends.
- **Second Defense.** If a Trailman is bullied, he should demand that the bully stop at once.
- **Third Defense.** If a Trailman observes someone bullying another person, he must tell the bully to stop at once.
- **Fourth Defense.** If an adult leader sees someone bullying another, the adult must tell the bully to stop at once.

Once a Trailman has engaged in bullying behavior, he must make immediate amends to the victim, including a Trailman handshake with an eye-to-eye sincere apology that includes saying "I'm sorry" and making good on any damages. If the bully does not carry this out to the spirit and letter of the rule, it will be handled like any other misbehavior. It will be taken to the Patrol Leader and progress normally as needed to the First Officer, then the adult leader, with appropriate action to be taken by the Troopmaster. The exception to this is dangerous bullying behavior, which goes straight to the Troopmaster for action.

NOW... *LEAD!*

You may feel like your backpack is overstuffed for the leadership journey.

It probably feels like there is so much to remember. So much to do.

Don't sweat it. Your growth in leadership skills will take place over your entire life, as long as you commit to learning all you can and put it into practice. Like with anyone pursuing mastery of a complex and important skill, it's the rare man who will master leadership in one short guidebook.

Seek out leadership mentors. Read great books on leadership. And commit to making consistent improvements in the way you handle the challenge and opportunities of leadership. Your role in your Trail Life USA Troop and patrol is designed to give you a great start.

You'll get there. And who knows? Maybe YOU will write the next great book on leadership!

APPENDIX

APPENDIX

OFFICER'S CONFERENCE 3-MONTH PLANNING

In January, Trailmen are actually doing planning for January, February, and March. If their planning meeting is the first Saturday of the month, they're putting the final touches on the January meeting plan. They're getting close to nailing down plans for February events. And they're confirming that they're still on track with the annual plan to do whatever their annual dream session slotted for the March outing. In an hour-long meeting, January should require 15 minutes or so, February will take 30-45 minutes, and March will only require 5-10 minutes. This teaches advance planning, establishes responsibilities for youth, and requires them to remain connected with the annual plan.

	January	February	March
Meeting activity	1st	1st	1st
	2nd	2nd	2nd
	3rd	3rd	3rd
	4th	4th	4th
Meeting Topic	1st	1st	1st
	2nd	2nd	2nd
	3rd	3rd	3rd
	4th	4th	4th
Event of the month			
Annual Event Prep			

OFFICER'S CONFERENCE ANNUAL PLAN

Sample from the Trail Life USA Patrol Planning Guide, available in the Trail Life USA online store.

April (cont.)
Program Topics (Branch/Trail Badge)

May 2019
Date   Activities
Program Topics (Branch/Trail Badge)

June 2019
Date   Activities
Program Topics (Branch/Trail Badge)

Don't forget! Don't forget to include faith-building activities like the Worthy Life Award in your plan.

January 2019
Date   Activities
Program Topics (Branch/Trail Badge)

February 2019
Date   Activities
Program Topics (Branch/Trail Badge)

March 2019
Date   Activities
Program Topics (Branch/Trail Badge)

April 2019
Date   Activities
Program Topics (Branch/Trail Badge)

September (cont.)
Program Topics (Branch/Trail Badge)

October 2018
Date   Activities
Program Topics (Branch/Trail Badge)

November 2018
Date   Activities
Program Topics (Branch/Trail Badge)

December 2018
Date   Activities
Program Topics (Branch/Trail Badge)

STEP THREE
Plan Program Topics & Activities

Write down your program topics and activities for each month to cover desired achievements for the year.

July 2018
Date   Activities
Program Topics (Branch/Trail Badge)

August 2018
Date   Activities
Program Topics (Branch/Trail Badge)

September 2018
Date   Activities

NAVIGATOR/ADVENTURER PATROL MEETING PLAN PADS

Sample page—pads available in the Trail Life USA online store.

Navigator/Adventurer Patrol Meeting Plan

Meeting Date: _____
Leader: _____
Patrol Name: _____
Level: ☐ Navigator ☐ Adventurer
Topic: _____

	What	Time	Who	Supplies Needed
Set-Up:				
Gathering:				
Opening/Devotion:				
Business:				
Skill Activity:				
Game:				
Closing:				
Clean-Up:				

These Meeting Planners can be reordered at the online store.

APPENDIX

CHECKLIST FOR OUTDOOR ADVENTURES

These lists provide suggestions of basic necessities. Use these lists to ensure you have evaluated all the possibilities given the scenarios and circumstances for your outdoor adventure. These lists were created to cover both Front Country (Campground) Adventures as well as Backcountry Adventures (Backpacking). Any specific differences will be noted accordingly.

1. Shelters and Packs

___ Sleeping bag(s) (Temperature appropriate)
___ Sleeping pads/cots
___ Daypack/Backpack

2. Food and Water

___ Wet/cold box for cold foods
___ Dry food box
___ Stove and Fuel
___ Dutch ovens and charcoal
___ Pots/pans/griddles
___ Specific utensils (peelers, whisk, etc.)
___ Measuring utensils
___ Serving/cooking utensils
___ Lighters/matches
___ Personal mess kit (plate-bowl, bottle/cup, utensils)
___ Food (enough for all participants and length of adventure)

*For Backcountry Adventures, you will need to rethink your cooking and food arrangements. You will want as few cooking items as possible, and your food will need to be non-perishable lightweight foods (just add water types). Consider using the following Backpacking options:

___ Nesting pot/pan set*
___ Personal backpacking stove w/ fuel*
___ Dromedary bag(s)*
___ Bear bags w/rope*
___ Bottle filter w/ purification tablets or other bacteria killing device*
___ Separate dirty water container*

3. First Aid

- ___ Gauze pads
- ___ Moleskins
- ___ Band-Aids, multiples of all sizes
- ___ Basic medicine (aspirin, Tylenol, etc.)
- ___ CPR mouth cover
- ___ Self-adherent wrap
- ___ Disinfectants
- ___ Tweezers
- ___ Emergency blanket

This list of First Aid materials includes suggestions for the basics of a First Aid Kit. Each Troop will need to adjust and/or add items to its First Aid Kit based on the specific activity and area.

4. Clothing and Hygiene

- ___ Season appropriate clothing (layers)
- ___ Sturdy shoes/hiking boots
- ___ Moisture wicking socks (several)
- ___ Hats/Beanies/Gloves/Coats (if needed)
- ___ Rain clothing
- ___ Packable towel
- ___ Toilet paper
- ___ Trowel
- ___ Toothbrush/toothpaste
- ___ Biodegradable soap
- ___ Swimming Suit/Trunks

5. Other Items

- ___ TLUSA Handbooks/ Field Guides
- ___ Flint & steel
- ___ Firestarter (lint, fat lighter, hemp rope, etc.)
- ___ Flashlights/lanterns/headlamps
- ___ Extra batteries
- ___ Charging method for phone/radios
- ___ Insect repellent
- ___ Sunscreen
- ___ Extra clothing
- ___ Compasses & maps
- ___ Radios and/or phones
- ___ Camping shovel/rake
- ___ Pocketknife(s)/Sharpener/Multi-tool (Mt. Lions with Woodsman card and older)
- ___ Axe/Hatchet/Saw
- ___ Hammers
- ___ Rope/bungee cords/paracord
- ___ Duct tape

DETAILED PATROL CAMPOUT SCHEDULE

Here is some idea of what you should know in advance:

ARRIVAL DAY
- Meeting location and time
- Load vehicles
- Drive to event location
- Arrival at event and check in
- Set up camp or activity
- Activities (skills, games, free time, etc.)
- Dinner
- Lights out

ACTIVITIES DAY
- Flag raising
- Breakfast
- Activities
- Service project
- Lunch
- Activities
- Free time
- Games
- Flag lowering
- Dinner
- Campfire
- Lights out

DEPARTURE DAY
- Flag raising
- Free time
- Breakfast
- Worship service
- Flag lowering
- Pack up and checkout
- Drive back to meeting place
- Unload vehicles
- Clean and inventory gear

DUTY ROSTER EXAMPLE

	JOB	Patrol 1	Patrol 2	Patrol 3	Patrol 4
TIME:	Lead Cook				
	Assistant Cook				
	Campsite Manager				
	Cleanup Crew				
DAY:	Fire Tending				
	Misc. Errands				

	JOB	Patrol 1	Patrol 2	Patrol 3	Patrol 4
TIME:	Lead Cook				
	Assistant Cook				
	Campsite Manager				
	Cleanup Crew				
DAY:	Fire Tending				
	Misc. Errands				

	JOB	Patrol 1	Patrol 2	Patrol 3	Patrol 4
TIME:	Lead Cook				
	Assistant Cook				
	Campsite Manager				
	Cleanup Crew				
DAY:	Fire Tending				
	Misc. Errands				

	JOB	Patrol 1	Patrol 2	Patrol 3	Patrol 4
TIME:	Lead Cook				
	Assistant Cook				
	Campsite Manager				
	Cleanup Crew				
DAY:	Fire Tending				
	Misc. Errands				

LOW IMPACT CAMPING

There are more people on Earth than there were a century ago, but we still have to operate in the same amount of room. That makes caring wisely for the wild areas we have left all the more important.

There are a few simple things Trailmen can do to walk more softly in the wilderness while still having a great time. If you remember from this chapter, deserts, mountains, prairies, and forests are homes. Just as you would take off muddy boots before entering your house, taking similar precautions in nature's houses will become a habit that demonstrates respect for God's creation.

Prepare in Advance

Know what you will need to bring, what you should leave at home, what you should do, and what you should avoid doing. The best way to do this is to ask the land manager for suggestions.

No Trailblazing

It may require walking a few extra steps, but stay on the prepared paths and camp whenever possible in prepared campgrounds. These places were reserved for human wear and tear so that the surrounding areas could remain pristine for future visitors. Remember, when you blaze a new trail, other people will be tempted to use it after you.

Not all wild areas are as durable as the grass in your yard. Some delicate places will hold the scars of your passing for a long time.

Leave it Intact

If it belongs there, it stays there. If it doesn't belong there, pack it out. In National Parks and Monuments, removing natural objects is a violation of the Antiquities Act.

Even if it's not illegal, it is unethical to collect "souvenirs" of your visit that deprive future visitors the same experiences you enjoyed. Don't dam creeks, dig trenches, or leave trash. Don't leave "pioneering" projects, such as camp gadgets, behind.

Take nothing but pictures, leave nothing but footprints, and make nothing but memories.

Be Careful With Fire

Campfires have their place in the outdoors, and that place is a carefully prepared area set aside by the land manager. Consider using a camping stove if your aim is to heat water or cook food.

If you are camping in a prepared place with a fire ring, use the existing spot rather than building a fire in a new place.

If you do use fire, make sure the area around it is clear of twigs, branches, and anything that can catch fire; and always watch a fire carefully to prevent flames from spreading to the surroundings. It only takes a moment to start, but it may take years for nature to heal from it.

Remember never to run or horseplay around an open fire. A tragedy could occur if a Trailman were to trip or fall into a fire or onto hot coals.

Wise Sanitation

Water you use at home is treated before being released. Obviously, you can't return water to its source as clean as you got it, but you can take precautions to minimize your impact on the land.

For short stays, remove solids from dishwater and put them in the trash. Then take dishwater or rinse water at least 200 feet (75 steps) from open water and fling it out rather than pouring it in one spot. For longer stays, dig a sump hole. It should be about a foot across and two feet deep. Remove solids from dishwater before emptying it. Fill in the sump hole before you leave, and return the land to a natural appearance. Water used to wash your body should be treated with the same precautions as dishwater.

It is less adventurous but a lot more pleasant to use restroom facilities at campgrounds. If you must dig a cathole for human waste, it should be located at least 200 feet (about 75 steps) from open water, trails or campsites. Dig a hole about 7 inches deep. After using it, fill it in with the soil you dug. Leave the area as close to its original appearance as possible, but leave a stick in the ground to warn people against using the same spot. Sanitize your hands.

For longer stays with several people, dig a latrine. A latrine is a shallow trench about four feet long and seven inches deep. After each use, sprinkle a layer of dirt to abate odors and keep away flies. Return the area to a natural appearance before moving on.

Getting Along With Other Visitors

One of the greatest parts about camping is getting away from it all. Select your campsite in a way to protect your own privacy and the privacy of others. Do not make excessive noise or use brightly colored tents. Leave loud electronics behind. Make sure you do not enter another campsite without asking permission.

HIKER'S RESPONSIBILITY CODE*

Hiking is fun except when it's not. The quickest way to spoil everyone's fun is to make easily avoidable mistakes.

You are responsible for yourself, so be prepared:
- **With knowledge and gear.** Become self-reliant by learning about the terrain, conditions, local weather, and your equipment before you start.
- **To leave your plans.** Tell someone where you are going, the trails you are hiking, when you will return, and your emergency plans.
- **To stay together.** When you start as a group, hike as a group and end as a group. Pace your hike to the slowest person.
- **To turn back.** Weather changes quickly. Fatigue and unexpected conditions can also affect your hike. Know your limitations and when to postpone your hike.
- **For emergencies.** Even if you are headed out for just an hour, an injury, severe weather, or a wrong turn could become life-threatening. Don't assume you will be rescued; know how to rescue yourself.
- **To share the Hiker's Code with others**.

*Developed and endorsed by the White Mountain National Forest and New Hampshire Fish and Game. See www.hikesafe.com for more information.

BACKPACKING METRICS

Metrics are used in the route and camp planning process to lay out reasonable-effort days of hiking and interesting places to camp. Guidebooks for your hiking area are also helpful for planning a trip. In order to use the metrics, you will need to read off the topographic map distances along the trail and the high and low point elevations of each up and down along the trail. The total elevation gain increases the hiking time and the aerobic effort involved in the hike whereas the total elevation loss increases the leg strain and the hiking time for steep descents.

The Backpack Time Metric (BTM) is computed as the sum of ½ hour for each mile and 1 hour for each 1,000 feet of total elevation gain and is used to estimate backpacking time to complete a particular segment of the trip.

$$BTM = \frac{1}{2}\left(\frac{hour}{mile}\right) \times Distance(miles) + 1(hour)\frac{Total\ Elevation\ Gain\ (feet)}{1000(feet)}$$

The Backpack Effort Metric (BEM) is computed as the sum of the BTM and ½ hour for each 1,000 feet of total elevation loss and is used to estimate the overall effort or impact to the body to complete a particular segment of the trip. This metric is primarily used for trips longer than a week to ramp up and equalize effort over the duration of the trip.

$$BEM = BTM + \frac{1}{2}(hour)\frac{Total\ Elevation\ Descent\ (feet)}{1000(feet)}$$

Example: Overnight in and out backpack trip that does the following over 5 miles (1-way) and then returns the same way (where the descents become the climbs and vice versa)

    1.1 miles - gain 600'
    0.5 miles - loss 300'
    1.9 miles - gain 1,000'
    0.9 miles - loss 700'
    0.6 miles - gain 400'

The total elevation gain for day 1 is (600 + 1,000 + 400) = 2,000 feet and the total elevation gain for day 2 is (300 + 700) = 1,000 feet. Using the equation for BTM:

$$BTM = \frac{1}{2}\left(\frac{hour}{mile}\right) \times Distance(miles) + 1(hour)\frac{Total\ Elevation\ Gain\ (feet)}{1000(feet)}$$

The BTM for day 1 is calculated as follows:

$$BTM(day\ 1) = (0.5)*(5) + (1)*(2{,}000/1{,}000) = 4.5\ hours$$

And the BTM for day 2 is calculated as follows:

$$BTM(day\ 2) = (0.5)*(5) + (1)*(1{,}000/1{,}000) = 3.5\ hours$$

The total elevation descent for day 1 is (300 + 700) = 1,000 feet and the total elevation descent for day 2 is (600 + 1,000 + 400) = 2,000 feet. Using the equation for BEM:

$$BEM = BTM + \frac{1}{2}(hour)\frac{Total\ Elevation\ Descent\ (feet)}{1000(feet)}$$

BEM(day 1) = 4.5 + (0.5)*(1,000/1,000) = 5.0 hours
BEM(day 2) = 3.5 + (0.5)*(2,000/1,000) = 4.5 hours

ADVANCEMENT 101

As you have grown in stature and maturity and left the Woodlands Trail for the higher/more difficult terrain of the Navigators, you are being entrusted with more responsibility as you hone your skills. One new responsibility that you have been entrusted with is keeping your own Advancement records. While Troop leaders may track this with you, **this Handbook is your place to record your attendance, service hours, Trail Badge Completion, and leader signatures.**

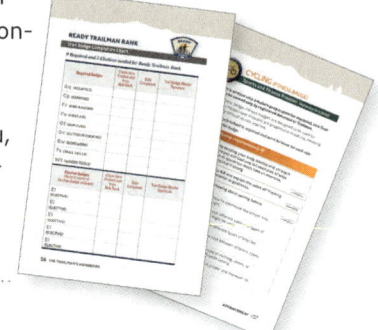

Navigator Advancement

The Navigator Program contains three Ranks that you as the Trailman are working to earn: Recruit, Able, and Ready Trailman. Each Rank has its own set of requirements and is earned by completing certain skills and service requirements, a certain number of Trail Badges, completing the Navigators Worthy Life Award, and passing leader conferences and Boards of Review. Most of your work as a Navigator will be focused on earning Trail Badges. Both the Required and Elective Trail Badges that you earn as a Navigator are foundational and will be required in order to earn your future Adventurer Awards.

Your time and work as a Navigator is essential for building the habits and patterns that will ultimately lead you successfully through the Adventurer Program and on to earning the Freedom Award.

Adventurer Advancement

The Adventurer Program is different from the Navigators in that you will be actively practicing your leadership capabilities as you earn Awards instead of Ranks, specifically the Journey, Horizon, and Freedom Awards. As an Adventurer, you have the freedom to set and achieve your own goals and Awards. It is your responsibility alone to know and track in this Handbook all of the detailed requirements and timelines for each Award.

The Adventurer Awards require that you complete certain skill requirements, Troop Involvement, Servant Service, Leadership experience, personal growth experiences, and community involvement. Your earning of these Awards will depend upon successful completion of Advancement Conferences and Boards of Review at your local Troop and the Area/National level.

The Awards in the Adventurer Programs are true Awards that you must complete correctly to earn. Participation efforts or simply doing "work" will not suffice for successful completion. You must take ownership of ensuring that all of the requirements are met correctly and in the correct order, in the same manner as you would when applying for a job or college.

> **Keep good records. You must take ownership of ensuring that all of the requirements are met correctly and in the correct order.**

From new Recruit to completed Freedom, your Trail Life Ranks and Awards are true awards! All acheivements in Trail Life are those you earn through learned skills and proven character development.

APPENDIX 319

PERIODIC TABLE OF

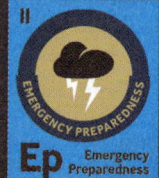

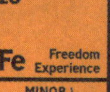

The printed poster of this Periodic Table of Advancements is a handy visual for tracking your acheievements. It is available to order at the www.TrailLifeUSA.com

ADVANCEMENTS

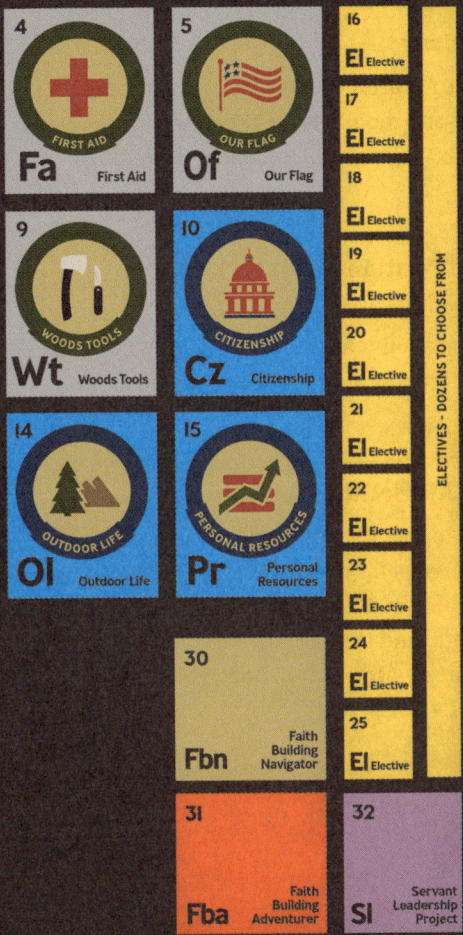

DESIGN YOUR OWN TRAIL BADGE

There are three paths to Design Your Own Badge:

Design Your Own Badge: Analogy

This is one of the easiest ways to draft a "Design Your Own Badge." Simply find an analogous badge and modify it for the new topic. For example, a Paddleboarding Trail Badge can be modified from the Canoeing or Kayaking Trail Badges.

Design Your Own Badge: Certification

Find a significant certification (Scuba, Jr. Lifeguarding, etc.), and after getting approval from your adult leader, earn your certification. The certification should take at least 8 hours in order to qualify as a complete Elective Trail Badge.

Design Your Own Badge: CLEAR Method

Choose, Learn, Explore, Apply, Report (CLEAR) is a formulaic Elective Trail Badge method that will work well for many topics, no matter how general or specific. The youth Trailman designs a Trail Badge that takes a minimum of 8 hours to complete, and the CLEAR method requires that the Troop Advancement Coordinator or Trail Badge Mentor approves each phase of your badge design.

The method is as follows:

C *Choose:*
- A topic of interest for your Elective Trail Badge
- A registered adult leader to serve as your Mentor

L *Learn:*
- Basic facts and broad concepts of the topic
- The history or development of the topic

E *Explore:*
- Details and gain mastery of key elements of the Topic
- Hands-on or practical experience

A *Apply:*
- Complete a personal project of at least 3 hours duration (advanced experience, career, certification, group activity, mentoring, or service type requirement)
- Demonstrate acquired knowledge or skills (advanced experience, exam, paper, presentation, or other method approved by your adult leader)

R *Report:*
- Trailman shares his report and experience with Design Your Own Badge with his Troop or patrol members.
- Troop advancement leader documents completion in the online Advancement Module.

Design Your Own Badge Elective Trail Badges give you the ability to make your Trail Life USA experience unique to you. With your interests and imagination in the driver's seat, the possibilities are endless for the kind of Trail Badges you can create.

More detailed instructions on creating and recording your Design Your Own Badge Elective Trail Badges can be found on www.TrailLifeUSATrailBadges.com.

APPENDIX 323

BAND OF BROTHERS
GROUP BIBLE STUDY & DISCIPLESHIP PROGRAM

The purpose of the Band of Brothers is to provide the structure for a Christian group Bible study and discipleship program that is satisfactory for completing the Bible Study requirement of the Adventurers Worthy Life Award and aimed at spiritual growth through Bible study and faith mentorship. The Band of Brothers program has young men disciple each other in Christian growth under the advisement of adult mentor(s). Your mentors must be Christian adults who have signed the Trial Life USA Statement of Faith and Values. Activities must be completed in conformity with Youth Protection Guidelines.

Youth Participation Requirements

All youth in the group must be professing Christians. This program is specifically for Christian young men that have a special heart for Jesus and a desire to take their walk to a higher level of Christian growth and discipleship. You must be approved by your Troopmaster and Adventurers Advisor to participate.

Group Structure

- Each group should develop a list of "ground rules" to guide the group's discussions and conduct.
- Groups should meet at least twice monthly during the school year for approximately 90 minutes per meeting.
- Each group may include Trailmen from any Troops within your Area.
- The group meets outside of normal Troop meeting times.
- Groups should be small enough in size for everyone to participate (6-10).

Programming

- Each group selects their own discussion topics and meeting format. One suggested format is a small group Bible study with a youth leader fostering discussion and dialogue.
- Each group, with adult advisement, will periodically determine their focus of study (a Christian book, a book of the Bible, topic or personality study from the Bible, a Bible study guide, etc.).
- Provide a social time at the beginning of each meeting.
- Provide meaningful corporate discussion time surrounding the study selected by the group.
- During meetings, groups may break up into smaller groups as accountability partners.
- Groups may plan additional events including fun, service, and spiritual activities with Mentor and Advisor approval.

UNIFORM INSIGNIA PLACEMENT

Trailmen wear their current level award on their right pocket. They may wear a previously completed award patch on the left pocket, if they wish.

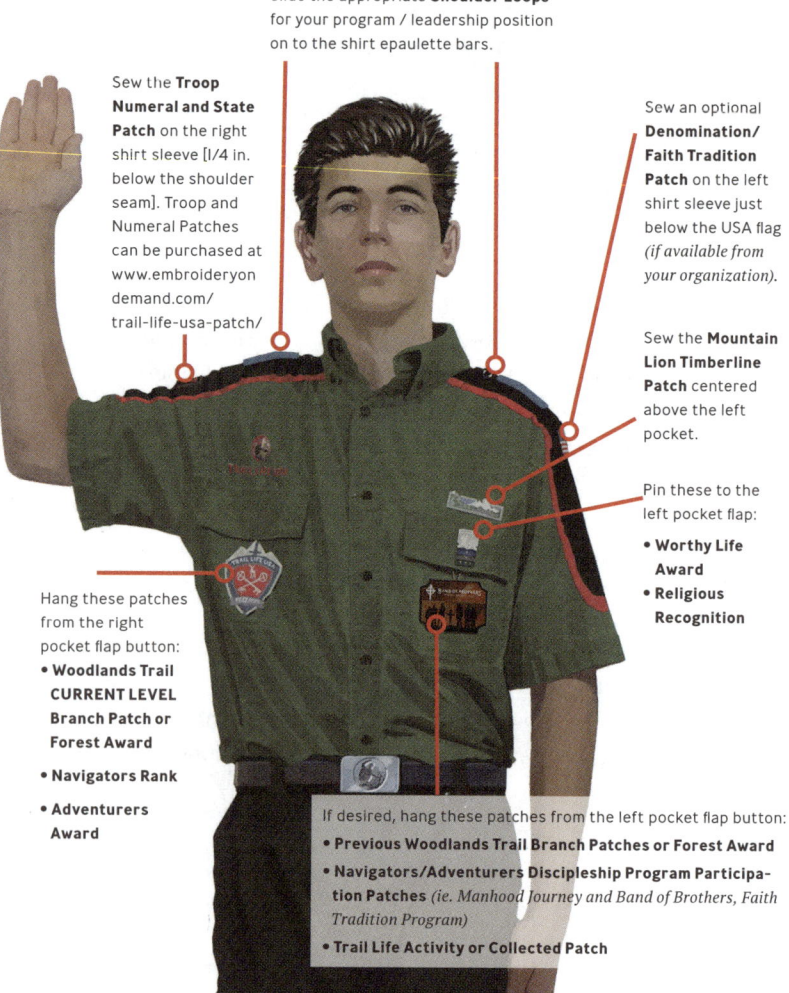

Slide the appropriate **Shoulder Loops** for your program / leadership position on to the shirt epaulette bars.

Sew the **Troop Numeral and State Patch** on the right shirt sleeve [1/4 in. below the shoulder seam]. Troop and Numeral Patches can be purchased at www.embroideryondemand.com/trail-life-usa-patch/

Sew an optional **Denomination/Faith Tradition Patch** on the left shirt sleeve just below the USA flag *(if available from your organization)*.

Sew the **Mountain Lion Timberline Patch** centered above the left pocket.

Pin these to the left pocket flap:
- Worthy Life Award
- Religious Recognition

Hang these patches from the right pocket flap button:
- **Woodlands Trail CURRENT LEVEL Branch Patch or Forest Award**
- **Navigators Rank**
- **Adventurers Award**

If desired, hang these patches from the left pocket flap button:
- **Previous Woodlands Trail Branch Patches or Forest Award**
- **Navigators/Adventurers Discipleship Program Participation Patches** *(ie. Manhood Journey and Band of Brothers, Faith Tradition Program)*
- **Trail Life Activity or Collected Patch**

All items can be purchased at TrailLifeUSAStore.com

WOODS TOOLS SAFETY GUIDELINES

To ensure safety, the following guidelines should be used whenever handling Woods Tools.

Rule	Knife	Saw	Ax
Covering blade when not in use	Close safely (fingers away from blade)	Blade sheathed	Blade sheathed
Carrying	Carry with blade closed	Carry with blade sheathed	Carry with head down and blade sheathed
Passing	Pass with blade closed	Pass with blade turned away	Pass with head down and blade turned away
Safety region	Safety circle (no one within arm's length)	Safety circle (no one within arm's length)	Ax yard 10' in diameter with no overhanging obstructions
When using	Cut away from yourself	Hold log on single chopping block and saw on the other side of the block	Chop/split logs on a chopping block
Use protective gear	Safety glasses recommended	Work gloves and safety glasses	Heavy boots, long pants, work gloves, and safety glasses
To sharpen	Whetstone or diamond stone – push blade away on stone at a 30-degree angle	Replace blade	Use file on secured ax head

Keep your woods tools sharp and do not use if dull, damaged, or loose. Never throw, strike with another tool, or misuse any woods tool.

TROOP SAFETY 101 – HOW YOU CAN HELP

Practice Youth Protection

Know and expect youth and adults to follow the 1-2-3 rules of Youth Protection at all Trail Life activities.
- **No One-on-One:** youth may never be alone with an adult not in their family.
- **Two-Deep:** two leaders must be present at each outing for proper supervision. Leaders can be identified by their required Member ID displayed in their lanyard.
- **Buddy system of Three:** three or more youth of the same level (Woodlands Trail, Navigator, or Adventurer) stay together at events and when tackling tasks, treks, or chores on their own.

Stay Alert for Strangers

Alert leaders to strangers on site.

Respect Others

Avoid bullying behavior and alert leaders of observed bullying in the Troop.

Follow the Rules

Follow the rules for your meeting or outing location such as avoiding bodies of water, restricted areas or activities, or regarding traffic patterns/playing in the parking lot, etc.

Prepare for Emergencies

Know where first aid supplies and AED's are kept at your location.

Safety Always First

Follow diligently fire, knife, and shooting sports safety practices and policies.

Protect Yourself

Always wear safety equipment required by the Health and Safety Guide as directed by your leader. This includes for example, safety goggles, secured life jackets on the water, and secured helmets when climbing or riding.

Protet Your Feet

Wear appropriate footwear. Closed toed shoes are required most of the time.

Avoid Disease

Wash your hands often including after every visit to the bathroom and before preparing or handling food.

Be Weather-Wise

Pay attention to weather conditions on outings and alert leaders to deteriorating conditions and dangers observed.

Be Water-Wise, Too

Follow water safety instructions of your leaders or lifeguards when near bodies of water. Take swimming lessons if you are not a strong swimmer.

Respect Other Creatures

Know how to stay safe around local wildlife (alligators, snakes, bears, insects).

Follow the Tent Rules

Follow Trail Life tenting rules — Navigators share tents with other Navigators, Adventurers share with other Adventurers.

Respect Privacy

Don't have phones out (cameras) near the bathrooms/showers/changing areas.

SWIMMING COMPETENCY TEST

Participants in swimming activities must demonstrate a minimum level of swimming ability. This competency may be documented using this Swim Test Form and kept on file at the Troop level or documented by a camp in a manner specified by their policies and also recorded on the "Trailman's Swim Card" for presentation at Troop water events. This test must be completed before a Trailman can participate in aquatics activities.

1 – Swimmer:

☐ Swim 100 yards without stops and with at least one sharp turn including the following:
- Jump feet first into water over the head, level off, and begin swimming.
- Swim 75 yards in a strong manner using one or more of the following strokes: side, breast, trudgen, or crawl.
- Swim 25 yards using an easy, resting backstroke.

☐ Demonstrate resting by back floating long enough to demonstrate ability to rest when exhausted.

2 – Beginner:

☐ In water in which he can touch the bottom, jump in and fully submerge head.

☐ Swim 25 feet on the surface without either considerable strain, touching the bottom, holding onto the wall or lane lines, etc.

3 – Non-Swimmer:

☐ Cannot complete either of above swimming tests without considerable strain, touching the bottom, holding onto wall, lane lines, etc.

Date of first test _____ ☐ Swimmer ☐ Beg ☐ Non-Swim

Name of person(s) conducting swimming competency tests and verifying swim classifications: _____
                                                Print Name

_____   ____ / ____ / ____
Signature   Certification Expires

CERTIFIED AS (please check): ☐ Certified Lifeguard
☐ Water Safety Instructor ☐ Aquatics Instructor ☐ Swim Coach

Certifying Organization, School or Team: _____

Date of retest _____ ☐ Swimmer ☐ Beg ☐ Non-Swim

Name of person(s) conducting swimming competency tests and verifying swim classifications: _____
                                                Print Name

_____   ____ / ____ / ____
Signature   Certification Expires

CERTIFIED AS (please check): ☐ Certified Lifeguard
☐ Water Safety Instructor ☐ Aquatics Instructor ☐ Swim Coach

Certifying Organization, School or Team: _____

Date of retest _____ ☐ Swimmer ☐ Beg ☐ Non-Swim

Name of person(s) conducting swimming competency tests and verifying swim classifications: _____
                                                Print Name

_____   ____ / ____ / ____
Signature   Certification Expires

CERTIFIED AS (please check): ☐ Certified Lifeguard
☐ Water Safety Instructor ☐ Aquatics Instructor ☐ Swim Coach

Certifying Organization, School or Team: _____

| **Date of retest** _____ | ☐ Swimmer ☐ Beg ☐ Non-Swim |

Name of person(s) conducting swimming competency tests and verifying swim classifications: _____

Print Name

_____ / /

Signature   Certification Expires

CERTIFIED AS (please check): ☐ Certified Lifeguard ☐ Water Safety Instructor ☐ Aquatics Instructor ☐ Swim Coach

Certifying Organization, School or Team: _____

| **Date of retest** _____ | ☐ Swimmer ☐ Beg ☐ Non-Swim |

Name of person(s) conducting swimming competency tests and verifying swim classifications: _____

Print Name

_____ / /

Signature   Certification Expires

CERTIFIED AS (please check): ☐ Certified Lifeguard ☐ Water Safety Instructor ☐ Aquatics Instructor ☐ Swim Coach

Certifying Organization, School or Team: _____

| **Date of retest** _____ | ☐ Swimmer ☐ Beg ☐ Non-Swim |

Name of person(s) conducting swimming competency tests and verifying swim classifications: _____

Print Name

_____ / /

Signature   Certification Expires

CERTIFIED AS (please check): ☐ Certified Lifeguard ☐ Water Safety Instructor ☐ Aquatics Instructor ☐ Swim Coach

Certifying Organization, School or Team: _____

SAFE AQUATICS METHOD

- All adults and youth who participate in aquatic activities must have a complete and up-to-date Trail Life USA Heath and Medical Form on file.
- All aquatics activities must have qualified and trustworthy adult supervision.
- Every person must have a buddy with him at all times.
- Areas approved for swimming and water games must be checked for obstacles and segregated into non-swimming (up to chest deep for your shortest non-swimmer) and swimmer area (up to 12 feet deep). An optional beginner area up to around 5-6 feet deep may also be established.
- Only those who have passed their Trail Life USA Swimming Competency test at the Swimmer level may venture into the swimmer area or participate in other aquatics activities.
- All water games and other aquatics activities require a safety orientation and a skill orientation or associated trail badge before participation.
- All aquatics activities other than swimming, water games, snorkeling, and scuba require the wearing of an approved personal flotation device (PFD).
- Proper discipline and adherence to the pool or waterfront rules are required at all times. No horseplay!

FLAG FOLDING

The traditional method of folding the flag is as follows:

Step A

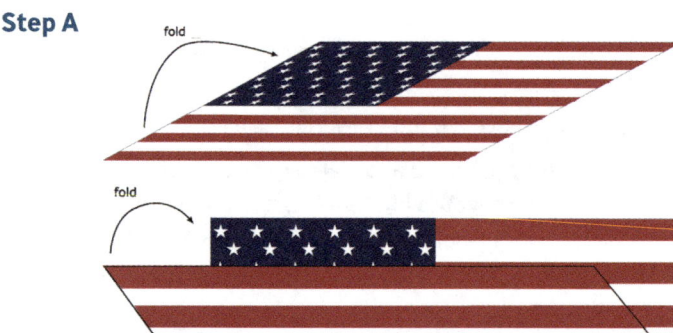

Straighten out the flag to full length and fold lengthwise once.

Step B

Fold it lengthwise a second time to meet the open edge, making sure that the union of stars on the blue field remains outward in full view. (A large flag may have to be folded lengthwise a third time.)

Step C

A triangular fold is then started by bringing the striped corner of the folded edge to the open edge.

Step D

The outer point is then turned inward, parallel with the open edge, to form a second triangle.

Step E

The diagonal or triangular folding is continued toward the blue union until the end is reached, with only the blue showing and the form being that of a cocked (three-corner) hat.

A properly folded flag.

INDEX

A

Able Trailman *32, 59, 318*
    rank requirements *70–76*

Advancement Conferences *65, 66, 319*
    Special Freedom Award Advancement Conference *66*

Advancements, Periodic Table of *320*

Adventurer Awards *33, 60, 318*

Adventurers Worthy Life Award *105–111*

Advisor *30, 31, 61, 274*
    in the Advancement Conference *65, 95*
    in the Freedom Award Advancement Conference *66, 113*
    in the Officers' Conference *277*
    in the Worthy Life final conference *106*

alcohol
    alcohol in First Aid *206, 209, 220*
    drinking alcohol *3, 14*
    drinking alcohol when diabetic *217*

Aquatics Badge *43*
    badge requirements & chart *118*

Aquatics, Safe Method *333*

B

Backpacking
    as an option for Outdoor Life Badge *162*

backpacking equipment checklist *308–309*

Backpacking Metrics *316*

Boards of Review *65, 318–319*
    Special Freedom Award Board of Review *66*

bullying *14, 328*
    Anti-Bullying Policy *302–303*

C

Camping Badge *44*
    badge requirements & chart *121*
    Camping as an option for Outdoor Life Trail Badge *165*

camping equipment checklist *308*

Camping, low impact *312–313*

Camping trips log *194–196*

Christian worldview *19, 20, 37*

Citizenship Badge *51*
    badge requirements & chart *123*

CLEAR Method. *See* **Elective Badges**

Cycling Badge *52*
    badge requirements & chart *129*
    Cycling as an option for Outdoor Trail Badge *166*

D

dangerous relationships *12*

Design Your Own Badge. *See* **Elective Badges**

Discipleship Square *284*

drugs
    abusing drugs *3*
    illegal drugs *14*

E

Elective Badges *57*
    Design Your Own Trail Badge *322–323*
    T.E.A.M. method *58*

Emergency Preparedness Badge *52*
    badge requirements & chart *133*

F

Family Man Badge *53*
   badge requirements & chart *136*

Fire Ranger Badge *45*
   badge requirements & chart *142*

First Aid
   epinephrine injection/EpiPen *219*
   poisonous plants
      poison ivy *250*
      poison oak *250*

First Aid Badge *45*
   badge requirements & chart *144*

First Officer *30*, *31*, *61*, **274**, **282**, *299*
   as award reqirement option *95*
   in the Officers' Conference *277*
   responsibilities defined **276**
   role in handling misbehavior *303*

Fitness Badge *53*
   badge requirements & chart *150*

flag *24*
   flag folding *334*
      folded flag illustrated *335*
      required for badge *68*, *92*
   flag patch on uniform *326*
   Our Flag badge *46*, *155*
   patrol flag *271*
   Pledge of Allegiance *24*
   salute to honor *24*, *25*
   showing respect for the flag *17*
   symbolism of the flag *46*

Flag badge. *See* **Our Flag Badge**

Freedom Award *33*, *34*, *61*, *112–115*, *318–319*
   Advancement Conference *66*
   award illustrated *35*
   award requirements **112–115**
   Board of Review *66*
   Freedom topper for Standard *30*

Frontiers *4*, **37**
   relationship to Woodlands Trail Branches *4*, *37*

G

guidelines for safety
   guidelines for woods tools *327*
   in relationships *13–14*
   Youth Protection *324*, **328**
   Youth Protection during meetings with mentor or leader *84*, *105*

Guidon Program *23*, *35*

H

handshake (for Trail Life) *25*
   as joining requirement *68*, *92*
   in apology *302*

Heritage Frontier *37*
   Citizenship badge *51*, *123*
   Our Flag badge *46*, *155*

Hiker's Responsibility Code *315*

Hiking Badge *54*
   Backpacking as an option for Outdoor Life Badge *162*
   badge requirements & chart *152*

Hobbies Frontier *38*

Horizon Award *33*, **60**, *318*
   award requirements *94–104*

J

Journey Award *33*, **60**, *318*
   joining requirements *92–93*

Junior Patrol Leader *31*, *81*, **273**
   as award requirement option *76*
   in the Officers' Conference *277*

L

Leader Conference *32, 92*
Life Skills Frontier *38*
   Emergency Preparedness badge *52, 133*
   Family Man badge *53, 136*
   First Aid badge *45, 144*
   Personal Resources badge *55, 176*
Low Impact Camping *312–313*

M

mission of Trail Life *iv, 15, 37,* **268**
motto: Walk Worthy *1,* **21**

N

Navigator Ranks *32,* **59,** *318*

O

Oath *26,* **269,** *278*
   as a joining requirement *68, 92*
   living by the Trail Life Oath *9, 10, 15*
Officers' Conference *31,* **273,** *276–278,* **277,** *282,* **289**
   chaired by First Officer *276*
   Officers' Conference, illustrated *277*
   suggested order for *278*
   voting during *278, 279*
Our Flag Badge *46*
   badge requirements & chart *155*
Outdoor Cooking Badge *47*
   badge requirements & chart *158*
Outdoor Life Badge *55*
   Backpacking Trail option requirements *162*
   backpacking trips log *164*
   badge requirements chart *160*
   Camping Trail option requirements *165*
   Cycling Trail option requirements *166*
   cycling trips log *168*
   Paddlecraft Trail requirements *169*
   Sailing Trail requirements *171*
Outdoor Skills Frontier *39*
   Aquatics badge *43, 118*
   Camping badge *44, 121*
   Fire Ranger badge *45, 142*
   Outdoor Cooking badge *47, 158*
   Outdoor Life badge *55, 160*
   Ropework badge *48, 185*
   Trail Skills badge *48, 189*
   Woods Tools badge *55, 192*
outings, types of *293*

P

Paddlecraft
   as an option for Outdoor Life Badge *169*
patrol *31*
Patrol Leader *31,* **61**
   as award requirement option *95*
   in the Officers' Conference *277*
   leadership skills and responsibilities *263-304*
   role in handling misbehavior *303*
   role in planning *289*
Patrol Method *265–267*
Periodic Table of Advancements *320*
Personal Resources Badge *55*
   badge requirments chart *176*
planning *289–301*
   at monthly meetings *278*

planning tools *305–311*
Pledge of Allegiance *24,* **47,** *156,* **278**
   as a joining requirement *68, 92*
privacy *13, 14,* **314**

Q

Quartermaster *30,* **61, 274**
   as award reqirement option *95*
   in the Officers' Conference *277*
   responsibilites defined **277**

R

Ready Trailman *32,* **59**
   rank requirements *76–83*
Recruit Trailman *32,* **59, 318**
   joining requirements *68–69*
relationships, dangerous *12*
Ropework Badge *48*
   badge requirements & chart *185*

S

safety, swimming *333*
   swimming competency testing *330*
safety, troop *328*
safety, woods tools *327*
Sailing
   as an option for Outdoor Life Badge *171*
salute (for Trail Life) *25*
   as joining requirement *68, 92*
Science and Technology Frontier *39*
Second Officer *30,* **31,** *61*
   as award requirement option *95*
   in the Officers' Conference *277*
   responsibilities defined **276**

sexual abuse *13, 15,* **302**
sign (for Trail Life) *25*
   as joining requirement *68, 92*
sleeping arrangements *13*
Sports and Fitness Frontier *40*
   Cycling badge *52, 129*
   Fitness badge *53, 150*
   Hiking badge *54, 56, 152*
   Swimming badge *187*
standard. *See* **Trailman's Standard**
Swimming Badge *56*
   badge requirements & chart *187*

T

TEAM Elective Trail Badges. *See* **Elective Badges**
tracking your progress *66*
Trail Guides *30,* **61, 274**
   in the Officers' Conference *277*
Trailman's Standard *30*
Trailmaster *30,* **31,** *65,* **274**
   in advancement conferences *65*
   in the Officers' Conference *277, 278*
Trail Skills Badge *48*
   badge requirements & chart *189*
Troop *30*
   offices *30*
   offices, illustrated *274*
Troop Structure, illustrated *274*

U

uniform *25, 28–29,* **280, 281**
   insignia placement on Troop uniform *326*
   uniform types *28*
   wearing your uniform properly *28*

W

Walk Worthy
   as a Trailman's worldview *21*
   the Trailman's motto: Walk Worthy! *27*

Woodlands Trail Program *23*
   instructing Woodlands Trail as a badge requirement *77, 81, 95, 101*
   Woodlands Trail and the buddy system *328*
   Woodlands Trail insignia on uniforms *326*
   Woodlands Trail Patrols *273*

Woods Tools Badge *49*
   badge requirments & chart *192*

Woods Tools safety guidelines *320*

worldview *viii, 18–21, 37*

Worthy Life *62–63*
   Adventurers Worthy Life Award ***105–111***
   as a rank requirement *77, 113, 318–319*
   Band of Brothers Bible Study *324–325*
   insignia on uniform *326*
   Navigators Worthy Life Award ***84–90***

Y

Youth Protection
   1-2-3 Rules *328*
   during all activities *324*
   during meetings with mentor or leader *84, 105*

Trail Life is grateful to the photographers at Unsplash for these photos:
Flag photo by Tim Mossholder on page 24
Half Dome photo by Pierre Le Vaillant on page 36
Mountain photo by Danka & Peter on page 64
Boys photo by Åaker on page 261
Yosemite photo by Laurel Balyeat on page 304
Panoramic by Rosan Harmens on page 312

PLANS & OTHER NOTES

PLANS & OTHER NOTES